ARSENIO

ARSENIO

A MEMOIR

ARSENIO HALL

with Alan Eisenstock

BLACK PRIVILEGE
PUBLISHING

ATRIA

New York   Amsterdam/Antwerp   London
Toronto   Sydney/Melbourne   New Delhi

ATRIA

An Imprint of Simon & Schuster, LLC
1230 Avenue of the Americas
New York, NY 10020

For more than 100 years, Simon & Schuster has championed authors and the stories they create. By respecting the copyright of an author's intellectual property, you enable Simon & Schuster and the author to continue publishing exceptional books for years to come. We thank you for supporting the author's copyright by purchasing an authorized edition of this book.

No amount of this book may be reproduced or stored in any format, nor may it be uploaded to any website, database, language-learning model, or other repository, retrieval, or artificial intelligence system without express permission. All rights reserved. Inquiries may be directed to Simon & Schuster, 1230 Avenue of the Americas, New York, NY 10020 or permissions@simonandschuster.com.

Copyright © 2026 by Arsenio Hall

All rights reserved, including the right to reproduce this book or portions thereof in any form whatsoever. For information, address Atria Books Subsidiary Rights Department, 1230 Avenue of the Americas, New York, NY 10020.

First Black Privilege Publishing/Atria Books hardcover edition March 2026

BLACK PRIVILEGE PUBLISHING / ATRIA BOOKS and colophon are registered trademarks of Simon & Schuster, LLC

Simon & Schuster strongly believes in freedom of expression and stands against censorship in all its forms. For more information, visit BooksBelong.com.

For information about special discounts for bulk purchases, please contact Simon & Schuster Special Sales at 1-866-506-1949 or business@simonandschuster.com.

The Simon & Schuster Speakers Bureau can bring authors to your live event. For more information or to book an event, contact the Simon & Schuster Speakers Bureau at 1-866-248-3049 or visit our website at www.simonspeakers.com.

All photos in the insert are courtesy of the author unless otherwise indicated.

Some names have been changed whether or not so noted in the text.

Interior design by Jill Putorti

Manufactured in the United States of America

1 3 5 7 9 10 8 6 4 2

Library of Congress Cataloging-in-Publication has been applied for.

ISBN 978-1-9821-9136-8
ISBN 978-1-9821-9138-2 (ebook)

 Let's stay in touch! Scan here to get book recommendations, exclusive offers, and more delivered to your inbox.

CONTENTS

I GROWING UP 1

1. An Old White Man with a Talk Show ... 3
2. My First Time ... 12
3. The Arsenio Show ... 16
4. I Make the Impossible Possible ... 25
5. A Handkerchief and a Glass of Water ... 38
6. Burning Down the House ... 47

II STANDING UP 55

7. Blood, Sweat, and Tears ... 57
8. I Wish You Love ... 65
9. Roach Motel ... 73

III STARTING OUT 77

10. Dining Out at the Supermarket ... 79
11. Q & A ... 90
12. Lady Marmalade ... 95
13. Desk Piece ... 102

IV TAKING OFF 107

14. Pryor Convictions ... 109
15. Better *Late* ... 122
16. Coming to America ... 135

V FLYING HIGH 151

17.	Woof Hall	153
18.	It's Hall or Nothing	158
19.	The First Show	166
20.	Phenomenon	173
21.	You're Gonna Be Around for an Awful Long Time	176
22.	Large and In Charge	184
23.	First Blurt	199
24.	Like a Virgin	208

VI LOSING GROUND 217

25.	Are You Going to Be Black Every Night?	219
26.	Down the Way	229
27.	You're Going to Help Me Live Forever	237
28.	Well-Known Balladeer and Homosexual	256
29.	Heartbreak Hotel	266

VII LETTING GO 273

30.	We Have to Get a Green Light for That	275
31.	I Gotta Do What I Gotta Do	287
32.	Daddy Coach	299
33.	All She Wrote	303

VIII GOING HOME 317

34.	Dream	319
	Acknowledgments	323

In loving memory of Nancy Wilson.
Without you, there is no me!
Rest in peace, Queen.

This is the story of a dream.

I
GROWING UP

1

AN OLD WHITE MAN WITH A TALK SHOW

FADE IN.

Los Angeles.

Sunday, January 15, 2024.

A typical January afternoon. Sunny and warm. Not like the east side of my beloved Cleveland, where I grew up. January is the rainiest, coldest, snowiest month of the year in *Believeland*.

Right now, two o'clock in L.A., sitting in a shiny black-on-black Escalade that still has the new car smell, I'm heading downtown to the 75th Annual Emmy Awards. I've been invited to be a presenter. First time I've been invited to attend the ceremony in, well, it's been a while. I'm giving out the award for Outstanding Writing for a Variety Series. I expect John Oliver will win because he always wins. I love John Oliver. I know what he does and how hard it is to keep that up week after week. He's won a million Emmys. He deserves them. I'm happy to hand him his next one.

When I had my show—*The Arsenio Hall Show*, from 1989 to 1994—we received six Emmy nominations. We won two—in 1993 for

Outstanding Technical Direction, and in 1990 for Outstanding Sound Mixing. We deserved those—we had a fantastic crew—but I would have loved to win for Outstanding Writing, like John Oliver, or for Outstanding Variety Series, like John Oliver, or Outstanding Talk Series, like John Oliver, but we never did. When you win for Outstanding Sound Mixing, but not Outstanding Series, it feels like Hollywood is saying, "We hear you perfectly, and we don't like you that much."

For the show tonight, I've picked out a blue-and-black tuxedo and a matching blue-and-black custom-made fedora. I like hats. My dad loved hats. He bought me a fedora at age three. He never left home unless he had on a dressy lid. He always took his hat off indoors. I'm not the gentleman he was. If not for the protruding brim, I'd sleep in a hat. My friend George Lopez turned me on to his hatmaker and this hat is at least ten fire emojis. It's all that, and extra butter. Dad would have loved it.

Shaved, made-up, and slapped with Burberry Hero, I slide into the backseat of the Caddy. The driver eases away from The Comedy Store—where I've met Kelly, my makeup artist—goes across Sunset, and turns down the treacherous La Cienega hill, heading toward the 10 Freeway and the Peacock Theater downtown. I'm going to the Emmy Awards solo, no date, no plus-one, just me. My choice. I have a wonderful son, Cheron, I've been in a relationship with my partner, Natalie, for twenty years, and I have a couple close friends, but when it comes to events like this one—when it comes to most work situations—I prefer pullin' up alone.

Some people call me a recluse. That sounds like I don't like people. I love people. I just prefer intimacy most of the time. Crowds and strangers intimidate me, make me anxious. If my friend Lon Rosen gives me Dodgers tickets, I start getting nervous at the thought of attending two days before the game. But I'm an actor, so I *act* like I'm comfortable in public. I handle my *bitness*, do what I need to do. But I'm a purebred homebody, and if I have my choice, I'd rather stay home with my woman, sipping a great bottle of wine, watching some bullshit like *Love Island*, or chillaxing with a good movie or documentary. That's a perfect evening. I have a nice little crib. I don't want it to go to waste. Okay, maybe I am a lightweight recluse. Whaaaatever!

As we drive down La Cienega toward the entrance to the freeway, I think about the past week. Super producer Jesse Collins called me out of the blue on behalf of the *75th Primetime Emmys* broadcast. They had an idea. Jesse asked me to speak for a minute or so before I presented an award. They want to honor me, he said. They want to pay tribute to *The Arsenio Hall Show*. They'd gotten access to my opening graphics, my crazy, stabbing signature—an *A* with a line shooting off into the air in blue cursive—that began each show. Then, as I come out, they'll play my theme song, "It's Hall or Nothing"—which I wrote—and Anthony Anderson, the show's host, will introduce me with the same exaggerated basso profundo that my announcer, Burton Richardson, did every night for six years, booming and elongating the *O* in Arsenio. The audience will love it, the producer said.

Hopefully, I think.

Hopefully, people will remember the show.

Hopefully, people will remember *me*.

I went through a lot during those six years.

In the beginning, nobody knew what we had, what the show would be. It debuted and took off like a rocket. Scorched the ratings. Blew *up*. Paramount had hopes, but they'd never expected anything like that. We were literally an overnight success. We were a star in syndication, which, for those of you who don't know, is a bunch of loosely connected stations all over the country, often fewer than a hundred total. We could be on in Boston or Butte, Montana, at different times—late at night, early in the morning, middle of the afternoon, or delayed or canceled for a city's MLB game. Our show wasn't on a network with hundreds of stations, all broadcasting the show at the same time, in late night, with an iconic mainstay like *Today* or *Good Morning America* waiting for my audience the next morning. All the more remarkable that we often went up against Johnny Carson, and knocked him back, a little bit. We at least got his attention. People heard my voice. People watched the show. Overnight I went from unknown to omnipresent.

Then time passed, things settled, reality hit, and reality bites. A year went by, two years, three, my champion at Paramount, Lucie, left, and I got caught in the middle of the late night wars, squashed between Leno and Letterman. The show lost its heat, the ratings fizzled, and we came down to earth. Meanwhile, I went from a leader of the pack to the man in the middle. I started to get slammed by both sides, Black and white. White people thought the show was too Black, and Black people wanted it blacker. I spent the last three years fighting for the show's life and my emotional and mental health. I kept trying to ride in that middle lane between Black and white America. It was difficult and exhausting because the lines kept blurring. Finally, I had enough. I decided to call it quits. I wrote a letter of resignation to the chairman of Paramount Television, Kerry McCluggage. I walked away. But the *Los Angeles Times* and some tabloids wrote false stories saying that Paramount canceled the show. Not true. They didn't. I resigned.

But the show did end. Six exciting, provocative, original years of comedy, conversation, and *music*—soul, R&B, gospel, indie bands, pop, hip-hop—hot sounds and hot talk, often with American artists and personalities not seen on any other talk show, like Bill Clinton, Robert De Niro, Prince, Michael Jackson, Madonna, Maya Angelou, MC Hammer, Snoop Dogg, and, huge controversy, Louis Farrakhan. I took my chair and went home, literally. I've basically stayed at home ever since, my choice.

But this afternoon, I've come outside.

I'm going to the Emmys. I'm a presenter.

I'm terrified.

The car pulls up to the artists' entrance of the theater, where my longtime assistant and friend, Corey Yamamoto, is waiting. I thank the driver and carefully exit the backseat. Don't want to wrinkle the suit, smash the hat, or bring attention to myself.

I make my way toward the door leading into the theater and I spot Kelsey Grammer and Ted Danson a few feet away. I love both of them. It's been years since I've seen them. I want to rush over and give them each a hug.

But I don't.

I'm too shy and insecure. I've always felt like a visitor to the world of stardom.

My nerves paralyze me. I veer toward the stage door, where I see one of my former stage managers wearing a headset. "Hey, boss," he says. I dap him, sign his iPad, then go inside, duck into a corner of the backstage area, and disappear into the darkness.

I close my eyes and think about what I'm about to say. Everything I wrote will be on the teleprompter, but I don't rely on that. I've got my minute memorized. I sway a little, whisper a prayer. *Be with me.*

The stage manager tells me ten seconds. I press my hands against my sides, feel the sweat on my palms as Anthony Anderson announces, "It's Arsenioooo *Hall*!"

I lower my head, step into the light. I raise my head and—

The audience is standing.

Applauding, cheering, pumping their fists—

Barking.

"Woof! Woof! Woof!"

They're *all* barking. The entire audience has become my "Dog Pound."

My throat tightens.

I nod, look into the audience, and try to make out faces. I recognize Tyler James Williams from *Abbott Elementary* and Ayo Edebiri from

The Bear. They're barking and pumping their fists. I spot Kieran Culkin from *Succession*. He's grinning, cheering, pumping his fist, and then I glance at the front row and see Hannah Waddingham from *Ted Lasso*, tall, blond, imposing. She's standing, applauding, and laughing, and a strange feeling comes over me.

They know me?

They're so freaking—

Young.

Then I hear myself say, "Hey, thank you!"

The ovation keeps coming. I bow, and when the cheering, clapping, and barking finally subsides, with my voice quivering slightly, I say, "As a kid, I idolized Johnny Carson. When most kids in Cleveland wanted to be football stars like Jim Brown, I wanted to be an old white man with a talk show."

Booming laugh.

Cracking the atmosphere like thunder.

I chuckle with the crowd, and I instantly feel calm. Relieved. Relaxed. I'm on a stage, telling jokes, talking to a crowd. To me, this is also home. I smile and say—

"I was a very weird ten-year-old. I even was a magician like Johnny. Check this out."

I point at a large screen to my right. A photo of me appears. I'm twelve years old, doing a magic trick called the Floating Zombie Ball. I'm wearing a suit and a tie. I'm holding up a large purple scarf with a skeleton in the center. I'm grinning.

The audience *awwws* at the old childhood picture.

"Yes. There I am in a black suit and tie, doing magic in the ghetto of Cleveland. Yes, I'm still alive."

The audience laughs.

"But I got my ass beat a lot. I loved Johnny so much I used to do *The Tonight Show* in the basement with my friends as guests. Eventually, I became a standup comic. I got my big break on *Late Night with David Letterman*. Then, on January 3, 1989, I debuted *The Arsenio Hall Show*."

Applause starts as a ripple, becomes a wave, then explodes.

"I was host now of that show I used to do in my basement, and I got to go head-to-head with the king, Johnny Carson, and his heirs to the throne, Dave and Jay. It was an honor to face off against that talented trio, but to be honest with you, I wished they sucked. But they didn't. And now here are some other folks who absolutely do not suck."

I announce the nominees for Outstanding Writing for a Variety Series, open the envelope, and read the winner—what a shock, it's John Oliver. After his acceptance speech, a tall woman wearing a glitzy gown whisks me offstage. She deposits me backstage, in a crowded, bustling pack of Trevor Noah writers and producers, taking photos as they continue celebrating his Emmy win for Outstanding Talk Series. Trevor is leaving *The Daily Show*, and this was his last chance for an Emmy. I'm excited for both Trevor and Oliver. They will head to the press room now, and afterward go to all the Emmy after-parties. I point to Corey and tilt my head to the left, my signal to call my driver and have him bring the car around so I can go home. That's where I have my after-parties. Home. With Natalie. I'll text her and ask her to open a Pinot from Napa and roll me a joint. With traffic, I should be home in about an hour.

Suddenly, John Oliver, clutching his statue, approaches me.

"I want you to know," he says.

His voice is low, hushed, and filled with a sort of—reverence. He looks at me. His eyes are bright, his accent thick, charming, British. He puts his arm around me and moves us away from the people near us.

"I am such a fan," he says. "You don't know how important you are to late night."

I blush, embarrassed, truly moved by his words, and then as if summoned, Trevor Noah, whom I've met many times, appears. He reaches past John Oliver, gives me a pound, and a hug.

"Arsenio," Trevor Noah says. "I am not here without you."

"You're our hero," John Oliver says.

For one of the few times in my life, I honestly don't know what to say. I nod and murmur thank you. Getty types and social media ninjas materialize, and we pose for pictures. I hug John, dap up Trevor, and then leave as quickly as I can, Corey hustling me out the stage door.

In the car, heading west on the 10 Freeway toward Pacific Coast Highway, I think about Trevor Noah and John Oliver, their genuine affection and gratefulness. I was so touched by them.

Hero, John called me.

I have been called so many names throughout my life. People in the 'hood always had trouble pronouncing *Arsenio*, I guess because the name seemed foreign. Every other kid on my block was Daniel or Alex. I don't think there was another Arsenio in the country. Now there are plenty, most of them named after me. The other day, a twenty-seven-year-old Coffee Bean & Tea Leaf barista named Arsenio took my order.

My dad, a pastor, never called me Arsenio. He called me "son" or "Little Buddy." Others called me "Little Rev" or "A-man" or "Senio." My mother, who named me, called me Arsenio, except when she was extremely angry at me. Then she called me A.H., her code for "asshole." My stepsister called me "Wang Wang." I have no idea why. Donald Harris, the star football player in my junior high school, called me either "Magic Man" or "Alakazam." I dropped everything and did my magic tricks whenever he wanted, usually in the school cafeteria. I doubt David Copperfield ever had to do magic in self-defense, the way I did. It always made me popular with neighborhood gang members and school bullies.

"Hey, Magic Man, come over here," Donald Harris would say. "Forget your lunch. You'll eat tomorrow. Somebody get this motherfucka a coin. Lou!" Lou Weaver, a badass bully, handed me a coin, which was poetic justice because he had taken my lunch money the day before.

"Here you go, Magic Man, okay, show them some shit."

To this day, people rarely call me Arsenio. Folks want to give me a nickname. Natalie calls me "A." My good friend Johnny Gill calls me "Hall." Eddie Murphy calls me "Mysterio." Tracy Morgan calls me "R." Jay Leno calls me "Brother Hall" and always has. Kevin Eubanks calls me "Ghost Dog" or "Ghost" because he says I always disappear without a trace. He even wrote a song for me called "Ghost Dog Blues."

But . . . *hero*.

Nobody had ever called me that before.

Not sure I deserve it.

I appreciate their kindness that night, at the 75th Emmys.

2

MY FIRST TIME

IN 1954, FRED HALL, a strict, conservative Baptist preacher, marries the lively, progressive, beautiful young church deacon's daughter, Annie Martin, who now officially becomes Annie Hall, just not *that* Annie Hall. Fred is sixty-five years old and Annie is twenty-one. The old song says opposites attract, and Fred and Annie confirm that. Annie, young, hip, loves popular secular music and has the radio blasting all the time to the R&B hits of the day—"I Got a Woman" by Ray Charles, "Ain't That a Shame" by Fats Domino, and the newest rock 'n' roll sensation Elvis Presley, who howls "Jailhouse Rock." Fred despises her music. He only listens to religious music, insisting on spirituals by Mahalia Jackson, the Five Blind Boys, or his favorite, Harry Belafonte. Annie likes to dance, swaying and twisting around the kitchen. Fred forbids dancing and calls Annie's music "hip-slapping music." Annie and Fred clash in other ways, too. Fred favors suits. Annie prefers wearing pants instead of long skirts or dresses. Fred says women should not wear *slacks*, his word for pants, it's in the Bible.

"Deuteronomy 22:5," he says. "A woman shall not wear a man's clothing, nor a man wear women's clothing, for whoever does this is utterly repulsive to the Lord your God."

"Sorry, I love *pants*," Annie says.

Whatever the subject, Fred and Annie each hold uncompromising, passionate beliefs about clothes, music, politics. Fred likes Nixon, Annie supports Kennedy. They fight daily over which radio station to tune in, Fred flicking the radio dial, changing Annie's pop music station to his gospel music, then Annie defiantly turns his gospel music station back to her pop music or R&B station. Fred, the older, strict reverend, and Annie, the youthful, hip progressive, dig in, neither altering their views, neither giving in to the other. Sometimes their arguments escalate into loud, screaming matches and one of them—Annie usually—leaves the room, and occasionally the house, going to her mother's, a few blocks away. Apparently, Annie and Fred manage to make up after some of their fights and focus their passion on each other. Two years after their wedding, Annie gives birth to a son.

Me.

When I'm five years old, I have an experience that changes my life.

On Sundays, my dad, mom, and I go to church. My mom sings in the choir and my dad works. He positions himself behind the pulpit and he preaches. But he doesn't just preach, he puts on a show. With handkerchief in hand, he prowls the pulpit, he gesticulates, he growls, he shouts, he whispers. He belts out the gospel and acts out his sermon, performing gospel theater, delivering a hypnotic sermon. When he concludes, he sings, "It will be glory, wondrous glory, when we reach that other shore," the congregation joining in. He electrifies the huge crowd in Elizabeth Baptist Church. People respond with shouts and applause. Women jump up, scream, swoon, some of them dancing in the aisles. My dad often allows me to sit in the pulpit, next to the associate pastor. I'm only five, but I know he dreams of me going into the family business. Some folks in the neighborhood even call me "Little Rev." I'm not sure I have the chops to follow in my dad's footsteps. But I am amazed at how he moves an entire audience to tears and joy with just his words, his voice.

On this particular day, my dad takes me to a wedding that he's officiating. I often go to weddings and funerals with him. For him, it's an introduction into the family business, starting at the ground floor. For me, it's precious time with my dad. We don't do much together that doesn't revolve around the church. We attend a church activity every day of the week and twice on Sunday, and we go to Sandusky's Cedar Point Amusement Park once during the summer for the church picnic. This time, the day of the wedding, we arrive at a private home. The host greets us and we walk into a house packed with people sitting and standing in the living room, an overflow of folks filling the dining room. I follow my father and find a chair off to the side in the living room. The ceremony starts. My dad stands next to the groom and then the bride begins walking toward them. My dad starts his wedding spiel. I'm bored so I decide to count all the guests in attendance—forty in all, crammed into two rooms.

Finally, my dad comes to the end of the wedding ceremony, the bride and groom proclaim their vows to each other, and my dad says, "I now pronounce you husband and wife. You may kiss the bride."

These two go at it.

Their faces smoosh into each other, the groom bends his new wife backward, and they kiss like there's no tomorrow.

"Kiss her, don't kill her," I say, loud.

The room explodes in a huge laugh.

A feeling shoots through me like a jolt of electricity. It's as if I've gotten shocked. At first, I'm stunned, and then I'm overwhelmed.

This feeling—I've never felt this—what is this *feeling*?

It is—I now realize—my first high.

I'm five years old and I am high.

The moment the laugh subsides, the instant it's gone, I want it back again. And again. And *again*. I *need* it back.

After that moment, after getting a big laugh in a room full of people, I will spend the rest of my life chasing that moment, in search of the charge I felt that first time.

One day, I come out of kindergarten and I see my mother waiting for me outside school. I stop at the school steps to make sure it's actually *her*. She never picks me up at school. I always walk home.

When I reach her, she says, "We're not going home. We're going to Grandma's."

I don't say anything. Once we're in the car, my mom says, "We're going to live with your grandma."

I start to ask why, but I don't have to. I know. I've heard the fights, the raised voices, the screams, the door slams. I've felt the chill throughout the house. The tension. The silence. I *know*.

"You can visit your dad anytime you want," my mother says. "You can walk over. It's not far."

I don't say anything. I'm five and I'm feeling the inevitable. The obvious. My dad is gone and we're starting over.

At my grandmother's, I find that my mom has moved everything I own over there—my clothes, my toys, my games, my books. She has moved my entire life. I lie down on what will now be my bed. I clasp my hands behind my head. *I woke up in one bed*, I think, *and I'm going to sleep in another.*

All in the same day.

This will be the beginning of a life on the move.

3

THE ARSENIO SHOW

SUDDENLY ON HER OWN, my mother starts working two full-time jobs to make ends meet. I hardly see her. After school, I go straight to my new home, my grandmother's house on Dawn Avenue, near the lumberyard and the old Kinsman Bridge. When I get home, I either hole up in my room or hang out with my grandmother, whom I call Mama. Mama and I quickly become tight, best friends. We bond over baseball.

I don't know much about sports yet—I will become a sports junkie—but Mama lives for the politically incorrectly named Cleveland Indians, today the Guardians. She can't afford to take me to any games, but I don't care because Mama creates the next best thing—bringing the game alive in my mind. We sit together on her small porch, tune in to the Indians on the radio, and root for the home team.

With the legendary play-by-play announcer Jimmy Dudley describing every pitch and creating a vivid picture for each play, I become hooked on the sport. The team isn't that good, but it doesn't matter. What matters is Mama and me sitting on that porch, eating hot, home-made, oven-roasted peanuts, shouting at the players as if they can hear us, losing ourselves in the game, imagining that we are at Cleveland Stadium, in person, the two of us.

After a year or so, my mom announces that we're moving.

"We can't stay with Grandma forever," she says, and we pack up and move to a small one-bedroom apartment, where, to my shock, my mom gives me the one bedroom. Mom buys another bed and turns the dining room into her bedroom. Easier for her to come and go when she works late or entertains. To keep me occupied, she provides a full-time babysitter—Emerson.

Emerson is a nineteen-inch black-and-white television that features a metal coat hanger instead of an antenna. Emerson becomes my new best friend, the perfect companion for a latch-key kid like me. I soon become obsessed with watching TV and with a certain type of show. Not cartoons or kid shows, like *The Jetsons* or *Captain Kangaroo*, like most six- and seven-year-olds. I become obsessed with talk shows.

After school, I run into my room and turn on *The Merv Griffin Show* and *The Mike Douglas Show*, which is shot right here in Cleveland. I'm enamored with these daytime talk show hosts, their style, how they socialize with their guests, and how much they love music. Both guys were big band singers, and they often sing with their in-studio bands. These shows are casual, loose, fun. It's like Mike and Merv are having a party and I'm invited. I don't like real parties, so watching a talk show party on TV is perfect.

Later, when I'm in high school, I get hooked on *Dinah!*, not what you would expect from a Black kid living in the ghetto. Something about Dinah Shore's breezy, welcoming style connects to me. And I love how the show starts by showing her signature, a "D" with a straight line shooting off into the air, like an arrow. I'm so taken by her signature that I copy it, starting mine off with the "A" for Arsenio and then sending a straight line upward, just like Dinah's. I will keep that as my signature for the rest of my life. I'll even start my show with my signature.

Back in elementary school, as I watch talk shows constantly, every day, hour after hour, I run into a problem.

I become fanatical about one particular talk show host. The king of late night—the king of all talk shows—Johnny Carson. The problem is Johnny comes on 11:30 at night and I'm six.

"Turn that damn TV off," my mother calls from the dining room. "It's too late."

"Okay, I'm doing it."

But I don't. I turn the sound way down, then crawl so close to the TV screen that I feel as if I'm practically inside *The Tonight Show* set, sitting next to Johnny.

"Arsenio, turn it *off*."

"It's off."

My bedroom door swings open.

"I can see the blue light underneath the door," my mother says.

My mom takes away my TV watching privileges for a week, not for watching TV so late, for lying. But I can't help myself. I can't stop. I'm addicted. In my neighborhood, you see people every day on the street, in your face, who are addicted to drugs and booze, so being addicted to *The Tonight Show Starring Johnny Carson* doesn't seem so bad. At least that's the argument I use on my mother. She knows a losing battle when she sees one. We compromise. I agree to turn the TV off at 11:40, after Johnny's monologue.

Around that same time in my life, magic happens.

It starts when my cousin Diane gets pregnant. A family scandal. She's fifteen years old and a sophomore in high school. Diane comes to live at Mama's house, too. Seems as if everyone moves in with Mama when life has them on the ropes.

Diane loves to read and goes to the public library every week. One day, she goes to the library and returns with a bunch of books, including one for me.

Magic for Beginners.

I devour the book.

I study card tricks, and coin, silk, and sponge ball sleight of hand. I try the card tricks and coin tricks, looking in the mirror, the way the book recommends. I practice in my room for hours. I like being in my room, alone, and now I have the perfect excuse to stay there indefinitely—magic.

The book becomes my bible. I never return it to the library. I still have it. I owe $37,000 in overdue fines.

My godmother, Idella Branham, teaches me how to ride the bus. Idella never learned to drive, but she's become a bus aficionado. She shows me how to ride the bus downtown and back. You need to take one bus, get a transfer pass from the driver, then get on a second bus, and on the way back, go in reverse. I go with her a couple of times and then I'm ready. I approach my mom. "Idella taught me how to ride the bus downtown. Can I go to the arcade?"

"Are you insane? You're seven years old. Absolutely not."

"I understand."

I'm hardheaded and determined, so I go anyway. The next day, I ride the bus downtown to the arcade. I stay for an hour or so, playing a few games of Skee-Ball, my favorite. As I come out of the arcade, I see Jean's Fun House and, next to it, Jean's Novelty & Magic Shop. I walk into the magic shop as if pulled by a magnet. Inside the store, a man—Jean himself—is performing close-up magic with another magician, doing a barehand appearing coin trick. I watch, mesmerized. He shows me both sides of his hand, reaches behind my ear, and produces a silver dollar. I stare, speechless.

"You like that," Jean says. Not a question. A fact.

I nod.

"Let me show you something else," Jean says.

He pours some coffee out of his cup into a shot glass, then makes the shot glass disappear into thin air.

"We sell that trick for nineteen ninety-five. Would you like to take it home and amaze your friends?"

I reach into my pocket, pull out a twenty I stashed from shining shoes, and hand it to Jean.

"Practice before you perform it," Jean says.

"Yes, sir, I will, I promise."

I never break that promise because from then on, pretty much all I do is practice magic.

I go to the magic shop exactly one month from that day. I would've gone sooner, but my mom put me on a one-month house arrest for taking the bus downtown without permission. Then, with her permission, I start going every Saturday and every day during holidays and school vacations. I always take the bus, just as my godmother Idella taught me, and I always go alone.

A year or so later, we move again, this time to a four-unit apartment building that my mother receives in the divorce settlement. She receives all the proceeds from the building, but she also becomes the landlord, a losing proposition, as she soon finds out, as well as an enormous pain in the ass.

Before we move into the apartment building, a new character arrives on the scene, my mother's new boyfriend, D'Light Davidson. I'm never clear about what D'Light does for a living. Let's just say that he's a Cleveland street hustler who introduces me to Kool & the Gang and teaches me life lessons my dad never taught me, things you don't find in the Bible. One day, I walk into my mother's bedroom and find a bulging Hefty bag giving off an odor you can smell from the hallway. Curious, I untie the bag and peer inside. It's packed full of weed. As I'm staring at the Hefty bag of pot, my mom and D'Light walk in. I look up at both of them.

"Is this—?"

"Oh yeah," D'Light says. "That's a big bag of weed. Not mine. I'm holding it for a friend."

He laughs and my mom shakes her head, then she laughs, too. It's hard not to like D'Light. He's handsome, roguish, with a tight medium-size Tito Jackson–like Afro, and a smooth way about him. He never raises his voice and his lips hardly move when he talks.

I like D'Light much more than my mom's previous boyfriend, the annoying State Farm insurance guy. We never got along. I still get a stomachache when that commercial comes on TV.

My mother likes the idea of being a landlord—for about fifteen minutes. Her enthusiasm then dribbles right down the drain, which like everything else in the building only works occasionally. In addition to her other two full-time jobs, my mother now has to be the building superintendent twenty-four hours a day, dealing with stopped up sinks and toilets, appliances that conk out, heating and air-conditioning units that shut off inexplicably, leaks in ceilings and floors, and most of all, *tenants*—those who pay their rent late, or not at all, and deadbeats who move out in the middle of the night, leaving their apartments filthy, piled with dirty clothes, broken furniture, old food, and all sorts of other disgusting crap. I'm too young to handle most landlord chores, so my mother assigns me one job, which I suck at—mowing the grass around the building. As soon as I start mowing, something attacks my sinuses—fumes from the lawnmower, pollen, swarms of miniscule bugs flying up my nose, and I go into a nonstop sneezing fit. I give my notice as in-house gardener after my first miserable day. Later, again pressed into service by my mother, I become a passable superintendent's assistant, my main talent being able to locate and replace blown fuses.

I have two passions. I live in two worlds.

Doing magic in the mirror and watching TV talk shows.

One day, my two worlds collide.

Or rather, I decide to *make* them collide.

The four-unit apartment building comes with a full basement—washing machine, dryer, furnace, incinerator, storage bins, and—most important to me—an open area wide enough for two or three chairs and a table, if you happen to have two or three chairs and a table, which we do, sometimes.

My mom, the neighborhood do-gooder, holds several "rent parties" for a neighbor who's fallen on hard times. My mother rents some tables and chairs from a party company and sets them up outside for guests to sit around and talk, play poker, and for her to sell sandwiches and drinks, all the proceeds going to the needy neighbor. Before and after each party, we store the tables and chairs in the basement where the party company will pick them up the next day.

One morning, I see the tables and folding chairs lined up along a wall in the basement, and I get an idea that grows out of a conversation I'd had with Wiggins, one of the kids in my grade. I had been telling him about the latest Johnny Carson monologue and Wiggins started taunting me, "Yeah, yeah, yeah, so when's *The Arsenio Show* going to be on TV? Ha ha *ha*."

Big joke. He laughs and everybody around joins him. But this gives me the idea.

I will do *The Arsenio Show*.

Obviously, it won't be on TV.

It'll be in my basement.

First, though, you have to understand that I am not merely obsessed with Johnny Carson. I want to *be* Johnny Carson. Especially when I read in magazines such as *Look, Time,* and *TV Guide* that Johnny used to be a magician.

That does it. I step up my game. I practice my close-up magic at home and then perform for my mother, D'Light, and any relative or neighbor who'll watch. I do card tricks, rope tricks, disappearing coin tricks, and my dancing cane trick, getting them to laugh at my constant patter, using words such as "ham hocks" instead of "abracadabra," while mystifying and amazing them. Then I take my act on the road and perform for my grandmother and my godmother. I hesitate showing my tricks to my dad, but I get up the nerve. He not only likes my tricks, he "books" me for a gig in the big church basement, opening for the junior choir's concert. He doesn't pay me, but his approval is payment enough.

I decide to host *The Arsenio Show* in the basement on a Sunday afternoon before the party company arrives to pick up their tables and chairs. I copy *The Tonight Show*'s set, putting out two chairs for my guests, and I set up a card table with a chair behind it as my desk.

I also devise a way to have a band. For Christmas, I received the hottest musical toy of the season, the Mattel Show 'n Tell, which comes with a TV screen on the bottom that enables you to project slides from TV shows, and a record player on top. I ignore the TV part and purchase several albums for the record player. For my talk show, I recruit Junior Brown from down the street to be my musical guest. He agrees to sing along to "Get Ready" by the Temptations.

I need an audience for my talk show, so I pass out invitations to kids in the neighborhood. I set up a couple rows of chairs, facing the two chairs on the "set" for my guest and the table where I'll sit. Right before the show starts, my audience arrives—seven kids.

I start the show by welcoming the audience. I follow with a couple of jokes and two magic tricks, a disappearing coin trick and something with a handkerchief. Then I introduce today's guest.

"Ladies and gentlemen, performing 'Get Ready' by the Temptations, let's hear it for *Junior*."

I turn on the Show 'n Tell, the song comes on, and Junior sings his *ass* off. He finishes, the audience applauds, and I bring him over for an interview, the same way Johnny does.

I don't remember what we talk about, but I remember bringing out my second guest, Wiggins, who can't stop laughing. I thank him and then I thank the audience for coming. I do a baseball swing, an homage to Johnny's golf swing, and end the show.

I perform my talk show in the basement once more a week later. I want to continue the talk show, but my mother doesn't have time to do any more rent parties, so I don't have access to the table or chairs. Then my mother gets rid of the apartment building and we move again.

4

I MAKE THE IMPOSSIBLE POSSIBLE

FROM FIFTH GRADE THROUGH high school, my mom and I live in at least a half dozen neighborhoods. We're always on the move and I'm always the new kid. I attend seven different schools—Charles W. Chestnut, Robert Fulton, Charles Dickens, Robert H. Jamison, Charles W. Eliot, John F. Kennedy, and Warrensville Heights High, where I graduate. I move so much I feel like an army brat or a fugitive. I keep sane by leaning into my four passions—magic, music, sports, and show business. Magic comes first because it's my career. Magic is my motor. Magic is my reason.

I put all the money I earn from odd jobs and my paper route into buying more elaborate magic tricks, including a freestanding, collapsible curtain backdrop tripod. I use all my babysitting money to purchase a used tuxedo at Goodwill. Every serious magician wears tails or a tux. Unfortunately, the one I buy doesn't fit so I also have to pay for alterations. I use the rest of my money to place an ad for "Arsenio the Magician" in the *Call and Post*, the local Black newspaper. Then I use the self-timer on my 35mm Olympus camera to take headshots and create a flyer that publicizes my availability for weddings, birthday parties, and Bar and Bat Mitzvahs. My mother allows me to use our home number. Different times back then.

My mom wants to get me out of my room. She looks at me and sees a twelve-year-old kid who spends every day alone, watching TV talk shows, doing impressions, or practicing magic tricks in three mirrors I've set up, while I wear my tuxedo. For some reason, she's concerned. She doesn't seem to understand that I have a career, magic, and I'm running a business, printing my weekly newsletter. My mother wants to be the mom of a normal twelve-year-old, even though I'm really not normal and she's questionable. She's a great mom—daring, liberal, supportive, my number one fan, ready to rent a car and drive me anywhere—but she's also working two full-time jobs and dating D'Light, street concierge, hustler, and hoarder of garbage bags stuffed with weed.

She works hard to force me out of my room. She signs me up for baseball, tae kwon do, church choir, theater workshops, and marionette classes at the Cleveland Museum of Art, and takes me to see plays and shows every chance she gets.

Meanwhile, thanks to those eye-catching flyers I create, I start to land a few gigs. I put a phrase on the front of the flyer, beneath "Arsenio The Magician"—"I Make The Impossible Possible"—and I think because I'm a kid, that intrigues people. I book a few weddings, birthday parties, and then somebody sees my magic act in a school talent show and I'm asked to appear on a popular local TV talk show—Barbara Caffie's *Rap*.

After that show, a Shaker Heights big shot who's tight with a bunch of the Cleveland Browns offers me a fortune—*two hundred dollars*—to perform at a cocktail party in his mansion. I ask my mom to drop me off and pick me up when I'm done. I may be twelve, but I'm a professional entertainer. I can't be accompanied at a gig by my mommy. She agrees, reluctantly.

I pack the trunk and backseat of her blue Ford with all my magic paraphernalia, and we leave the grid of mournful gray blocks in our neighborhood and head into the expansive and manicured suburbs. I gawk as we drive down streets lined with huge houses spaced luxuriously apart, all with green lawns big enough to be ballfields. We pull past some hedges and enter a hidden circular driveway in front of an imposing mansion. Two parking attendants wearing suits and ties sprint toward us, open my car door, and start unloading all my stuff. The next thing I know the Ford pulls away and I'm entering a foyer that's larger than our apartment. I crane my neck and see a dazzling chandelier—yes, a chandelier in the *hallway*. I have entered a world I do not know, but a world I want to know.

The host suddenly appears. He's one of those old rich men you look at and can't tell what race he is. He's either a light-skinned Black dude with a perm or a severely tanned white man with a second home in Florida. He leads me downstairs to a furnished, tricked-out basement—bar, buffet table, huge-screen TV, a DJ at a turntable in the corner, playing R&B music piped through speakers in the *ceiling*. The host steers me to my table set up in the center of the room, prominently located near the desserts. I sit down and begin a solid hour of close-up magic as the guests casually come and go, extremely well-dressed men with gorgeous, half-dressed women draped all over them. Some of them head over to a glass-topped bar where the guests inhale lines of white powder through rolled-up bills. I've heard about cocaine—everybody in my neighborhood knows about cocaine—but this is the first time I've actually seen it. These coke sniffers seem to be having a great time, laughing, talking loudly, whispering while they massage their gums with their fingers.

At one point, I glance across the room and through the center of a trick involving linking rings, I see one of the Cleveland Browns walk into the room. He wears an expensive-looking navy blue suit and he's chatting up three very hot women. I know him. I've seen him play on TV and I own his football card—star running back Leroy Kelly. I catch myself in mid-gape. I have to turn back to my rings because I don't want to mess up what could be my big break. I finish the trick and look for Leroy Kelly again, but he's gone. Did I imagine seeing him and the bevy of beauties surrounding him? Maybe. I don't know. I do know that for this one night, I am in the center of Cleveland royalty.

One day, as usual, I take the bus downtown myself. I plan to play Skee-Ball at the arcade and then hang out at Jean's Fun House. When I walk into the magic shop, I see Gertie, Jean's wife, sitting at the register, chain-smoking. She puffs, inhales, coughs, exhales, then swats a brown cloud of smoke away from her face.

"Hi, Gertie," I say. "Jean coming in today?"

"No," she croaks. "He's dead."

"Jean *died*?"

"Yeah, so he's not coming in."

She blows out another brown cloud of smoke and dissolves into a phlegm-filled, hacking cough.

"I might have to close this fricking place," she says between coughs.

I can't believe this. "Why?"

"I don't know how to do these things. I don't know these fricking tricks."

She frowns, then studies me as if she's just noticed me.

"You do," she says. "You know this shit."

"Well, I know some—"

"You know more than I do. Somebody has to run the magic department. Do the tricks, sell the tricks. Might as well be you."

"Am I old enough for a job—"

"Sure. You just gotta show people the tricks. I'll pay you cash. As part of the deal, I'll order magic tricks and any other equipment you want for your act, at my price."

From then on, after school, weekends, holidays, and summers, I work off the books at Jean's Fun House and Jean's Novelty and Magic Shop. I'm the new resident magician and manager of the magic department. I'm fourteen years old.

One day, over Christmas vacation, I take my lunch hour at the nearby Halle Brothers Co. department store (Halle Berry's parents named her after the store). I go to the store to check out the toy department and to catch Santa's hilarious elf, Mr. Jingeling, a local TV celebrity.

This day, after Mr. Jingeling finishes his elfish antics, a Herb Alpert track comes on and a magician, John Thompson, wearing black formal tails, appears. John removes a rose from his lapel and turns it into a long white silk scarf. Then he makes two live white doves appear, one on each end of the white silk, their wings fluttering on his outstretched arms. As the audience applauds, I realize I am watching, easily, the coolest white man ever to do magic. He's like James Bond doing a dove act. John performs a fifteen-minute set. His closing trick is what magicians call a barehand dove vanish. He somehow makes the doves disappear, right before our eyes, replaced on his hand by the white scarf.

I'm awestruck. I gape at John Thompson, then glance at my watch, realizing I have exactly two minutes to return to the register at the magic shop. I pop out of my seat in the audience and run out of Halle Brothers.

I come back the next day. And the next. On my fourth consecutive day in the audience, John Thompson winks at me. On the fifth day, John says to me, "Don't leave."

After the show, I follow him to his dressing room, a sort of oversize closet with a couch, chair, and table, upon which rests a wooden cage containing three doves. I stop, stare at the doves.

"You really love magic," he says.

"I'm a magician," I say.

"Are you now?"

"Yes. I work at Jean's Magic Shop. I've been on TV."

"Impressive," John says.

"I'm fourteen," I say. "I know I still have a lot to learn." Then I blurt, "How do you do the barehand dove vanish?"

John looks me over like I'm a suit he's considering buying.

"I'll show you how to do it. Next time I'm in town."

"When's that?"

"Next Christmas."

This is before cellphones, so I don't speak with John Thompson for an entire year. The following Christmas, I sit in the front row at Halle Brothers, waiting for him. He appears, nods at me, and smiles, as if we've seen each other the day before. Then he performs his barehand dove vanishing trick. I'm even more in awe. After his act, we go to the dressing room, and true to his word, John teaches me the trick.

"I need to get some doves," I tell my mother.

"*Doves?*"

"Yeah, for my act," I say. "I make them disappear. I turn them into stuff. It's great."

"How many?"

"Three."

"Three *birds?*"

"No. Doves."

"Where are you going to keep them?"

"In my room. In a cage. Actually, a coop."

I can tell by the look on my mom's face that this conversation is not going my way.

"We can't afford a cage," she says.

"I'll build it."

"Arsenio—"

"I'm not asking for a dog. Or a monkey. Just three harmless doves."

My mother gives in. "You have to take total responsibility. Keep them *inside* that coop. I can't have them flying around."

"Absolutely," I say.

So, at fifteen years old, I become the proud owner of three white doves. I build a cage for them in my closet. I never consider them pets. They're cast members, part of my act, the next logical step in my quest to become as my pamphlet advertises—*Arsenio the Magician*.

One day, my uncle Wallace Moore shows up at our apartment with three suitcases, a matching set of Samsonite luggage.

"What's all this?" my mother says. "You moving in?"

"It's luggage," Uncle Wallace says. "For Arsenio the Magician."

"For real?" I say.

"You need to show up in style at your gigs. You can't be lugging your equipment and your tricks around in paper bags and shit."

I don't know if it's because of the luggage or the doves, but I start booking gigs regularly, bringing in a hundred dollars per show, which is a fortune for a fifteen-year-old in the early 1970s. Then, my big break. Cleveland's Karamu Theater hires me to perform in the lobby during intermission of a play called *Day of Absence* written by Douglas Turner Ward, the celebrated playwright and cofounder of the Negro Ensemble Company in New York. Easy, fun gig. Fifteen minutes of jokes, card tricks with audience participation, vanishing lit candles, and an arm guillotine called "Disecto." I'm like an indoor street performer in the center of a crowd of matinee patrons as they run to the restroom or grab a beverage before the second act begins.

What I don't know is that as I work my magic, a Black magic woman—author and culinary anthropologist Vertamae Smart-Grosvenor—has her eyes fixed on me, watching me work the room. As the room lights blink signaling two minutes to go before the play resumes, she approaches me and introduces herself. She has flown in from New York to see the play but has been struck by how funny and unique I am.

"I've never seen a Black magician," she says. "I have a friend who I think would love your act. Do you have a card?"

Well, of course I do, and I do some sleight of hand and produce my business card.

Two days later, my mother gets a call from New York.

"My name is Anna Maria Horsford," the caller says. "I produce a show in New York called *Soul!*. I'd like your son to be a guest on the show. We'll fly him to New York and take care of his hotel room."

I don't know at that moment that I'm about to become part of television history. People have called me the first Black TV talk show host, but Ellis Haizlip, the host and coproducer of *Soul!*, which aired on PBS in New York from 1968 to 1973, owns that distinction. *Soul!* celebrates Black culture, Black music, Black writers and poets. Anna Maria Horsford will go on to star in many TV shows and movies, most famously *Amen* with Sherman Hemsley.

"Of course, Arsenio will need a chaperone," she says on the phone. "I assume you, or his dad?"

My dad, the preacher, will never approve of me performing my magic act on television. He's not a fan of show business. He believes it's the devil's business. He won't be my chaperone.

That leaves my mom. She would go with me to New York, but I know she can't give up a day of work.

But this is the biggest break of my life. I can't say no to *Soul!*. I have to go to New York. I have to find a chaperone.

On the plane, I sit on the aisle next to my chaperone.

D'Light.

"I'm giving up a day of work, you know," he says.

Work, in his case, being selling weed from his bulging Hefty bag stashed in the corner of my mother's bedroom.

"Thanks for taking a vacation day," I say.

"More like a sick day," he says, raising the shade and staring out the window. I swear his lips never move. He speaks to the tarmac. "Fifteen years old and you're on TV. Not bad."

"I guess," I say.

I'm trying to act nonchalant in front of D'Light, but in my head I'm screaming—*Not bad? It's fucking INSANE!*

Ellis Haizlip, producer and host of *Soul!*, looks more like a college professor than a talk show host—fly glasses, perfect 'fro, enormous, intimidating mustache. On each show, shot before a studio audience, Ellis presents at least four guests, Black cultural icons such as Muhammad Ali, Stevie Wonder, Aretha Franklin, Al Green, Bill Withers, and James Baldwin. I follow drummer Buddy Miles, who played with Jimi Hendrix and Carlos Santana. Ellis introduces me and tells the audience my age, fifteen. As I walk onstage, wearing a new suit my dad bought me for Easter, I hear the audience's muted, polite reaction.

I walk with purpose, strutting like a matador before a bullfight, holding a candle. I stop on my mark as instructed, give the audience a smile, and light the candle. A second later—*whoosh*—I turn the candle into a handkerchief. I casually stuff the handkerchief into my breast pocket as if I'm about to go out on the town. I don't remember the rest of the performance, but I do remember taking a bow, and walking off the stage, the studio audience applauding behind me.

I practice magic all the time now, inventing harder and harder tricks. I paint one of my doves blue, another one red, and place all three doves—red, white, and blue—into a box. I drape a cloth over the box, yank it off, and the doves are gone, replaced by an American flag. I try all my tricks on Mom and D'Light. I even interrupt them in bed. I don't think twice about what they're doing, or I don't notice, or I don't care.

"Think of a number from one to a hundred," I say to D'Light, as he and my mom scramble under the covers and D'Light jacks the sheets up to his chin. Another time, I barge in, unannounced, flick on the lights, and say, "Mom, write your name on this dollar bill."

I land several more gigs, many in the suburbs, which means I need transportation. My mom can't afford to leave work, so I always enlist D'Light to drive me. He always comes through and never really complains, although one time I hear him muttering through his immobile lips, speaking like a ventriloquist, "How did I become Arsenio the Magician's road manager? I work, too. I'm a *businessman*."

And then, thanks to magic, I find myself with two new friends, Howard Levine and Greg Victoroff, both around my age, both teenage magicians. We meet at the Cleveland Magic Society, where magicians of all ages hang out. I stand out because I'm the only Black teenage magician who attends the meetings.

On the surface, Howard, Greg, and I couldn't be more different. They are white and live in Cleveland Heights, a wealthy suburb, a million miles away—in *every* aspect—from whatever apartment I'm living in at the time. But the three of us start spending afternoons and weekends together, mostly at Greg's house. One time, Greg invites me to spend the night.

I arrive on a Saturday, around noon. My mom drops me off and Greg greets me at his front door. We walk through double doors and into an entryway the size of a Sheraton's. Walking down the hallway between twin curved staircases, we meet a man wearing a suit and white gloves. "Mr. Hall, may I take your bag?" he says.

I look at Greg.

Greg nods. The butler—my friend has a *butler?*—takes my bag and then says, "May I show you to your quarters?"

I don't speak. I've gone mute.

"You're staying in the guest room," Greg says. "I'll show you."

He leads me down the hallway to an elevator.

An elevator in a house? The only time I've seen an elevator before is in Halle's department store.

"What time will you be having lunch, Mr. Victoroff?" the butler asks.

Greg looks at me for confirmation. "One o'clock?"

"Huh? Oh, yes. One is perfect. Wonderful. Delightful."

"Excellent. I'll alert the cook."

Mr. Hall. Mr. Victoroff. A butler. A cook.

Now, this *is* over-the-top insane.

To be this rich becomes my dream. From that moment, I vow to make this dream come true. I live in a three-room apartment with one bathroom that I share with my mom. Greg has his own bathroom. *I now have my own bathroom. I always want to have my own bathroom.*

I make arrangements to attend the world famous annual magic convention in tiny Colon, Michigan, the "magic capital of the world," home of the legendary Harry Blackstone. The convention holds a contest for best amateur magician and I'm determined to win. Then, because it seems like a great idea, I write Mr. Harry Blackstone, Jr., a letter and invite him to dinner, my treat. I want to meet Mr. Blackstone and pick his brain. I don't even consider that he wouldn't accept my invitation. I'm sure he will. I'm not remotely surprised when he says yes.

Around this time, a friend of my mother's family from Alabama, Louis McKinney, comes into our lives. Sweet Lou, as everyone calls him, arrives with a reputation—a former pimp and a semi-celebrity in the neighborhood. I say *former* because like a few famous pimps from the 'hood, Sweet Lou has gone straight. He's banked cash from his previous illicit activities and has begun buying property. Sweet Lou has risen from pimp and hustler to successful real estate baron. He buys several buildings and businesses, including a small grocery store—a cross between a bodega and a 7-Eleven, which he names McKinney's Superette—next door to a bustling barbecue restaurant.

A year or two earlier, when my mom became overwhelmed with being both landlord and superintendent of the fourplex apartment building she got in the divorce settlement, Sweet Lou made her an offer.

"Annie, if it's all too much for you, go live over McKinney's Superette. I got a nice apartment there. Used to live there myself. I'll even give you a deal on the rent."

So, Mom sells the fourplex and we move again. I don't mind. The apartment is comfortable and I have my own room. The sounds and smells from McKinney's Superette and the barbecue restaurant next door fill the apartment—cash registers dinging, pinball machines pinging, shouts and laughter from customers, and every day around two in the afternoon, hickory smoke from the barbecue restaurant wafts up, curling into the apartment, making my nose tingle and my mouth water.

We settle into life above McKinney's Superette—my mom, me, my doves, and most evenings, D'Light. He rings the doorbell around eight and I buzz him up. A week or so before my mom and I are to leave for the magic convention, two men wearing suits approach me while I'm outside the store. One of the suits smiles at me. "Where's D'Light?"

I don't answer. D'Light has taught me the strict code of the street—*Say nothing*. Especially to people you don't know. In particular, men in suits.

"D'Light," the suit says again.

I scratch my head. "Who?"

"Cleveland Police," the guy says. He spreads his suit jacket and displays a badge he's wearing on his belt. He also shows me the gun holstered against his hip.

"D'Light Davidson," the other cop says. "Where is he?"

"I don't know no D'Light," I say.

"What's your name?" the first cop says.

"Arsenio."

The second cop smirks. "You Italian?"

"Ha, funny," I say. "Are you?"

"You don't know D'Light?" the first cop says, hard.

"Nah," I say.

"Where do you live?" the second cop says.

I tilt my head toward our apartment above McKinney's Superette. "Up there. With my mom."

"You sure you don't know D'Light?" the first cop says.

"Never heard of him."

The two cops stand there for a long time, blocking my way to the door of our apartment. I don't move, acting as if I have all the time in the world. Finally, one of them hands me a business card.

"Tell your mom we stopped by," the first cop says.

A few days later, the police arrest D'Light.

He gets convicted of some crime and goes to jail.

That's too much for my mom. Their relationship becomes shaky and she breaks up with him.

I never see him again.

5

A HANDKERCHIEF AND A GLASS OF WATER

NOW THAT I'M BOOKING gigs and about to go to a magic convention, I need to step up my style game. I decide to copy two of my idols, fashion plates David Ruffin, lead singer of the Temptations, and Johnny Carson.

Since my parents' divorce eight years ago, I don't see my dad all that much. But twice a year, at Easter and the end of summer, he takes me clothes shopping at Howard's Haberdashery in Shaker Heights, the top men's store in one of Cleveland's fanciest suburbs. He buys me the essentials—pants, shirts, shoes—but this year, because I've read that Johnny Carson is about to launch his own clothing line, I want to buy a suit like Johnny's. A blue suit.

"How do you know it's blue?" my dad asks. "You have a black-and-white TV."

"I read about it in *Time* magazine," I tell him. "I saw pictures."

I don't remember if my dad lectures me right then in the store about the horrors of Hollywood. He doesn't have to. He has made his point forcefully and often. He does not want his son to even think about going into show business, that den of iniquity. He still holds out hope that I will see some kind of divine light and become a preacher. But he relents and buys me the blue suit. I know he's thinking that preachers as well as talk show hosts wear suits. In any case, I don't know any other kid in my neighborhood who wears a suit.

I make another unexpected style choice a few days later. I hear that the Temptations will be performing nearby at Case Western University. I have to go. I buy two tickets and take my cousin Elaine. She's older, and while she loves the Temptations, I'm *obsessed* with them. Their songs are the soundtrack of my life.

The show knocks me out. Like everyone else in the audience, I'm on my feet for the entire concert, cheering, dancing, and singing along to every song. I accompany David Ruffin, the bespectacled lead singer, as he belts out hit after hit—"My Girl," "Ain't Too Proud to Beg," "Since I Lost My Baby."

After the show, Elaine and I head to the stage door to try to get a glimpse of the Temptations, maybe even snag an autograph. As we turn the corner at the back of the theater, I see a limo idling at the curb. In the backseat, his arm dangling out the window, sits David Ruffin, wearing incredibly stylish oversize glasses. He's chilling, listening to the radio, then David Ruffin and I make eye contact.

"He's so cool," Elaine says.

"I want his glasses," I say. "I need to get those glasses."

Elaine looks at me. "You don't wear glasses."

"I don't care. *I have to get those David Ruffin glasses.*"

I think I shout this because David Ruffin rolls up his window and waves to me. I give him a small wave back.

After that, I buy a pair of David Ruffin glasses with clear lenses to accentuate my style.

I don't need glasses even now, but I still wear those same fake David Ruffin glasses.

With my road dawg D'Light gone, my mom rents a Plymouth Fury and drives me to Colon, Michigan for the magic convention. I do meet up with Harry Blackstone and take him to dinner, to a small restaurant near the convention. I can't recall what we talk about except that he tells me I seem older than my age—must be the glasses—and that he likes my blue suit.

I kill at the convention. I'm one of the youngest magicians to enter the contest and I finish in second place. Every trick I do scores and I create a showstopper for my finale. I ask two audience members to join me onstage, a guy and a woman. I ask their names, joke with them, and then I present two colorful scarves, which we magicians call silks. I tuck the silks in front of the woman's turtleneck, then I tug on the silks, and tied in the middle of the two silks is a bra. The woman gasps, then laughs. The audience roars. It looks as if I've somehow unhooked and removed the woman's bra from beneath her blouse. Of course, it's not her bra. It's sleight of hand. I borrowed a training bra from Toni Lipford, a girl in my neighborhood. I promised to return it to her when I got back to Cleveland. It would have been too embarrassing to go into a store and buy a bra. Now, onstage, I pocket the silks and the bra, and bow as the audience applauds.

At the end of the convention, Hank Moorehouse, one of the featured magicians and a contest judge, comes over to me. Hank, distinguished-looking in a sport coat, bowtie, and impressively trimmed goatee, says, "Congratulations. You did very well. The trick when you had the bra appear between the two silks—"

He shakes his head in admiration.

"Great finale."

"Thank you, Mr. Moorehouse," I say. "That means a lot."

"But I want to tell you something, young man."

My stomach clenches. For a second, it feels as if everything in the convention center—everything in my entire world—goes silent. I can't explain how, but I know what Hank Moorehouse is about to say will alter the course of my life.

"One day you're going to get rid of the magic," he says. "The coins, the cane, the silks, the doves, everything. It's all going to go away."

"I love doing magic," I say. "It's my life."

Hank Moorehouse shakes his head solemnly.

"Listen to me. This is important. You're only a kid and you're out here making adults laugh. That's unique. There's something about you that goes beyond magic. You're going to talk for a living. You're going to be a standup comedian."

I'm not sure what that is.

"You did this card trick," Hank Moorehouse says. "You told this lady, 'Blow on the cards, and I'll say the magic words.' What did you say next?"

"I said, 'I know all the white magicians say *abracadabra*. I say *collard greens*.'"

"The audience went crazy," Hank Moorehouse says.

I remember the laugh. I remember the rush.

"You don't need props, you only need yourself. Just you and a microphone. Like Flip Wilson."

I know Flip Wilson. I've seen his show on TV.

"I'm sure of it," Hank Moorehouse says, rubbing his goatee, nodding at me. "You're going to be a comedian."

The three-and-a-half-hour drive home from Colon to Cleveland seems longer. I can't get Hank Moorehouse's words out of my head. After we get back to our place above McKinney's Superette, I tell my mom that I want to see a standup comedian perform.

"You can't go," she says. "They're in nightclubs. You're too young."

I don't argue. I'm still trying to process what Hank Moorehouse told me.

I know my mom has some old record albums by Redd Foxx, a famous—and famously filthy—standup comedian. A while ago, I came across the albums, and my mom snatched them away as if the records were so hot they'd burn my fingers. Now I *have* to listen to them. I need to hear what being a standup comedian is all about. One day, while my mom's at work, I put on one of Redd Foxx's "party" albums, *Laff of the Party*. I can't believe my ears. Though tame by current standards, what I hear then shocks me. Redd's voice is rough, almost hoarse. He's crass, *very* politically incorrect, and funny as hell. I giggle along with the club audience he's entertaining—"A girl's legs are her best friends . . . but even the best of friends must part"—and I crack up when he tells jokes about the blasphemous preacher, Reverend Eatmoore Bush.

My dad would flip out.

But the more I listen to Redd, the more I know I need to see a standup comedian in person.

Meanwhile, on the street below and inside McKinney's Superette, I am getting a different kind of education, taught by my professor, Sweet Lou. He and his contemporaries see me as a young man they can mold in their image, which is frightening because most of them are former pimps, hustlers, drug dealers, thieves, and con men. They seemingly know everything and hold intractable opinions about every subject—life, love, money, and especially, women. Helpful because I've been with exactly one woman in my life.

Recently, my godmother Idella Branham introduced me to Claudine, the smoking hot daughter of a pious churchgoing friend of hers. Claudine, way older than I am, a high school *senior*, attends church regularly and is active in several church clubs. My godmother hatches a plan. She figures if I become friends with this very religious daughter of her very pious friend, I, too, will spend more time reading the Bible and participating in church activities. My godmother's plan backfires. Claudine does enjoy going to church, but she enjoys receiving oral sex a lot more. Every afternoon, we spend time playing house in her bedroom. Because she is so deeply religious, she often cries out, "Oh, *God*."

One day, I go into the store to buy a few slices of ham for sandwiches to make for dinner while my mom works. I take out the small stash of bills I've earned from my paper route and plop it down on the counter.

"Nah, *nah*."

Sweet Lou, who's been standing near the magazine rack and watching me, slides over, scoops up my money, and steers me into a corner.

"Let me talk to you for a minute, pimp," he says. "Look here. Don't ever take your knot out like that."

"My knot?"

"Your roll. Your wad. Your money, pimp. You have to *prepare* before you come into the store. Figure out how much you'll need and keep that separate. Never take out all your money. You feel me?"

"I think so."

"Dawg, in this neighborhood, you're a mark. We're all watching you. We see your knot, we'll rob you ten minutes from now."

I nod. "Don't take out my knot."

Sweet Lou flashes his golden grin. "That's right. Hear that."

Thanks to Sweet Lou, I keep different amounts of money in separate pockets. I never take out my knot.

One night, while I'm in bed reading the latest *Time* magazine, my mom knocks on my bedroom door and pops her head inside. "You still want to see a standup comedian?"

I sit up straight. "I really do."

"Okay," she says. "Al Green's coming to town."

"I love Al Green but he's not that funny."

She shakes her head. "He has a standup comic opening for him. I got us tickets."

I feel like flying out of the bed and wrapping my arms around her. I'll say this. As crazy as I can be, as insane as my dreams may seem, my mom always hears me, always supports me.

"Saturday night," she says, producing two tickets. "Herb Jubirt. He's the opening act."

"I might wear my suit," I say.

She smiles and closes the door. A count of three. The door opens and my mom sticks her head in again. "By the way, how do you like those Redd Foxx albums?"

As my mom and I take our seats in a downtown arena to see Herb Jubirt, the opening act for Al Green, I notice that the houselights are on and the first six rows are empty.

"Nobody's here," I say.

"They don't know Herb Jubirt," my mom says. "Everybody's coming later for Al Green."

We settle in. I lean forward and focus on the stage, which is bare except for a stool and a microphone. A few more people arrive and after about fifteen minutes, the houselights dim and an announcer's voice booms over loudspeakers, "Ladies and gentlemen, please welcome—Herb Jubirt!"

A man wearing a suit slowly walks onstage to scattered, polite applause. He holds a handkerchief and a glass of water and places both on the stool. He removes the hand mic from the microphone stand and looks at the audience. He appears to be checking us out, gauging us. Then he smiles. A warm, genuine smile. He seems to be enjoying us, enjoying where he is, enjoying the stage, the arena, the crowd. Even more, he seems to be enjoying *himself*. I watch this man—this stranger—alone on that stage, loving his place, loving his power, and I think, *He could be my dad. That's what my dad does.*

Then Herb Jubirt delivers his first joke.

The audience laughs.

The arena—this dim, half-empty, soulless space—suddenly feels filled with light.

Herb Jubirt delivers a second joke, and the entire atmosphere in the arena shifts. The mood changes.

More people arrive, take their seats, Herb does another joke, and the laughter builds.

He delivers his fourth joke. The audience roars. Herb laughs with them. He backs up toward the stool, takes a sip of water, and pats his forehead with the handkerchief.

He comments, the crowd laughs, and he grins again.

He's got them.

He *owns* them.

He's accomplished that with nothing but his voice. And when he's done doing his standup, he'll just leave. When I'm done with my magic act, I can't leave. I have to do an entire breakdown. I have to pack all my stuff into my suitcases and then I have to deal with my doves. I got to walk them, feed them, clean up their shit. Herb Jubirt doesn't have to deal with any of that. He must feel so—free.

This is how my dad must feel when he preaches.

Herb Jubirt prowls that stage, alone, doing nothing except speaking, and the audience roars. This standup comedian—the opening act for a megastar—destroys this crowd that didn't know him before, a crowd that didn't even want to see him. They absolutely love him now.

That's exactly what this is. I identify it. I know what I'm experiencing. What I'm feeling.

Love.

I am feeling the love between a man on a stage and hundreds of *strangers*.

It's so much like preaching.

After thirty minutes onstage, alone, Herb Jubirt ends his set and says, "Thank you."

The audience—the arena has filled by now—applauds, shouts, cheers, some people stand. Herb Jubirt has not only turned this crowd around, he has made them his.

Herb Jubirt bows, picks up the stool, and leaves the stage. At that moment, I know.

I know who I am.

I know what I want to be.

I want to be a comedian. I want to be the opening act for stars.

6

BURNING DOWN THE HOUSE

I ENTER HIGH SCHOOL with a résumé—magician, drummer in the marching band, and founding member of the Soul Sophistications, a Kool & the Gang funk-jazz knockoff. I'd started fooling around with the drums at a friend's house because I read that Johnny Carson plays drums. Eventually, I get my own drum set, then a "friend" of my mom, jazz musician Paul Weeden, gifts me his old guitar with only three strings. I turn that into my version of a bass guitar. In the Soul Sophistications, I play drums and occasional bass. We also have a trumpet player, Johnny Britt, a saxophone player, and another bass player, but he can't sing and play bass at the same time so I sing whenever he plays bass. We hold rehearsals in my mother's bedroom because it's the only room big enough to hold my drums. It's also the smelliest. The room reeks of D'Light's weed. Our band gets high just by being in the bedroom. Incredibly, we book a bunch of paying gigs, achieve some local notoriety, and even accumulate a small but enthusiastic gaggle of groupies.

I reluctantly reveal my standup comedian secret in English class.

The teacher gives us a homework assignment—write down one of our dreams. The night before, as usual, I had watched *The Tonight Show*. One of Johnny Carson's guests had been jazz singer Dee Dee Bridgewater. I hadn't heard of her, but she was attractive and she could *sing*. She would go on to win a Tony award for her performance on Broadway in *The Wiz*, and I would have her as a guest on my show. Back in high school, for my English class, I start writing the assignment on a yellow legal pad, and my thoughts pour out on the page. I write about how I dream to be a standup comedian and open for Dee Dee Bridgewater in Las Vegas.

The English teacher calls on us to read our dream papers aloud, and as I do, the class starts laughing. The kids, especially my friends, *kill* me—"You fucking idiot. You, a standup? You gonna open for Dee Dee Bridgewater? Who the fuck *is* Dee Dee Bridgewater? Las Vegas? You going to bring *The Arsenio Show* to Las Vegas, take over for Wayne Newton? HaHA*HA*."

Merciless.

Let them laugh. Only motivates me more.

Around this time, my mother announces that she is going back to school for a year and that I will be living with Idella Branham, my godmother. Idella lives in a nice area of Cleveland, so I don't mind moving there. But Idella is very religious and has dreams of her own for me. She carries my father's dream in her heart. She wants me to be a preacher.

"You're going to be a great preacher," she tells me, daily. "You know why? You can *talk*."

Now that I've gone public with my dream of being a standup comedian, my godmother decides to pull me away from that and steer me toward the church. She sees a clear connection between standup and preaching. Both involve being in front of people, talking, entertaining, grabbing an audience's attention, and moving a crowd. *Preaching.* To my godmother, all it will take for me to go from comedy to religion is a little nudge. I understand her logic. I even go along with her when she tries to get me to learn all the books of the Bible by heart. I do my best. When it comes to standing onstage and entertaining, I'm all in. But I know I'm not made to be preacher.

I don't have many opportunities in school to perform standup, so I rely on my magic to entertain and avoid ass whippings. All the hard-ass guys love me because I mystify and amaze them. I'm a weirdo but I'm their weirdo. Study hall becomes my show and I am the host. I set up at a table in the back of the classroom and the kids crowd around me. Donald Harris, the roughest and scariest guy in school, a first-string varsity linebacker, becomes my assistant.

"Hey, Magic Man, show this motherfucker that trick with the tooth. You bring your cards? Your coins? Do that disappearing coin trick. You know the one, that coin roll. Hey, motherfucker, give my man a quarter. Now. *Now.*"

I pull my deck of cards out of my pocket, fan them out, do two one-hand cuts, and the kids cheer. After a while, the study hall teacher ends the show. "Okay, Arsenio, you have to put your stuff away."

I look at Donald, shrug, and start packing up my shit, but the next day, I'm back at it, doing my magic, hosting my show, with Donald, my enforcer, my cohost, my sidekick, my Ed McMahon.

A year goes by. We move again. I leave my godmother's house, and John F. Kennedy High, and my mom and I move to Warrensville Heights, a Cleveland suburb, where I finish high school. Along the way, I acquire a serious girlfriend, Joyclyn, a year younger, smart, gorgeous, a cheerleader. At first you might think this doesn't track. I'm nerdy, a kid who does card tricks and coin rolls in study hall. But I'm also in a band, I've been on TV twice, and with a running start, I can dunk a basketball. Not every cheerleader ends up with a varsity football player. Some choose magicians who can dunk.

After I graduate, I enroll at Ohio University. I throw myself into campus life. I go to concerts, become a DJ on the radio station, play intramural sports. But I miss Joyclyn. Ohio U is three and a half hours from Cleveland. Then Joyclyn tells me she's going to Kent State University, which is less than an hour from Cleveland. One night, some friends and I go for a drive in the countryside and practically plow into a Klan rally. I can't believe what I see. A scrum of angry white guys in hoods, a cross burning, your typical stomach-churning, bloodcurdling racist fun fest in the woods. That does it. I transfer the *hell* out of Ohio U.

Around the same time I enter Kent State, my mom finds a great job working in the office for the Teamsters Union—in Chicago. She packs up and moves to the Windy City and I claim my old bedroom at my grandmother's house on Dawn Avenue. My mom gifts me her car so I can drive back and forth from Kent State to Cleveland whenever I want.

Meanwhile, I'm back with Joyclyn and rocking college life. I join the debate club and I land the lead in the campus production of *Purlie Victorious*, in which I play, of course, a preacher. I score a two-hour show on the campus radio station, which I call "Arsen*io* on the Rad*io*." The radio station owns a limited number of records, all by white artists, so I bring my own collection, lugging them to the station in a wooden crate. I play the Temptations; Earth, Wind & Fire; Johnny "Guitar" Watson; and I play comedy albums by Dick Gregory and Franklyn Ajaye, both of whom are coming to perform on campus.

I also form a new band, which we call Rare Element. We play dances and talent shows and we kind of blow up, at least at Kent State and the surrounding area. Incredibly, we book a major gig. Eddie Kendricks, the first tenor of the Temptations, has left the group and is doing a solo concert on campus. We open for him. A huge break for us. Then because of a lack of chemistry—and talent—Rare Element dissolves.

I become friends with another aspiring standup comic, Steve Harvey. Steve and I hang out, hoop daily, and dream. We talk about life after college, performing standup in comedy clubs, getting discovered, becoming famous. Steve and I go to see standup comedian Dick Gregory when he comes to Kent State. Dick is a little older, political, heady, and I respect the hell out of his unique material. He makes me think, shows me a cerebral side of comedy.

One day, after playing ball in the gym, I sit in the bleachers with Steve Harvey. I want to talk about the future. I want to make plans.

"I've been thinking," I say. "There's nothing for us in Ohio. We both know that. We should go to Hollywood after we graduate. It's only a year away. Not that far off."

Steve shakes his head. "Can't do that, dawg. I'm on academic probation. I didn't make it. I'm not coming back next year."

We don't say much after that. I'm so stunned that Steve and I forget to exchange contact information. I won't connect with him again until years later, in Hollywood, when we're both working as standup comedians.

Meanwhile, Franklyn Ajaye, who's promoting his movie *Car Wash*, starring Richard Pryor himself, arrives on campus. On my radio show, I've been wearing out Franklyn's new album, *Don't Smoke Dope, Fry Your Hair*, playing it until the grooves practically meld together. Now he plays the gymnasium at Kent State and *kills*. He confirms my goal to become a comic. His set inspires me. After the show, I introduce myself to Franklyn backstage, mention that I'm the campus radio station DJ who's been playing his record nonstop, and say, "Hey, we got a really good party happening tonight. I can take you."

Franklyn perks up. "Show me where it is, man."

I take him to the party, then we find another, and as we leave for a third frat party, I say, "Hey, can I ask you a couple of questions? I'd like to pick your brain."

"Sure," he says, "go for it."

"I want to be a standup comic. Have you ever been to The Comedy Store?"

"I go all the time," he says. "I was there two nights ago."

"Would you recommend that I go to Hollywood after I graduate?"

"It's not even a question. You *have* to."

It's settled. I'm going to Hollywood.

I just don't know how or when.

I will graduate at the end of summer of '77. A bittersweet time. I'm the first to graduate college in the Hall family and my dad is extremely proud. But he hasn't been feeling well lately and I keep warding off thoughts of the inevitable.

The summer is hot and lazy, a time for contemplation, planning my future, or at least plotting my next move. For now, I have a good living arrangement. I live in a small studio apartment at a reduced rent because I've signed on as the janitor for the Kent Village apartment building. Days, I work out at the campus gym with my friend Cortez Brown, star of Kent State's basketball team, and coach a Little League baseball team. At night, I continue my DJ gig at the radio station and perform with my band weekly in the lounge of a Ravenna, Ohio bowling alley. I keep thinking about my future as a standup. What will I do at the end of the summer after I officially graduate? How do I get to Hollywood? I can't seem to formulate a plan. So, for now, I simply dream.

One hot, dry, windy night, as I chill out at home in front of the TV, breaking news interrupts the show I'm watching. A fire is blazing through a neighborhood in Cleveland. The camera pans down a street, past a few houses that are burning ferociously and I recognize a house on my grandmother's street. I get as close to the screen as I can, trying to identify the exact group of houses that are on fire, and I know it's my grandmother's block. It hits me then that my mother is in Chicago and my grandmother is in her house, alone, with the fire roaring up her street.

I call my grandmother's house and get no answer. Within seconds, I'm in my mother's car, driving like a fiend toward Cleveland. I drive the 480 East like an Andretti instead of an Arsenio. It normally takes an hour to drive to my grandmother's house. I get there in thirty minutes.

I park my car and race toward her street. I run as fast as I can, but police, firefighters, EMTs, and a throng of residents and onlookers block my way. I scan the crowd. I don't see my grandmother. I push through the people gawking at the burning houses and stand on the sidewalk across from my grandmother's house, which is engulfed in flames. I stay riveted to my spot on the sidewalk, unable to move a muscle. Suddenly, I hear wood splintering from the second floor of her house. I look up. A bathtub rips through the upstairs wall, the pipes still attached, slithering behind like a metal tail. The tub sails through the air and crashes to the ground. A second later, the air-conditioning unit I'd placed in my window blasts through the wall. I watch, my mouth open, gaping, as wood crackles and the sickening stench of ash and soot stings my nostrils. I feel like I'm inside the walls of a roaring fireplace.

I try to squeeze past a cluster of people, but a police officer stops me. I shout that my grandmother might be in that house and then someone calls my name. I spin, do a one-eighty, and Barbara Robinson, a neighbor I used to date, approaches me. We hug.

"She's safe," Barbara says.

I fight back tears. "Where is she?"

"She's with some other neighbors on the next block behind Miss Hickman's house. We took them all over there."

I still need confirmation. "She's all right?"

Barbara nods, and I hug her again.

My grandmother escaped the fire with the clothes on her back and not much more. I'd kept some stuff at my dad's place, but I left clothes, books, and especially magic tricks and props at my grandmother's, including my trophy for finishing second in the young magician's contest in Colon, Michigan. Those losses make my former life of magic feel somehow distant and final, a dream literally gone up in smoke.

A few days after the fire, I return to the charred and empty lot, the remains of the house now rubble and piles of ash. I walk the perimeter of the lot and something on the ground catches my eye—my grandmother's .38 Smith & Wesson revolver, almost totally melted, only a piece of the black handle left intact.

After the fire, my grandmother moves in with her daughter Maggie, my aunt. I return to my Kent State apartment to consider my options. I could move in with my dad. I could become a permanent Kent, Ohio resident. Or I could let luck take the steering wheel and drive me wherever it may go. Given my choices, I pack up my car, head west, and join my mother in Chicago.

II

STANDING UP

7

BLOOD, SWEAT, AND TEARS

CHICAGO.

Comedy paradise.

Home of the Comedy Cottage, the Comedy Womb, Zanies, Mister Kelly's, the Comedy Bar, and the biggest launching pad of them all, Second City.

I haven't actually performed any standup—yet—but I've made notes, I've started writing jokes, I've worked out in the mirror, and I have checked out a lot of these places. I even get my courage up and apply to Second City. Might as well start at the top, go for broke. I know I have to move fast because I don't have a lot of money to support my dream. To be honest, I don't have a lot of support, period.

My dad isn't even aware of the dream I'm chasing. I know how he feels about Hollywood and show business, so we don't discuss it. When I call him, he asks *how* I'm doing, but I avoid any conversation about *what* I'm doing. In a perfect world, I'm sure he'd like me to be in Cleveland, preaching, serving as his assistant pastor. But he always taught me, "God

CALLS a man to preach." Until God calls, I'm gonna keep working toward a star on Hollywood's Walk of Fame. At least I have my mom.

"You want to do *what*?"

I sit at her kitchen table. She stands with her back pressed into the sink. Her mouth has dropped open. She waves at me, brandishing a soup ladle like a weapon.

"I heard from Bernard Sahlins," I say. "My audition went well. I've been accepted to work out at Second City."

"And this Bernard man will pay you how much?"

I clear my throat. "You don't get paid anything. It's like college for comedy. That's how it works. At first. Then later—"

"*Later?*"

I lower my voice. "Mom, it's Second City. It's a big deal. I want to do comedy. It's my dream."

"Dream all you want, but you got to pay your rent."

"I know, but—"

"But *what*?"

She takes a breath, exhales, then raises her voice, slightly at first, then higher and higher until she hits full scream.

"Why did you *go* to college?"

I start to answer. She cuts me off.

"I'll tell you why. To prepare you for life so you can get a good job. What are you doing? Your dad wanted you to be a preacher. No? Not for you? Okay. But at least that pays!"

She shakes her head.

"A standup comedian. A standup *comedian*. Please. Arsenio, I'm asking you. Be normal. *Be. Normal.* Do normal shit. Dream when you go to sleep. Dream for all eight hours. But the rest of the time, when you're awake—GET. A. JOB."

So, I park my dream of becoming a standup comedian and attend a two-day job fair. A company called Noxell likes me, but they only have openings in their Detroit office. I pack my bag and head to The D, a brand-new employee of Noxell, maker of Noxzema cold cream, Rain-Tree lotion, and CoverGirl makeup. I am the district sales rep in charge of displays in the Detroit region. There is actually a science to displays. I don't know that until I work at Noxell. My job is to position our products in the best locations in stores, the loftiest goal to grab the attention of customers as soon as they enter the store, or try to steer them left instead of right, and subconsciously move them in front of the Noxzema cold cream display.

Full disclosure.

I cannot stand the smell of Noxzema, meaning that I am totally wrong for this job.

I mention that in a drugstore to a store manager to make him laugh. He doesn't. My mouth gets me fired right after I start.

With no Noxell company car and my rent due, I quickly find another job within walking distance of my apartment.

I'm now the manager of the toy department in a department store in Inkster, Michigan. I'm still in charge of product and displays, but I add shipping and receiving to my job description, and every so often, I add Lenora the shipping and receiving clerk, to my bedroom.

I have my own family challenges with my mom and dad, but Lenora's family is legit soap opera crazy. She finds out one night that her dad is actually gay and has a husband and a whole other family in another city. Lenora and her brothers, two musicians in a band, had no idea. To take her mind off her family drama, she and I go to see her brothers perform at a club in Detroit.

Lenora and I take our seats in the audience, her brothers begin playing their set, and their Marshall amplifier smokes, hisses, and blows up right onstage. The audience gasps, the brothers scramble to fix the amp, and within two minutes, the crowd gets restless and people start to leave. Lenora grabs my arm.

"Go up there," she says.

"Where? Onstage?"

"Yes. Cover for my brothers. You can do it. You're funny."

So, I do.

I climb onto the small stage, greet the audience, "Hey, looks like we got some audio problems, that's okay, the mic works," and I go into fifteen minutes of standup comedy, unplanned, unrehearsed, untested, completely off the top of my head. Within thirty seconds, I'm rolling, in a zone, half here, half somewhere else, but all in, and getting laughs. Finally, the brothers replace the amp and I return to my seat, the audience applauding.

"That was great," Lenora says. "You've obviously done that before."

"Once or twice," I say.

"You should be a comic," she says.

"And give up managing the toy department in Inkster, Michigan?"

Lenora laughs and her brothers begin playing, but my mind—my entire being—has entered a different *realm*. I'm somewhere else, thinking, planning, projecting, imagining. I have been adrift in Detroit for a year, and I finally ask myself—what the hell am I doing here?

I quit my job the next morning. I say goodbye and thanks to Lenora, wish her luck with her family *mishegas*, and move back to Chicago.

Joyclyn, my college girlfriend, graduates Kent State, and joins me in Chicago. We get an apartment together, she finds a job, and we agree on a plan. I'll work on my act and start seriously looking for paying gigs, while she brings in rent money and supports us until I get my career going. My mom is aghast. She hates that I quit my steady job in Detroit. But I simply can't put off my dream any longer. Thankfully, Joyclyn is all in. We're young and determined. I know I can do this. I knew it back in Detroit, even before I did that spontaneous fifteen minutes of standup while Lenora's brothers replaced their amp.

That night, I tuned into *The Tonight Show* and watched a new young comic do a tight, hilarious five minutes. He did so well that Johnny invited him to sit on the couch next to him. I said aloud, to the empty room, to the universe, "That should have been me." I know I can do this. I *have* to do this.

I bring that fire with me to Chicago.

Joyclyn urges me on, my mother wants to kill me, but I put my head down, block out every distraction, and go to work. I write and polish ten solid minutes of material, keep another ten minutes in my back pocket if I need it, and hit the clubs.

I start at the Comedy Cottage. I do well and I get paid, twenty-five dollars. Then I go to the Comedy Womb, get paid there, too, and then I go back to the Comedy Cottage and cash another paycheck. I become a regular working the Chicago comedy club circuit, twenty-five dollars here, fifty dollars there, all of which I hand right over to Joyclyn for a share of the rent and expenses. It's not close to equal, but it's a beginning. My mother remains unconvinced and unhappy.

"I wish you were using your college education," she says. "You can't be bringing in much money working these clubs."

"Mom, I'm just starting out. The money will come."

"When?"

I can't answer that. But her uncertainty—her wanting me to give up standup and get a steady job—drives me even harder.

Then I break through. I score a gig opening for the rock band Blood, Sweat & Tears. The band is chilling in their dressing room, but their hit song "Spinning Wheel"—*What goes up must come down*—plays in a loop inside my head as I bound onstage, the houselights in the theater still on. I smile and hit the half-empty audience with my first joke.

Nothing. Silence. The sparse crowd, with a few people now starting to trickle in, hates me. They would hate any opening act, I realize. They consider me an annoyance, an intrusion, an unwelcome surprise. I shake it off and press on. It doesn't get any better. I'm bombing. I wish they would turn off the houselights. I wish they would turn off *all* the lights. I'd be better off performing in the dark.

Somehow I finish my set, and sweat pouring off my forehead, I stagger backstage, feeling as if I've been beaten up, and then someone hands me seventy-five dollars in cash, my biggest payday yet. I say thank you and tell myself, it happens, you win some, you lose some, but you have to keep going, do not stop, push forward. Never give up.

One day, I bump into Johnny Britt, my friend from high school who played trumpet in the marching band and was part of our crazy jazz-funk band, the Soul Sophistications. Johnny and I haven't seen each other in six years. We reminisce about the old days in Cleveland and being musicians together. I bring him up to date about my standup and beginning to work regularly, and he tells me that Otis Williams, the founder of the Temptations, has just hired him to be the group's musical director. I invite Britt to see me perform at the Comedy Cottage. I'm hot the night he comes, the laughs rolling over each other like waves. After my set, Britt tells me that the Temptations use comedians to open for them sometimes and says, "But they don't do as good as you just did." *Click.* A lightbulb comes on.

My cousin Diane, who gave me my first book about magic from the library, knows Otis Williams. Diane calls Otis and tells him about me. Otis tells Diane that the Temps will be appearing at the Hyatt Blue Max for a four-night run. I ask Ed, the owner of the Comedy Cottage, for a favor. He talks the talent coordinator for the Blue Max into coming to see me on a sold-out Saturday night. I *murder* the Cottage that night and the talent coordinator books me for the Temptations' entire run.

I remember the night. I remember the call.

April 1.

Ever since, I've refused to do April Fool's jokes. Nothing about April Fool's feels funny to me.

It's late, around three a.m. I'm exhausted. I've just worked three shows at three different clubs, the last one the Comedy Cottage on River Road, same street as my mom's place. Too wasted to drive home, I decide to stay at my mom's apartment that night. I see myself yawning, opening the door with my key, and then crashing onto the couch. I fall into a deep sleep.

The phone jars me awake. Pisses me off. Why would anyone call this late? Must be some jerk pulling an April Fool's prank. The phone keeps ringing. Shit. They're going to wake my mom. Then I hear her pick up the phone and in a muffled voice, say, "Hello?"

Within seconds, her door swings open and my mom steps into the living room.

"Arsenio," she says. "You awake?"

"Yes," I say, sitting up.

"Your uncle's on the phone."

Her voice drops, and then she says, her voice cracking, "Reverend Hall passed."

That's how my mother always refers to him.

Reverend Hall.

My dad.

I don't believe it. I spoke to him a week ago. I talk to him regularly. I knew he had been sick—

"Did you hear what I said?"

My mother speaks softly, gently.

I nod.

And then I wonder—

Is this real? Am I dreaming?

I rub my arm. I feel my flesh. This isn't a dream.

I look at my mom. I blink, feeling my eyes fill up. I need to let out my tears, but I hold myself back. My dad always taught me that men don't cry.

"He was eighty-nine," she says.

I don't know where to look. At her? At my hands? I blink again and raise my eyes to the ceiling. My mom turns and slowly leaves the room.

Reverend Hall passed.

My dad is gone.

He desperately wanted me to be a preacher. He disapproved of my becoming a comedian. He hated Hollywood. I can hear his voice as we sat in front of the TV—

"Hollywood is a horrible place. Look at those shorts Chaka Khan is wearing. Sinful. Hollywood is a den of iniquity. A *horrible* place."

I also think he was afraid I couldn't make a living. I wanted to show him that I could. I never told him I was starting to get work, that I was making money, slowly but surely. That might have changed his mind. I think he would've smiled when he saw how the audience laughed and applauded for me. It would've reminded him of how his congregation swooned when he preached. Maybe then he would've felt better about my career choice. Maybe he wouldn't have worried so much.

Maybe he would've been proud of me.

I think he would have. He was proud when I performed my magic act on that TV show. Maybe I would've become his favorite comic. I knew how to make him laugh, doing jokes and imitating a visiting preacher from another church. He would've been proud of me. I know it.

That's all I wanted, then and now.

I wanted my dad to be proud of me.

8

I WISH YOU LOVE

CHERRY HILL. PHILADELPHIA. ATLANTIC CITY.

Sometime after the Blue Max four-nighter, I hit the road with the Temptations. Between gigs, I regale Otis, Melvin Franklin, and the other guys with anecdotes from Cleveland, including the story of my David Ruffin glasses and tales of my talk show in the basement and how I made "Get Ready" my theme song. Melvin, especially, loves my stories and we connect. He becomes the big brother I never had. He looks out for me, teaches me about the road, watches my back.

He tells me which barbershop I should go to at each stop. He knows the best and cheapest places to eat. He introduces me to his friends backstage, identifies who are merely hangers-on, who want something from you, and shields me from the cocaine dealers. Thanks to Melvin, I learn who to trust, who to avoid, and how to tell which is which.

After I finish my tour with the Temptations, I return to Chicago on a high, but still missing my dad. I lose myself in my standup. I hook up with a local Chicago agent and I land gig after gig, opening for the Emotions, working the ChicagoFest at the pier, the *Playboy* Clubs in Chicago and Lake Geneva, Wisconsin, and doing the Raleigh Hotel in the Catskills. I'm bringing in decent money, contributing more and more to rent and expenses. One night, after my set at the Comedy Cottage, my agent and I go into the greenroom, or as the owners more accurately call it, the kitchen, and she says, "I think I have a good gig for you. A one-nighter. I'll know tomorrow."

Tomorrow comes and the gig happens. She books me to open for TV star and Grammy Award–winning singer Nancy Wilson, who's headlining a corporate gig in the ballroom of the Conrad Hilton Hotel on Michigan Avenue.

I love me some Nancy Wilson. I watched her on *The Andy Williams Show* and I remember her appearances on *The Carol Burnett Show*. I love her songs "I Wish You Love," "Guess Who I Saw Today," and "(You Don't Know) How Glad I Am." She's sultry and sweet and can sing anything from jazz and pop to rhythm and blues. I can listen to her all day. This gig is a gift.

Nancy's working a convention and I'm told to do a longer than usual set, twenty minutes. I hit the stage in the hotel ballroom and after a couple of minutes, I am slaying. The conventioneers are drunk, happy, and into me. At the twenty-minute mark, as I'm wrapping up, I see the stage manager gesturing frantically from the wings. He's spreading his arms and mouthing, "Stretch!"

I go to my "back pocket" material and do another five minutes. The crowd stays with me. But I don't have a lot of material left. I look over at the stage manager. He shrugs. Nancy is *late*.

I do five more minutes, use up the last of my saver stuff, and ad-lib some material about what it's like being a Black comic working the Catskills. Now I'm dry, got no jokes left. I begin to riff, saying anything that pops into my mind, pulling stuff off the top of my head, out of my *ass*, and I'm still killing. I do odd impressions, Jimmy Carter visiting a Black neighborhood, one of the Pips performing alone when Gladys Knight goes solo. The audience is roaring, applauding, loving everything I say but—*where is Nancy?*

I look over at the stage manager again and incredibly, I see—

Nancy.

Standing there, in her stunning full-length royal-blue dress.

She laughs at something I say, and then she blows me a kiss. I introduce her, saying, "Ladies and gentlemen the two classiest words in the business of show—Nancy Wilson."

After her show, Nancy invites me to meet her in her hotel suite.

"I'm really sorry I made you go past your twenty minutes," she says. "But you are so funny. I wish my manager were here. We have to figure something out."

She pauses, thinks, then says, "I'm coming back to Chicago. I'm playing the Blue Max at the O'Hare Hyatt. I want you to open for me and maybe I can get John Levy to see you. No promises."

A few days later, I get a call from John Levy's assistant. John makes me a formal offer—opening for Nancy Wilson at the Blue Max, a free room, and seven hundred dollars for the run.

I nearly choke.

Seven hundred dollars?

And a chance to meet her manager?

I shout a thank-you to the assistant. Then I pace in my bedroom, my heart racing. I stop dead, realizing, "I need a new tuxedo."

I still wear the same tux I bought from Goodwill to do my magic show. The tux has become too tight, too short, too worn.

Before opening for Nancy—even before getting paid—I buy one.

On time.

Right on time.

I do four nights at the Blue Max, Thursday through Sunday.

Before my show the first night, I peek out from behind the curtain to see if anyone is sitting in Nancy's house seats.

How will I know John Levy? Who am I looking for? A really successful-looking guy. I read about him in *Ebony* magazine and learned that he's Black and was married to Gail Fisher from the television show *Mannix*.

John Levy doesn't show on Thursday. He doesn't make it Friday or Saturday, either. On Sunday, the last night, I peek out from behind the curtain, and in Nancy's seats I see an older guy in a beautiful suit, smoking a cigarette in a cigarette holder. I do a double take.

I feel as if I'm seeing a ghost.

The man in Nancy's seats—John Levy, her manager—looks like my dad. My dad with a cigarette.

My dad never smoked, but he was dapper and handsome, just like John Levy.

I shake off the sad, unsettling feeling that shoots through me and somehow get through my set.

Afterward, John Levy and I talk backstage.

"Nancy's right," he says. "You're hilarious."

I try to smile, but I keep staring at him. I want to turn away, but I can't. John Levy looks like my *dad*. But this dad loves instead of loathes show business. Hard to get my head around *that*.

"I'm semi-retired but I can get you some work," John Levy says. "You can open for Nancy and some of my other clients and friends, Joe Williams, for one, and maybe some dates with Aretha. But you have to move to L.A. You can stay in my guesthouse until you find your own place. You will need a full-time manager and an agent. I'll help you with that. I'll get you rolling. I think you'll do well—"

"Wait. Did you say I have to move to L.A.?"

"Sooner the better. That's where all the work is. By the way, what are you doing in two weeks?"

"Nothing."

"I want you to open for Nancy at Carnegie Hall, then go on the road with her for another week."

In my head, I'm screaming, *CARNEGIE HALL*, but I say, cool as I can manage, "Thank you, Da—Mr. Levy."

"John," he says. "Call me John."

I need to prepare for Carnegie Hall. For the next two weeks, I perform at the Comedy Cottage, Zanies, and other clubs, working up new material, sharpening the jokes I have, perfecting my timing. After my spot at the Comedy Womb, a comedian I've seen on TV comes over to me.

"Good set," he says. "You're funny, Hall."

I thank him. The comic has thick, wavy brown hair, a strong chin, and a distinctive Boston accent.

"Jay Leno," he says, offering his hand.

"I've seen you on *The Tonight Show*. I really love your stuff."

Since his appearance with Johnny Carson a year or so ago, Jay seems to be on TV constantly. His career is blowing up.

"How's it going for you?" he asks.

"Good. I just opened for Nancy Wilson."

"No shit. I used to open for her, too. I opened for her in Denver."

"I'm opening for her in two weeks at Carnegie Hall."

"That's a good gig. Hey, are you ever in L.A.?"

"I'm moving there," I say.

"Here's my number."

Jay pulls a pen from his shirt pocket, writes his phone number on a napkin, and hands it to me. "When you get there, call me."

I slide the napkin into my back pocket.

"I will," I say.

He's just being nice, I think. Why would a comedian who's on TV all the time want me to call him? I'm sure the number he wrote on the napkin is bullshit, a joke, the number for "Dial-a-Prayer" or some shit.

* * *

I can't move. I stand at the corner of 57th Street and Seventh Avenue in New York City and gawk at the building across the street.

Carnegie Hall.

Its multistoried, majestic Neo-Italian Renaissance presence looms above. Carnegie Hall is no mere music venue. Carnegie Hall is a musical cathedral. I feel dwarfed by its size, its scope, its significance. The week Carnegie Hall opened its doors in 1891, Tchaikovsky conducted here. Fucking *Tchaikovsky*. Tonight, I will step onto the historic stage of Carnegie Hall and do twenty minutes of jokes. I feel—

Fantastic.

Nancy's using a full orchestra—horns, strings, wind instruments, all of it. She leaves after her sound check, but I stay, watching her young musical director, Michael Wolff, as he puts the final touches on her arrangements. I take a seat in the front row and just watch. I'm mesmerized as Michael moves from section to section, from musician to musician, a wide smile on his face, pointing out charts to the bassoon players, the drummers, the violinists.

"Here, look, I'm putting a crescendo there, and then I want you guys to rest four beats, *then* the horns come in, like so—"

Michael, longhaired, a whirl of motion, connects with every musician in the orchestra as if he or she is a close friend. He's also a magician with the charts, constantly sticking the baton between his teeth and scribbling revisions and additions on sheet music. Michael is both a people person and musical prodigy.

When he takes a break, I walk over to him and introduce myself.

"It's amazing watching you," I say.

Mike thanks me and smiles.

"I'm about to say something crazy," I say. "Try not to laugh."

He laughs.

"Some day, man," I say. "I'm going to have a talk show on TV and I want you to be my musical director."

Mike keeps smiling. "A talk show, like Johnny Carson?"

"Exactly. I want you to be my Doc Severinsen."

His laugh fades, but he keeps his eyes on me.

"I know, you think I'm a dreamer, this is never gonna happen, but I'm serious."

"Well, I'm gonna say something crazy, too," Michael says. "I believe you."

I offer Michael Wolff my hand. We shake. An agreement. A pact.

We're on the road, in some Waffle House, when I first hear it.

A quick high-pitched squeak, coming from Michael Wolff.

I hear it and I dismiss it.

Nancy and I have killed at Carnegie Hall and now we're in the middle of another ten days on the road. She's gone to her room and I'm sitting with a few of the musicians, a bass player, a keyboardist, a drummer, and Mike. I often hang out with members of the band, usually these same guys. We go out after midnight for a very early breakfast, pancakes preferably. Tonight, I sit next to Mike. He picks up the bottle of maple syrup and pours some on his pancakes, and I hear it again.

That high-pitched squeak.

Unmistakable.

Then he spreads some butter over a pancake and he squeaks again.

He doesn't seem to notice.

He catches me looking at him, and says, "What?"

"Nothing, I just, nah."

I don't hear the squeak again that night.

I hear it the next night.

This time we're having midnight breakfast again, and subtly, but distinctly, Mike squeaks.

I don't know if I should say something to him or ignore it.

I ignore it.

We never discuss it.

It will be years until I find out that Michael has Tourette's syndrome. He actually doesn't know what it is, either. It appears randomly and relatively infrequently and I don't think it bothers him. It certainly doesn't bother me. It never affected Michael Wolff's ability to conduct or play with my posse, which is what I call the *Arsenio Hall Show*'s band. It will, however, nearly prevent the studio from hiring him.

I finish my two weeks on the road with Nancy Wilson and call John Levy to solidify my plans to move to Los Angeles. I break the news to Joyclyn, my girlfriend.

"I have amazing news," I say. "Nancy Wilson is arranging for me to move to Hollywood. Pretty exciting. You're coming, too, right?"

"Not unless you marry me," she says.

Okay, truth. For some time now, Joyclyn and I have been drifting apart. We've never really gotten back the closeness and heat we had in high school. We've grown up and grown apart. The intense young love we had has gone and we've become more like roommates. I'm certainly not interested in getting married to her, or anybody else.

"Lyn, I'm not ready to get married," I say.

Joyclyn storms off into another room and closes the door. End of a chapter. I'm turning the page. Joyclyn and I had a good thing when we were fifteen, but show business is my woman now.

9

ROACH MOTEL

I MEET TAYLOR AT one of the comedy clubs I'm working. She's older, divorced, and dreams of moving to Hollywood to become a writer. She hangs out every night at the club and we share our stories. Taylor's story beats mine by a mile. A former madam, she opened a brothel with her ex-husband, who somehow pissed off the mob. They dropped him down a trash chute in a tall apartment building in Chicago and killed him.

"You should write that," I tell her after we have incredible sex in the back of a rented truck. The sex should have been incredible. Taylor is not only a former madam, she used to train her hos. She introduces me to sex that goes way beyond what I learned in high school, beyond what I could ever imagine—"Quick, get a nine-volt battery and when the basket swings in your direction, touch my clit with it!"

I'm exaggerating.

A little.

After we have sex again, this time indoors, she agrees to share the driving on the two-thousand-mile trek to Los Angeles.

We leave Chicago on New Year's Day. Four days later, we hit the 101 Freeway, drive through Studio City, pass Universal Studios, and approach the Hollywood Bowl, which is flanked by palm trees on either side, a far cry from Cleveland.

"I've never seen anything like this," I say. "Orange trees and palm trees everywhere. I feel like one of *The Beverly Hillbillies* arriving here with Elly May."

As we turn off the freeway, I see a sign, "Next Exit, The Braille Institute."

I picture a group of blind blues singers wandering aimlessly on the freeway.

I write that line on a piece of paper, the first joke I write in Hollywood.

I drop Taylor at her friend's house in Laurel Canyon. We promise to stay in touch, but we won't see each other much after the trip. Right now, it's close to midnight, too late to call John Levy. I drive slowly down Hollywood Boulevard, taking it all in, feeling uneasy. The real-life Hollywood I'm driving through is far sleazier than the glamorous Hollywood I've seen on TV. I'm low on cash so I look for a cheap place to stay. I find a motel on the corner of Sunset Boulevard and La Brea called the Paradise. Perfect. I leave Chicago and two days later I'm in Paradise.

The motel room is tiny and smells of bleach. The rug squishes as I walk from the door to the bed. I decide to keep my clothes on, including my shoes. I lie down on the bed. The mattress buckles and dips to the floor. I feel like I'm lying in a divot.

I'm so tired I immediately drift off to sleep. I wake abruptly to a woman screaming and a man shouting. I hear a slap, someone running, then gunshots. I reach over and turn on the bedside lamp. I start to sit up. I stop. I feel something tickling my palm. I look down. A roach crawls over my hand.

"AHHHH!" I clap my hands, killing the roach. "FUCK!"

I jump out of bed, flush the roach down the toilet. I move to the center of the room, not knowing what to do, where to go. I don't know whether to get back into bed, or—

BLAM!

Another gunshot. Louder. Closer. Then a scream. A siren. Then voices of police squawking through a loudspeaker.

"I can't escape," I say, then my mind goes to—

Roaches.

I hate roaches. When I was a kid, living at my grandmother's, I killed a roach that crawled onto my face while I was sleeping. I freaked out. I told myself, "I have to get away from this. I have to get out of here."

Now in this roach motel, I shout, "Did you roaches follow me from Cleveland? Are you all part of the same family?"

Outside I hear, "Police! Let me see your hands!"

Screams. Shouts. Gunshots.

Welcome to Hollywood.

III
STARTING OUT

10

DINING OUT AT THE SUPERMARKET

FIRST THING IN THE morning, I call John Levy from a pay phone in the Paradise parking lot. John answers on the first ring, and, my voice quivering, I tell him I've arrived in Hollywood and ask him if his offer to stay in his guesthouse still stands. Those are the words I hear coming from my mouth. Inside my head, I'm screaming, *Help!*

That afternoon, I move into John's guesthouse. He lives off a twisty road above Sunset Boulevard, in Beverly Hills. This seems like the real Hollywood to me, a neighborhood where the stars apparently live. I assume that because I passed a guy on the side of the road, holding a sign offering "Tours to the Stars' Homes—Only $15." I'm tempted to take a tour myself, but I'm about fourteen dollars short of the tour price.

John and his new wife, Cora, greet me at his front door and walk me to his guesthouse. As soon as I put down my bags, I catch myself staring at him. I'd forgotten how much he looks like my dad. Salt-and-pepper mustache. A similar blueish ring around his brown eyes. Same smile, same mannerisms.

"Long trip?" John says.

"Stressful night," I say.

"You need to relax," he says. He produces a joint, lights it, inhales deeply, and passes it to me. I accept it gratefully. We sit on the couch in the guesthouse, passing the joint, talking about my trip and possible gigs he may have lined up for me—opening for Nancy again, doing a few nights with Joe Williams and a young jazz keyboardist named Patrice Rushen. He mentions something in the future at a club called the Roxy.

But as he talks, I just keep staring.

He is my father's twin.

That's where the resemblance between the talent manager and the Baptist preacher ends.

I suddenly crack up.

"What's funny?" John asks.

"I look at you and it's like I'm smoking weed with my *dad*. And that would never happen."

"Your dad didn't smoke weed?"

I try to conjure that image. I picture passing a joint to my dad, the strict, straight Baptist pastor, and mildly stoned now, I lose it. Then John loses it.

"No smoking, no drinking, no music, no TV, no movies," I say after we stop laughing. "But when I was five years old, he taught me how to clean a gun, a rifle, and a squirrel."

Now John stares at me.

I stare at the slightly smudged numbers written on the napkin I hold in my hand.

Jay Leno's phone number.

I'm sure he wrote down some random numbers, but I rapidly dial them anyway.

Jay answers the phone.

"Hello?"

"Jay, hi, it's Arsenio."

"Hey, Brother Hall. Where are you?"

"I'm in L.A."

"You made it. Give me the address. I'll come get you."

Jay arrives on a motorcycle, one of many he owns. I hop on the back, Jay hands me a helmet, I put my arms around his waist, we tool down toward Sunset, and end up having dinner at the Spaghetti Factory. We talk comedy, the Hollywood life, show business, working the road, opening for certain stars and how they treat you, some with respect, some with attitude, some as if you don't exist. And we talk motorcycles. Jay is obsessed with them and is a wealth of knowledge. I am intrigued and want to learn more.

From then on, Jay and I spend most of our free time hanging out together. At night, he introduces me to the comedy club circuit. We go to comedy clubs in Hollywood, Hermosa Beach, and Pasadena. We play the clubs and then either go out or hang out at his house high in the hills, right below the Hollywood sign. During the day, we haunt motorcycle dealerships. I go from being interested in motorcycles to longing to have one of my own. But I don't know how to drive a clutch, so Jay takes me to an empty parking lot and gives me motorcycle driving lessons.

"By the way, Hall," he says. "These bikes have handles behind you, see? When you're riding on the back, you don't have to put your arms around me like we're a couple."

One afternoon, we both buy motorcycles. I want to get matching ones, but Jay splurges and buys a Ducati, gorgeous, classic, and light-years out of my price range. I only have moped scooter money, and not even that. I have more like Schwinn money. At Jay's suggestion, I buy a Yamaha Vision 550, a bike that meets with his approval, meaning he can be seen with me when I ride it. I honestly don't know how I'll afford the payments.

One night, after we perform at the Hollywood Improv, having arrived on our bikes, Jay invites me to his house for dinner and video games. Jay, his wife Mavis, and I hang out in the kitchen for a while, talking, laughing, drinking wine, ice tea for Jay, who doesn't drink. While Mavis checks on dinner, Jay brings me outside to show me his pool and jacuzzi illuminated by overhead lights. I'm not merely impressed, I'm hopeful. A successful standup comedy career can bring you a house like this? A beautiful, manicured, lit-up outdoor area with a pool? I feel even more inspired, more driven.

"Man, your own pool, and jacuzzi."

"Unbelievably relaxing. Comes with a remote—"

I smell smoke. More than someone grilling. I look at Jay. "Do you smell that?"

I whip around. A black cloud of smoke rises from a neighbor's house two doors away. Flames shoot up the far wall, licking the roof.

"Holy shit," Jay says.

We race into his house.

"Mavis, call the fire department!"

Jay and I run out the front door and sprint to the burning house. He presses the doorbell and I pound on the door. No one answers. In tandem, we kick the door and break it down. We rush into the burning house, shouting for the neighbors. We burst into a back bedroom and find an older couple asleep.

"You wake them up," I say to Jay. "They need to see you first, not a random Black guy standing over them."

"Good point. You'll give them a heart attack."

We wake them up and lead them out of their house. A few minutes later, sirens wail and firefighters arrive. Jay and I watch the firefighters dousing the sides of the house, saving most of the structure, then we head back to his house, walking past several neighbors who have come outside. A few of them start clapping and the applause builds. I lower my head, feeling uncomfortable, but the crazy thought does occur to me, *Tonight Jay Leno and I saved two lives.*

I can't take advantage of John's graciousness and hospitality forever, so after a couple months, I move into my own apartment, a one-bedroom on Poinsettia Place near Hollywood Boulevard. John's working on lining up gigs for me. I'm not Jay Leno, but I am surviving. My dad left me five thousand dollars in his will and my mom sends me Hallmark cards from Chicago, with cash or checks stuffed inside. I'm beyond grateful to her, but her money comes with a price—her constant suggesting that I need to find a steady job. *I will*, I tell her. *I'll find a steady job—working as a comedian.* I say that part under my breath.

I work out every night I can, at any club who'll put me onstage—comedy clubs, disco clubs, jazz clubs, even a strip club. I earn anywhere from the low end—nothing—to the high end—twenty-five dollars a set, not a living wage, but where I am until John starts getting me more work. As I walk through each day, my body feels as if it's crackling with electricity. Excitement? Anxiety? Probably both. I blow off steam by roller skating from one end of Hollywood Boulevard to the other—roller skating has become all the rage—and playing pickup basketball at nearby Poinsettia Park.

No matter where I go, I bump into stars. I play basketball with Roger Mosley, who costars in the hit TV show *Magnum, P.I.* I do my laundry in the basement next to Steve Railsback, who played Charles Manson in the TV movie *Helter Skelter*. And while roller skating along Hollywood

Boulevard, I spot Carol Burnett coming out of a department store, about to step into her car. I skid to a stop in front of her.

"Miss Burnett, hi, my name is Arsenio," I say. "I'm a huge fan. Any chance I could get a quick picture?"

"Sure, Arsenio, of course."

I produce a small instamatic camera from the fanny-pack I always have with me and snap a flick of Carol Burnett flashing her warm, signature smile.

In a strange way, I feel as if these stars are unconsciously taunting me and inspiring me at the same time. This mantra bangs inside my head—*you could be a star, too, you will be a star, someday*. But right now I'm living in a small one-bedroom apartment on Poinsettia Place, adjacent to success, skating on the outskirts of show business.

I dominate at Poinsettia Park. Well, Mark and I dominate. Mark is Mark Jackson, starting point guard for St. John's University, who's home for the summer. Mark will become the New York Knicks' first-round draft pick, the NBA Rookie of the Year, an all-time great player, then a coach and TV announcer. At Poinsettia Park, he and I can pick any three random guys—it doesn't matter if they've never seen a basketball before or if they're old guys on a bench feeding the birds—and we'll dominate. We always call "winners," and thanks to Mark, we hold the court for hours.

One day, Mark leaves early and I play a final game on my own and I start to exit the park. I sidestep a group of people, kids mostly who are clustered around someone who's caught their attention. I get closer and see, incredibly, Muhammad Ali. He holds a Kleenex in his hand, which he flutters at the crowd.

"Okay, see, I have this Kleenex, right here in my hand. Now, I'm putting it into my palm. Watch very carefully. Don't turn away. Nobody look away—"

And the Greatest—Muhammad Ali—slowly, dramatically, begins stuffing the Kleenex into his enclosed palm and I think—

I am watching Muhammad Ali doing a magic trick.

Not only is he doing a magic trick, I know the trick.

I won't reveal it because I'm still a magician at heart. I'll say this. We used to sell the trick at Jean's Magic Shop back in Cleveland.

Now Ali opens his hand and the Kleenex has vanished.

The kids and adults watching applaud. The champ then does the trick in reverse, easing the Kleenex out of his hand, making the Kleenex reappear. Again, the crowd applauds. Muhammad Ali tosses the Kleenex to a kid who snatches it and clutches it to his chest. The champ bows, grins, and exits the park.

Years later, when he's a guest on my show, I'll remind Muhammad Ali that I once saw him entertaining a group of people at Poinsettia Park, by doing a magic trick—the disappearing Kleenex. The people watching him were riveted. I was one of them.

I continue to do shows with Nancy and I open for a jazz artist at a club called Concerts by the Sea in Manhattan Beach, and I do a night opening for Joe Williams at the Parisian Room, a jazz club on South La Brea Avenue. Joe is kind and supportive and, man, that buttery *voice*, but the crowd and I don't mesh. They're drunk and hostile and annoyed that they have to endure an opening act before Joe comes on. They've come to hear jazz, not an unknown comic. After my set, I stand in the back and listen to Joe, too. I know his records. Johnny Carson always puts him on as a guest. But his golden voice is even more dynamic and thrilling in person. Afterward, I tell him how much I loved hearing him sing. He thanks me and says, "Tough crowd tonight."

"Part of the game," I say.

Joe reaches into his pocket and brings out his knot. "The club pays you a hundred for tonight?"

"Yes," I say.

"You're worth a lot more than that." Joe peels off four one-hundred-dollar bills and slaps them into my palm. "I hope we work together again."

John hatches a plan to bring me more exposure. He puts together a showcase for industry insiders at the Roxy Theatre on Sunset Boulevard, which he calls, "Nancy Wilson Presents Arsenio Hall."

"I'm inviting everyone," he tells me. "Regency Artists agents, William Morris agents, Quincy Jones, Mitzi Shore, who owns The Comedy Store. It'll be your coming out party. I want you to do a whole hour."

Bold move, I think. *A golden opportunity.*

I better not suck.

I start working on new material, adding observations from the entertainment news I consume voraciously, and I start taking notes on what happens in my daily life. I hope this showcase brings me some work because my cash flow is on the verge of drying up. I cut corners everywhere. I'm down to eating my meals a few blocks away, at Ralphs supermarket.

I have a system. I grab a shopping cart and pretend I'm shopping, staring intently at items on shelves, moving slowly down every aisle. I put a few things in my cart to make it look like I'm seriously shopping. I even pause to read the ingredients on labels. It's all fake. I'm just biding my time until I get to the front of the aisle leading to frozen foods. Because standing there at a table, wearing an apron and a chef's hat, is a young woman grilling Jimmy Dean sausages on a portable grill. She has arranged a dozen or so pieces of sausage on a plate in front her, each one stabbed with a toothpick for easy sampling. I smile at her, pretend that I'm not interested in her sausages, push my cart past her, and then, acting as if I've had second thoughts, I double back, shrug, and casually grab one of the perfectly grilled pieces of sausage on the plate in front of her.

"Um," I say, after I scarf the sausage, giving her a look indicating that I'm both delighted and surprised. "Delicious."

She beams, I beam, and I swing my cart up the aisle to finish my "shopping." But a second later, I back up, slide next to the plate of sausages, and grab another.

"So good," I say.

"They're on sale this week only," the young woman says.

"Oh? I will definitely—"

I speak with my mouth full and grab another piece of sausage.

"One more for the road," I say, and then I look at my wrist, at my nonexistent watch, roll my eyes as if I'm late for an important appointment, and speedily move the shopping cart by her and up the next aisle.

I don't want to overdo it with the free sausage samples, or as I call them, dinner, so I hold off for a solid two minutes before I loop around and come back to the young woman who is now looking at her real, actual watch.

"Cannot resist these," I say, snagging another piece of sausage. "Um *um*."

I beam.

She doesn't.

She glares at me. She gives me a withering look that indicates I've been made. I'm a sausage thief. She narrows her eyes as if she recognizes me from *America's Most Wanted*.

"One more for dessert," I say.

I reach for the plate. She blocks my hand.

"This is your fifth piece of sausage," she says. "I keep track."

"It's only because you're such a good cook," I say. "I can't resist you, I mean, your delicious sausages."

She tries not to smile, but she can't help herself. And she is kind of cute—

"What time do you quit, you know, grilling sausages?" I ask.

"Fine, you can have one more," she says.

I grab another piece of sausage before she changes her mind.

"Thank you," I say. "I'll stop now. I think I reached my limit."

"Six," she says.

"That's my limit, six?"

"No, that's the time my shift ends."

For the record, we do go out that night.

I do my hour at the Roxy. I perform a bit about being so hungry that dinner for me is sneaking Jimmy Dean sausage samples at Ralphs supermarket while I push a shopping cart and pretend to shop. It goes over well. I also talk about current events and show business news. I do the bit I wrote about Gladys Knight and the Pips. I say, "Gladys is coming out with a solo album. If that happens, I'm not worried about Gladys, but I am worried about the Pips. Especially Bubba Knight. What is he going to do? All he knows is the background to the songs. He'll be in a Vegas lounge, doing choreography and singing, "'Leaving . . . ,'" and then I do some Pips steps, and sing, "'Whoo whoo, yours, mine, midnight train to Georgia, whoo whoo . . .'"

After my set, people swarm me backstage, I accept compliments and hugs and pocket countless business cards, and then, appearing in my peripheral vision, I see John, my father figure, grinning proudly.

Monday morning my phone rings.

"Hello?"

"Hey, Pip."

I hold the phone away from me for a second, then return it to my ear, having no idea who this could be.

"It's Q. Quincy Jones. I saw you at the Roxy Saturday night. You were funny as hell. I love the stuff about Cleveland."

"Come on, is this really Quincy Jones?"

"Yes it is. My good friend John Levy gave me your number. I loved your whole set. The supermarket stuff. I know what it's like to be hungry like that. And your Pip stuff was hilarious. That thing about Bubba. Ha! I know Bubba."

I don't know if it's him, but I go with it.

"Thank you very much, Mr. Jones. I had no idea you were there."

"I had to leave right after. So, I was wondering, have you ever been in a recording studio?"

"Never."

"Come by tomorrow. Hang out with me. Spend some time. I want to meet you. Does tomorrow work?"

"Absolutely, Mr. Jones."

"Good. And call me Q."

11

Q & A

SOMEONE BUZZES ME INTO the lobby of the recording studio. I sign in at the front desk then someone buzzes me through another door. I close it behind me and enter a maze of hallways. As instructed, I turn left, right, take another left, and then I find Quincy Jones engaged in deep conversation with another man, who I soon learn is the studio engineer. Quincy sits in front of a massive control board, an angled slab of electronics with rows of buttons, dials, knobs, and levers. He looks as if he's about to pilot a plane. I freeze in the doorway of the control room not sure what I'm supposed to do, where I'm supposed to go. Q sees me and waves me over.

"Come in, come in," he says.

He stands and rolls a chair next to him.

"Sit here. I got something I want you to hear. You're from Ohio, right?"

"Yes. Cleveland."

"We're going to listen to a guy from your way, Toledo, actually. New guy. That's next. First, I want you to hear what I'm doing now."

Q points to two large tape reels facing us. In black marker, the label reads, "Off the Wall." Q caresses a lever with one finger and the large reel whimpers, whirs, and rotates.

"Listen to this," he says.

A soulful, catchy intro to a song comes on, a sort of *ting-ting-ting*, then a male voice begins singing, but in a different way than I've ever heard, almost as if the singer's voice is a percussion instrument, then the singer howls, "*Owww*," and infectious dance music kicks in. My head bobs. I tap the side of the control board. I look at Q and I grin.

"You like that?" Q asks.

"Oh, *yeah*. That is funky, man. I really like that."

Quincy turns a different dial and brings the bass up. The funky dance music fills the room.

"Man, that is so good, *so* good," I say. "Who is that?"

"That's Michael, man," Quincy Jones says.

It takes a few seconds to register.

He's talking about Michael Jackson.

Michael like I've never heard before. Michael like no one has ever heard before.

The Jackson Five have gone their separate ways.

This is Michael solo, no Jermaine, no Tito.

"I'm working on something with Michael," Q says, tilting his head toward the large reel in front of us. I remember the inscription on the label.

Off The Wall.

Q brings the music up louder, and this 1980s funk sound washes over us, electrifying me. Michael attacks this song full on, a song called "Workin' Day and Night," his voice achy and strong at the same time, " . . . you got me workin' day and night . . ."

"Incredible," I say.

"Michael, man," Quincy says, shaking his head. "He's going to come back harder than ever."

Q plays several songs from the album—"Don't Stop 'Til You Get Enough," "Rock With You," "I Can't Help It," and "She's Out of My Life." I feel like he's giving me a sneak preview into greatness, which, of course, he is. *Off the Wall* will establish Michael as a megastar, selling twenty million copies. It will be the first of Quincy's three collaborations with Michael, the others being *Thriller* and *Bad*.

This seems otherworldly. Here I am, sitting at a control board in a recording studio next to Quincy Jones as he plays Michael Jackson's soon-to-be monster hits for me—me alone—not a record executive, not a music promoter, *me*, a twenty-three-year-old standup comic from Cleveland, who a week ago was stealing pieces of sausage for dinner at Ralphs supermarket.

"So, that's Michael," Quincy Jones says. "Probably releasing that end of this summer." Q hits a dial, stops the music, then reaches over, removes the large reel in front of us and replaces it with another. "Now, I want you to listen to this guy. He's one of the singers I'm putting on an album called *The Dude*."

"The Ohio guy," I say.

"Yeah, I'm gonna play you the scratch track."

"I'm sorry, the what?"

"It's a crude demo of someone singing. No corrections. No improvements. Really raw. Here we go. Brand-new guy."

Q eases up a lever, the new tape spins, and an absolutely angelic voice comes on, singing a song called "Just Once." I *feel* this voice. Exquisite. Honey-soaked. I hear Joe Williams as a tenor.

"Who is this?"

"His name is—" Q scans a piece of paper in front of him. "Here it is. James Ingram. Listen to this next one."

I lean back, close my eyes as James Ingram from Toledo, Ohio, sings, "One Hundred Ways." He scorches that song.

"He's got something, doesn't he?" Q says.

"Absolutely."

Q and I listen without speaking until James Ingram finishes singing on the scratch track. For a long time, neither of us speaks.

"Gorgeous," I say.

"Perfect word," Q says. He studies me for a second. "Question for you. Do you rap?"

"No, no, I don't."

"Ah, too bad. I'm working on the title track for *The Dude* and it has rap in it. I thought if you rapped, I'd let you try."

"I've never rapped," I say. "I only do comedy. I might try rapping someday, but, no, I don't rap."

"Okay," Q says. "Thought I'd ask."

I wonder if he's disappointed. Or if I've blown an opportunity. Q turns away and focuses on some dials on the control board. He seems preoccupied. I guess I could've lied and faked it. Maybe I can salvage the moment and say, "Well, you know, I rap a little," but I can't do that. I'd rather tell Quincy Jones the truth than try to rap for him and suck.

Then Q spins in his chair and faces me.

"By the way, I got rent for you," he says.

"I'm not sure I understand—"

"Meet me at A&M Studios tomorrow. I set something up for you. They're going to give you a voice-over job."

"For the record, I've never done a voice-over. Not even sure what that is."

"It's easy. All you have to do is read a sentence or two into a microphone. It's your first time so it'll be scale."

"That's fine. That's great. Thank you."

I have no idea what scale is.

I don't dare ask. I'll take scale. Scale is fine.

We listen to a couple more tracks, then Quincy breaks for a lunch meeting. I thank him and head home.

The next day, I meet Q at A&M Studios on La Brea Avenue, where he's producing an album by an R&B group called Atlantic Starr. He takes a seat outside a small glass booth that has only a chair and a microphone inside. He hands me a sheet of paper.

"Here's your copy," he says. "Go in that booth. When the engineer points to you, read it."

"Aloud, right?"

Q starts to speak, sees the grin on my face, and laughs. I go inside the glass booth and gently push the chair away. For my first paid Hollywood voice-over gig, I need solid footing.

Outside the booth, the engineer raises his hand, holds for a beat, then points at me. I take a deep breath, exhale, and read as convincingly as I can, "Atlantic Starr. Available on A&M records and tape."

"Nailed it," the engineer says.

I come out of the booth and Q hands me a check for six hundred dollars.

Scale.

Rent.

12

LADY MARMALADE

JOHN KEEPS BOOKING STANDUP gigs for me, but money remains tight. I fill out my taxes for 1979 and calculate that I grossed eleven thousand dollars. I try to cut down my expenses, stretch out that eleven grand. To save on gas, I walk or roller skate as much as possible. I limit my meals. I eat once a day, a habit I've kept even now. I no longer pilfer sausages at Ralphs. That habit I've given up.

To boost my career, John sets me up at the Roxy again, this time opening for jazz keyboardist Patrice Rushen, a stunner with a stunning voice. A few years later, in 1983, Patrice will receive a Grammy nomination for her song "Forget Me Nots." After my show at the Roxy, a young woman, Cynthia Gilbert, searches me out, finding me in the dressing room upstairs.

"You were so funny," she says. "I want you to meet Roy Gerber. I'm his assistant. I think we can help you take the next step in your career."

By now, in 1980, I've become a student of show business. I know who's who, what's happening, who's hot, and who's not. I'm very familiar with Roy Gerber. He manages Jack Jones, Diahann Carroll, and a host of other big-name singers. He even once managed The Beatles. Everyone respects and knows Roy. I later learn that Roy was the inspiration for Oscar Madison, the role Walter Matthau played in Neil Simon's smash Broadway play and hit film *The Odd Couple*. At the Roxy that night, I tell Cynthia that I would be interested in meeting Roy, but first I have to talk to my manager, John Levy. John encourages me to move on to Roy.

"Like I told you, man, I'm getting ready to retire. I can't do this shit the way I used to. I wanted to get you going. We did that. Now you got to move on. I can't hang out at The Comedy Store every night. It's tough. A waiting game. You go there, you work every night, they don't pay you, it's a showcase. It takes time to get you to open for bigger stars and get into TV. I don't have that kind of time."

I'm so touched by John. At the most critical moment of my career, John doesn't act like a manager or an agent. He speaks to me the way a father would speak to his son, the way I dreamed my father might have spoken to me.

I do move on to Roy—and Cynthia—but informally. I'm too impatient to sign with them or any manager. I play the field in a way, taking any gig that comes along, from Roy, or anyone who shares my dream, my drive. I land a good gig right away, opening for Jack Jones, a well-known pop singer and Grammy Award winner whose hits include "Lollipops and Roses" and the Burt Bacharach–Hal David smash "Wives and Lovers." We play an army base in Grand Forks, North Dakota, and a cruise ship in Acapulco. I come back to L.A. after opening for Jack, then hit the road almost immediately, playing gigs across the country, coast to coast. Over the next few years, I open for Natalie Cole, Tina Turner, Wayne Newton, Robert Goulet, Lynda Carter, Neil Sedaka, Lou Rawls, the Pointer Sisters, Vicki Carr, Dionne Warwick, Stevie Wonder, the "Queen of Soul herself" Aretha Franklin, and the R&B icon who becomes my pal, the glorious Patti LaBelle.

Patti.

The sister I never had and always wanted.

First, I'm a huge fan. For years, her giant hit, "Lady Marmalade," has taken up residence inside my head, the closest I've ever gotten to speaking French fluently. Live, onstage, no female vocalist moves me like Patti.

I don't remember how our relationship escalates to a fast friendship, but it happens easily and organically. I remember a night that may be the beginning. During a down night on our tour, while visiting Patti at her home in Philly, she and I decide to see Lionel Richie and Sheila E. at the Spectrum. After the show, a bunch of us congregate in Sheila E.'s dressing room. Patti is a force, but a quiet force. She comes across as shy, reserved, but somehow she makes everyone around her feel comfortable and at home, as if we're members of her family. This night she says, "If you all come back to my house, I'll cook for y'all."

We form a caravan heading to the LaBelle compound, Patti's limo the lead car, with Sheila E. following in her tour bus. That evening at Patti's house is a fog of delicious food and rivers of drink, then more food, all punctuated by constant, nonstop laughter. Patti and I bond to the point that I feel like a member of her family.

Back on the road, after almost every show, Patti and I go out. Patti loves food and restaurants, and so do I. We also discover a chardonnay from California called Patz & Hall. The wine is delicious, but we choose it because of the name.

That first time we go out to dinner, Patti waits until after the waiter serves our main courses, and then she reaches into her purse.

"Where'd I put that?" she says.

She digs into her purse. She angles it toward me and as she rummages around inside, I see several bottles of spices.

"Here we go," she says.

She pulls out a bottle of some special hot sauce. She removes the top and begins dribbling hot sauce liberally over her food. She catches me staring. "What?"

"You have a whole spice rack in your purse," I say.

"These places never spice things right. You know I like this hot sauce better than anything they're going to have. There. That should do it."

She replaces the cap, returns the hot sauce to her purse, and clasps her handbag shut. The second time we go out to dinner and she reaches for her bottle of hot sauce or one of the other spices in her purse, I lower my head, praying that the chef doesn't burst out of the kitchen, screaming that Patti has ruined his world-class pheasant and truffles under glass recipe, and kick us out of the restaurant. The third time she goes for her extra spice, I expect it. The fourth time, I hardly notice, and don't care. I've even adopted her practice. As a nod to Patti, now I, too, carry my own bottle of Tabasco whenever I fly or go to a restaurant and order a Bloody Mary. As Patti says, they never spice it right.

Patti likes to gamble.

Blackjack—"Twenty-One"—is her game.

One night, in Atlantic City, after dinner in one of the hotel's restaurants, we decide to hit the casino. Patti reaches into her purse and hands me a stack of money.

"Is this for dinner?" I say.

"No, no, no. Hold on to that. That's my gambling money."

"Your knot."

"My what?"

"Your knot. Back in Cleveland that's what Sweet Lou, my friend the pimp, called your money roll. He'd say, 'Just take out what you need. Never bring out your knot. That's how you get robbed.'"

"Okay, take my *knot*," Patti says. "But this is for my gambling."

She peels several bills off her knot, stuffs them into her purse, and hands me the rest.

"I want you to hold on to that, okay? I don't want it on me. When I gamble, I have a limit. I never go past it. Never. If I lose my limit, that's it. I go back to the room."

"Smart," I say.

"I want you to hold on to the rest of my knot. Here's the important part. No matter what I say, do not give me any more money. Do not give me the rest. Okay?"

"Got it," I say. "I will not give you any more money."

"No matter what I say."

I pocket Patti's knot and we go to the casino. Patti and I exchange a knowing look and she sits down at a blackjack table. I decide to scope out the casino. I wander toward the roulette wheel, watch red come up instead of black, move on to the craps tables and watch a young woman in a flimsy dress throwing dice. The dice land on her number, and the crowd of people crammed around the craps table roars and applauds. I continue toward several rows of slot machines. I make a right turn and Patti appears out of nowhere, blocking my way.

"Give me that money," she says.

"You lost your limit already?"

She holds out her hand and rubs three fingers together. "I need the rest of my stash. Give me my *knot*."

"No," I say, and move past her.

Patti comes after me. "It's my money. Give it to me."

I turn around and say, quietly, "No."

"Hall, give me my *money*."

"Patz, *no*."

"Are you serious right now?"

I turn to her and say, calmly, "Patti, you said do not give you any more money, *no matter what*. So, that's what I'm gonna do—not give you any more money."

"I don't care what I said. It's my money and I want it. I need to have it. NOW."

"Ms. LaBelle," I say. "You can have your money—when we go back to the suites. Now, if you'll excuse me."

I practically run to the bank of elevators at the far end of the casino. I don't look, but I can sense Patti behind me, desperately trying to keep up. We rush into the elevator at the same time, right before the doors close. We don't speak on the ride up to our floor. We don't speak when we get out of the elevator or in the hallway on the way to her room. When we get into the room, I smile at her, reach into my pocket, and hand her the rest of her money. "Here you go."

She snatches the money away from me. "I can't believe you listened to me."

She looks at the cash in her hand, then takes a long, almost lustful look at the door. I know she's thinking about going back downstairs to the casino. I also know that she won't go to the casino alone.

"I don't suppose you want to go back downstairs—"

"Nah," I say. "Kind of tired."

"Yeah," she says, "me, too."

She folds her remaining bills and slides them into her wallet.

"Hall," she says.

"Yeah, Patz?"

"Thanks."

I have long dreamed of doing standup and opening for a star like Patti LaBelle. But in my wildest dreams, I never imagined Patti and I would become so close that I would stay at her house. I not only have my own room, I become a sort of surrogate uncle to her ten-year-old son, Zuri. When Patti sleeps in, Zuri and I hang out. I take him to breakfast, shopping, and to get a haircut, just like any uncle would. Except we pull up to IHOP or the mall or the barbershop in a limo.

The folks around Patti—her staff and security—all get to know me and accept me as a fixture in Patti's life. I hear people describe me as "Patti's opening act and a very nice young man." One night in Vegas, though, I lose my mind and go all-out action movie star.

I love watching Patti's show. I especially love her version of "Over the Rainbow." During the song's intro, Patti, who's into clothes, comes out wearing a stunning fur wrap. Before she starts singing, she shrugs out of the fur, kicks off her shoes, and tosses the fur and shoes to fans in the front row, asking them to hold her stuff until she finishes the song, when the stage manager will retrieve them. This night, she tosses her fur wrap and shoes and a guy in the audience snatches them and takes off. He shoves past the people in the front row and runs up the aisle.

"Get him!" I shout, running after the thief, the stage manager running behind me.

I put my head down. My forehead burns. I'm insane. I'm going to get this guy. I find another gear, kick into a sprint. "Come back here! That's my sister's shit! Give it back!"

I pump my legs even harder and catch up to the guy right before he's able to exit the theater. I grab him at the same time the stage manager catches up to us. The stage manager, a big, burly Jelly Roll–looking dude, wrestles the thief to the floor, and pulls the fur wrap and shoes away from him, just as two security guards descend, haul the thief to his feet, and escort him away.

Breathing hard, I bend over and lean my hands on my knees. I look up to see the stage manager in the same position.

"You got some wheels," the stage manager says.

I huff, shake my head. "What the hell was I thinking? I'm not *John Shaft*. I'm a comedian."

"Patti's right," the stage manager says. "You are a very nice young man."

13

DESK PIECE

1982.

The Hollywood Improv.

I wait in the wings. The MC introduces me and I jog to the mic on the small stage of Budd Friedman's famous club. I hear polite applause, a tick above tepid. I smile at the audience. I hold for a beat to settle myself because I can feel my heart pounding.

"Good evening," I say, calming myself. "My name is Arsenio. It's a very unique name for a Black guy. In Greek it means Leroy."

The audience roars.

My heart settles.

I move on to my second joke about going to a rough high school in Cleveland that had the world's toughest cheerleaders—"I dated one named Bubba Ann." Ten minutes later, I conclude my set to an explosion of applause. I'm surprised, gratified. I wave and say God bless, as I always do, and dart off the stage.

Incredible because I'm not even supposed to be here tonight.

DESK PIECE

The only reason I got this chance to appear in front of a full house of talent bookers, agents, and studio executives, some representing shows such as *The Merv Griffin Show* and *The Tonight Show*, is that at the last minute Billy Crystal couldn't make it. Budd—or Roy or Cynthia or whoever's managing me at the time—thought of me.

It doesn't matter how I got here. I got here.

And, thank God, I *killed*.

Opening for Aretha, Patti, and all those other superstar singers has seasoned me. I know the road. I know how to play clubs. I know audiences. I've honed my jokes and I know which ones work. I have had years of experience now. I was so ready for this night. I had prepared for this opportunity for years. But I never expected this opportunity to come right now, out of the blue. Like so much else in life, nothing happens according to plan.

After this set at the Improv, my world opens up.

Everything changes.

TV comes calling. I get cast in game shows, a TV pilot, and get a shot on a couple of talk shows. I do a hot five minutes on *The Merv Griffin Show*. I dress to kill, wearing a dope new three-piece suit and tie. Merv, a gracious, sincere guy, corners me afterward, pumps my hand, and tells me how much he loved my set.

Then I fly to New York for a major breakthrough. I do *Letterman*, my first late night talk show. Always conscious of style and aware that Letterman draws a young, hip audience, I don't wear a suit. I go with a colorfully patterned pink-and-white sweater over a blue button-down shirt. Dave introduces me, his last guest that night, and I come on calmly, feeling surprisingly relaxed. I don't push. I don't rush and the jokes land. I start to roll, and I go into a joke about not being able to understand announcements spoken over the PA system in airports. I follow that with an impression of the guy who does that muffled announcement at LaGuardia and I get heckled. Yes, I have a *heckler*—on the *Letterman* show. A guy in the back of the studio audience begins doing his impression of the airport announcement. The fucking guy *mimics* me. Unreal. Who gets heckled on a late night TV show? Nobody. Never happens. But I've done a million clubs and I'm ready. I deal with it.

I laugh, shake my head, and say, "I work all my life to get on the *Letterman* show and I get a fat man who does impressions up there. Man, oh man."

The audience takes my side and roars.

I don't understand it. My friend backstage thinks this guy confused me with comedian Michael Winslow from the movie *Police Academy*, known as the "man of 10,000 sound effects." I'll never know.

I take it in stride and move right along, ending my set to a large round of applause. I wave to the audience and start to go offstage, but Dave gestures for me to take the chair next to his desk. He apologizes that he's run out of time and invites me back. As the show ends, he leans over and tells me that I handled the heckler well.

"We don't usually have hecklers," he says.

"My luck," I say.

After *Letterman*, my luck does change for the better. First, I go back on the road, opening for Aretha, Patti, and Dionne Warwick, and then I land a coveted quiz show—a primo spot, top row, center square. I'm among six celebrities starring in the new one-hour game show mashup, *Match Game/Hollywood Squares Hour*. Gene Rayburn hosts the *Match Game* portion and Jon "Bowzer" Bauman hosts *Hollywood Squares*. We shoot a week of shows in two days at NBC studios in Burbank. I'm styling, wearing a black suit and pink tie, sitting between impressionist Fred Travalena, who breaks into an impression and routine every time

Gene speaks to him, and Shawn Stevens, a young heartthrob on the soap opera *Days of Our Lives*. As I scribble words that match the contestants' answers to Gene's double-entendre questions, I attempt to coax laughs from the staid studio audience. At times I wonder if they understand English. Fred is on much firmer comic ground with his frenetic impressions of Frank Sinatra and Gerald Ford.

We shoot three shows, then break for lunch. I pass on eating in the commissary and go off by myself, taking my own private tour of NBC. I amble through the lot and then wander toward the soundstages housed inside what looks like a massive airplane hangar. I pass by people painting scenery, walk by a few offices where writers work on current NBC shows, until I arrive at a door marked, in small letters, "The Tonight Show."

I look left, right, and then I try the door handle, which I know will be locked.

The door opens.

I step inside the studio.

The lights are on. I walk down a narrow hallway with signed black-and-white photos on the wall—Bob Hope, Phyllis Diller, Dean Martin, Flip Wilson, Jimmy Stewart. I slide by the bleachers where the audience sits, pass an area at the side of the stage where trumpeter Doc Severinsen leads *The Tonight Show* band, and step toward the stage where every night Johnny Carson entertains America.

I stop at the edge of the stage. I breathe in the set as if it's air. The famous couch and coffee table that I've seen every night on TV face me. A painter's tarp covers Johnny's desk. Sprinkles of sweat bead up on my forehead. I hear a noise. I whirl around, expecting to see a janitor or security guard, but the studio is empty. The noise I hear must be the thumping of my heart.

I exhale, then I step onto *The Tonight Show* stage, and with my hands trembling, I yank the tarp off Johnny's desk.

I can't move. I'm in thrall. I stare at Johnny's chair. At his desk. At his famous pencil case and blotter. I feel my feet move. I'm walking slowly around the side of the desk.

I take a few more steps and then I ease behind Johnny Carson's desk and sit in his chair.

The chair fits me perfectly. It feels as if my ass is made for this chair. I shift, get comfortable. I pull a pencil from Johnny's pencil case, drum on the desk the way he does, replace the pencil, and say, "Well, this has been a great show. Good night, everybody."

I smile. Then I stand, look down at Johnny's desk, and instantly I feel lightheaded. I lean on his desk with both hands, waiting for the feeling to pass. After a few moments, I swallow, stand straight, look at my watch, and see that I'm about to be late for the shooting of the next two *Match Game* episodes. I push off from Johnny's desk, pick up the tarp, and cover his desk. I move to center stage, to Johnny's mark, where he performs his monologue every night.

"Hi, my name is Arsenio," I say. "It's an unusual name for a Black guy. But in Greek, it means Leroy—"

I teepee my hands in prayer, smile, and bow.

I step off the stage, begin to head out of the studio. I halt halfway and turn back. I take in *The Tonight Show* set again from this new angle, look at the tarp I put back over Johnny's desk, and with an edge of defiance, determination, and promise, I say, "Yeah, my name is Arsenio and I'll be back."

IV

TAKING OFF

14

PRYOR CONVICTIONS

IN 1982, THE FAMOUS TV programmer Fred Silverman, called "The Man with the Golden Gut," who had successfully run all three television networks, forms his own company and partners with MGM Television. He wants to launch this new company with a bang. He decides to produce a syndicated late night show to compete with *The Tonight Show*. He envisions a wackier version of the Carson show that will appeal to a younger audience. To host the show, he brings in Alan Thicke, a well-known Canadian TV and radio personality. Later, the show hires a little-known Cleveland comic as Alan's cohost.

Me.

Thicke of the Night debuts with a splash in September 1983. But the ratings drop precipitously and the show lasts less than a year. The show tries everything—sketches, singers, dancers, a recurring cast of comedians including Jim Carrey, Fred Willard, Richard Belzer, and Gilbert

Gottfried, controversial conversations with L.A. talk show host Wally George, even female mud wrestling. Nothing sticks except maybe the mud, and the ratings drop week after week. But Alan and I bond. We find we have a lot in common, from our addiction to macadamia nuts to our love of R&B music. At one point, I ask him, "How come you don't book any R&B? I know how much you love it."

"I keep getting pushback from the studio."

"Alan, I was in Cleveland last weekend and I saw this kid. Johnny Gill. He's eighteen years old. Man, can he sing. He's like a baby Levi Stubbs of the Four Tops. Why don't we step out of the box? Do the stuff Carson isn't doing. Offer an alternative. What do we have to lose?"

Alan books Johnny Gill. Johnny comes on the show, the third guest out, following an actress from the prime-time soap opera *Dallas*. Not only does Johnny do well, he gets ratings, which causes commotion, confusion, and possibly panic in the next studio executive meeting. Someone leaks this conversation to me—

"What are we going to do? We can't have Alan Thicke from Canada doing *Soul Train* the talk show."

They don't have to worry. The ratings return to terrible and *Thicke of the Night* dies the slow death of viewer indifference. But some good comes out of it. Johnny Gill and I hang out in L.A. while he's doing the show, we click, and have remained best friends, confidants, brothers, ever since, for more than forty years. Alan more than survives the cancelation of *Thicke of the Night*. The next year he stars in the hit sitcom *Growing Pains*.

Ultimately, the show helps me, too. I earn a decent paycheck, allowing me to stash enough cash to buy my first home. I purchase a condo within walking distance of both the Hollywood Improv and The Comedy Store for a hundred thousand dollars, the going rate, but a financial stretch for me. I can afford the condo. I just can't afford furniture.

I become a regular at The Comedy Store, the famous haven for both up-and-coming and well-established comedians. Mitzi Shore, who won the club in her divorce settlement from comic Sammy Shore, runs the Store like a benign dictator. She controls your spots, your times, your *life*, all while paying you twenty-five bucks a set. If Mitzi likes you, you work, and the town, meaning show bookers and producers, notices. If she doesn't like you, you die. Thankfully, she likes me.

Like other young comedians on the rise, my friends Howie Mandel, Sam Kinison, and Keenen Wayans, I work the Original Room. We all long to work the Main Room, but that's reserved for the big names—Letterman, when he's in town, Robin Williams, or legends like Richard Pryor. When Richard performs, Mitzi goes all out. She actually books both rooms for him—he performs in the Original Room and she reserves the Main Room for him to entertain his invited guests and entourage afterward.

Before or after our sets, Keenen and I hang out in the parking lot, adjacent to the Continental Hyatt House where movie stars and rock bands stay. One night, a car pulls into a parking space and a thick, imposing bodyguard in a suit climbs out and opens the driver's door for Richard Pryor.

"Excuse us, coming through, excuse us," the bodyguard says, leading Mr. Pryor into the club.

Seconds later, a Trans Am pulls alongside Richard's car and Burt Reynolds and Sally Field emerge.

"Park my car, will you," Burt says, handing the parking attendant a one-hundred-dollar bill.

"You see that?" I say to Keenen. "Mitzi pays us twenty-five dollars. I'll park fucking cars for a hundo. Let me park your car!"

After Richard arrives, I hustle inside, disappear into a dark corner against the back wall, and watch him do five brilliant minutes. Richard Pryor performs comedy as a kind of profane poetry, painting ferociously funny images leading to punchlines that tear into you. He jokes about

Africa, sex, the Mafia, fatherhood, and marriage. He pummels you with his genius. After his five minutes, Richard moves to the back, lights a cigarette, and murmurs to his bodyguard, "I got guests?"

"Yes, sir. Mick Jagger, Charlton Heston, Burt Reynolds, and Sally Field."

I saw Mick, Burt, and Sally. I somehow missed Moses.

Richard starts performing every night at The Comedy Store. He's working up new material for a concert film that will be called *Richard Pryor Live on the Sunset Strip*, adding five new minutes every set. And every night after he works, he entertains—Mick Jagger several times, Charlton Heston often, and Stevie Wonder, whom Richard's bodyguard leads by the arm into the Main Room.

"Richard's holding court," I say to Keenen as the bodyguard closes the door behind them. Soon laughter, loud conversation, and Stevie Wonder playing the piano drift through the Main Room's thin walls.

Man, I would love to be invited inside that inner sanctum to hang with Richard Pryor, but until now, the closest I've come is my nightly exchange with him in the parking lot.

"Hi, Richard," I say.

"How you doing?" he says.

Well, it's not nothing.

I do become tight with Johnny Witherspoon, a funny, seasoned comic we all call "Spoon," who always opens for Richard, and after a minute or so introduces him. I learn he's from Detroit and we share a family connection.

"I had an uncle in Detroit," I say. "He was a carpenter."

Spoon says, "I was a carpenter. I made cabinets."

"You wouldn't know Jethro McGee, would you?"

"He was my boss."

We laugh at the coincidence. It feels as if Spoon and I are now somehow related. After that, I gravitate toward him even more. I seek out his wisdom and soak up the stories he tells me about being a comedian and actor. One night, after a mediocre set, I say to Johnny, "I need some advice, man. I'm struggling here."

"You don't need any advice. Your comedy is good. Keep doing it. Get your hours in. The more you do it, the better you'll get. Just keep at it."

"I hear you. Thank you."

"Only thing I'll say is stay away from white women."

"What?"

"You heard me. Stay away from white women. That's the only advice I'm ever going to give you."

After that, whenever I come into The Comedy Store, Johnny makes sure to repeat his advice, "Good set. You staying away from white women?"

I assure him that I am. I have no idea why I should avoid white women, but I follow his advice—until I fall off the wagon. I go on a date with a young model, Pamela Anderson, who becomes a *Playboy* magazine "Playmate of the Month," an honor accompanied in the magazine by a glossy centerfold. I can describe Pam in two words—"hot" and "white." We go to dinner at Geoffrey's in Malibu. We sit on the roof at a private two-top called "the nest," enjoying a panoramic view of the Pacific Ocean from the Santa Monica Pier to Catalina Island. Then we hit a recording studio where Johnny Gill is working on a new track, and then on to The Comedy Store so I can do a late set.

When I walk into The Comedy Store, I sit Pam at a corner table in the back and go onstage for my set. I immediately lock in, blast off, and *destroy*. One of my best sets ever. I know I'm going to score twice this night. With thunderous applause roaring behind me like a tidal wave, I take Pam's hand. She's still laughing as I strut toward the back door of the club.

"You were so funny," she says, and then I see Spoon, arms crossed, standing at the back door, nodding at Pam, glaring at me. He shakes his head. "What did I tell you?"

One night, while I'm hanging out in the parking lot, Richard's bodyguard approaches me.

"Your name Arsenio?"

"Yeah."

He extends his hand. "Rashon Khan."

"Wait. Not Maung Gyi's Rashon Khan?"

"How do you know Maung Gyi?"

"I'm from Ohio and I knew him back then," I say. "I worked out with him for a year."

And then Rashon Khan, Richard's bodyguard, a guy so feared that everyone scatters out of his way when he approaches, bows to me and daps me up. "Did you study *bando* with Dr. Gyi?"

"Honestly, Mr. Khan, a little bit. Not like you. But I heard all about you. Your tournaments."

Rashon Khan shakes his head, smiles at me. "I can't believe you know Doctor Gyi."

The next night, Rashon corners me and whispers, "Richard said you can come in and say hello."

"What? Really?"

"You're a good brother, and you're funny," Rashon says. "You and Richard should know each other."

After Richard's set, I follow actor Bernie Casey and Burt Reynolds into the Main Room. Rashon nods to me and closes the door behind us. I slide against the wall, find a seat, and sit silently, my hands folded, not believing that Richard has allowed me into his inner circle while he holds court. I don't say a word. I don't dare. I'm not sure Richard even knows I'm there, but the next night, and the night after that, Rashon escorts me into the Main Room, and afterward, Rashon and I head outside. We talk about how I met Doctor Gyi at Ohio University, and we talk about Hollywood. Rashon doesn't trust people in general and definitely trusts no one in show business.

"How's it going for you?" he asks.

"Really good," I say. "I've been on the road with Nancy Wilson and I did Harrah's in Reno with Aretha. And I just bought a condo."

"That's nice," he says. "Now, next time Richard asks you how it's going, tell him all that. Stop that shy shit. Fuck that he's a legend. Talk to him like you would talk to anybody. He may give you some good advice. He's done all the shit you're doing."

"Thank you. Rashon, can I ask you a question?"

I wait for him to respond. He nods.

"The doorman said you were Richard's cousin. Is that true?"

"These peckerwoods get shit all mixed up. I'm Flip Wilson's nephew. Khan is my Muslim name. My very first job, I worked security for my uncle Flip. You ever meet him?"

"No, man, but I idolize him."

"You have to meet Flip one day."

"I would love that—"

As I speak, I see Rashon stare past me, and straighten his shoulders. Work mode. Battle ready. I turn and see Richard coming out of the back door of The Comedy Store.

"Hey, Arsenio, how's it going?"

I clam up. I try to say, "Good," but it comes out "Gfff."

Rashon jumps in. "Mr. Hall just bought a condo. His first place."

"You bought a condo? That's wonderful. Congratulations."

"Thank you."

"I want to see it," Richard Pryor says.

"Really? It's not far from here. I'd be happy to show it to you. I don't have any furniture yet—"

Rashon shoots me a look that says—

"Stop talking."

"Great," I say. "I would love to have you over."

"We'll drop by one day," Richard says as he gets into his car.

"I really don't have any furniture," I whisper to Rashon.

"Doesn't matter," he says. "Just get some Courvoisier. That's all you need."

One afternoon, someone knocks on my door. I look through the peephole and see Rashon.

"It's Richard," Rashon says.

How the hell did he get past our state-of-the-art security system? I don't want to know. There may be three dead rent-a-cops in the bushes.

I open the door and Richard bounces in. Rashon stays back, finds a spot in the entryway, and stands there at attention.

"Come on in," I say to Richard. "Sorry, I don't have a couch or anything—"

"You got something to drink?"

"Courvoisier."

"Good man," Richard says.

I bring out a bottle of the cognac and two glasses, and Richard Pryor and I sit on my living room floor. We sit there, in the barren living room in my empty condominium, for the next two hours, talking, laughing, sipping Courvoisier, and listening to Miles Davis on the stereo I've had since college.

"I love your place," Richard says. "I remember when I bought my first place. A lot like this. That's back when I was happy. Life was simple. Then everything changed. Now I got a big ass mansion in a gated community, pool, guesthouse, tennis court. I bought it for other people, not for me. Bought it for who I'm *supposed* to be. That's the house I'm *supposed* to have. No. I didn't buy that house for me. Not at all."

Richard and I hang out a lot more after that afternoon, most often at The Comedy Store. He keeps fine-tuning his live show—*Tonight I want to talk about something serious. I want to talk about fucking.* Richard is raw, real, and knows no limits. I'm inspired by his process, awestruck by his creative courage.

Richard always asks about my work. He monitors my career. He supports my every move. He watches over me like an older brother. One time, after his set in the Main Room, I say, "Richard, I got a gig. I'm opening for Chaka Khan at the Universal Amphitheatre."

"I love Chaka Khan's music," Richard says. "And she's fine as a motherfucka. Set me and Rashon up with some tickets. We're going to come early to see you."

As the opening act, I work the amphitheater with the houselights on and half the crowd walking in. I do fairly well at first, but during my last fifteen minutes, I catch fire. When I end my set, the crowd leaps to their feet. Chaka comes on and I head to my dressing room. I find Richard waiting in the hallway.

"You killed," he says.

"Great audience," I say. "They were into it."

"Nah, man, you were good. People stood up when you finished."

"Anything I can do better? I'll take any criticism you got, tips, advice, anything."

"Advice? I can't give advice to a motherfucka getting a standing ovation. Don't change shit. Keep doing what you're doing."

"Thank you. Sometimes I can't believe all this is happening for me."

"Stop questioning it and just live. It's yours. You're doing it. You're making it. Now live it."

From then on, Richard and I become closer and closer, through all the stages of his career, and mine, through his fights with heart disease and finally multiple sclerosis, diagnosed in 1986. During this time, Richard writes and directs an autobiographical film, *Jo Jo Dancer, Your Life Is Calling*, detailing his freebasing accident. He invites me to the set and I watch him direct, which is like going to film school on the fly. I shadow Richard as he deals with cameras, lighting, sound, blocking, script revisions, and the actors. Then I get cast in a six-episode summer sketch comedy show for ABC and I write a piece for me and Richard in which he plays his famous character Mud Bone, a wino philosopher from Tupelo, Mississippi. As always, Richard performs brilliantly, but even with him in the cast, the pilot doesn't sell. A few years later, Richard, Redd Foxx, Eddie Murphy, and I appear together in the gangster comedy film *Harlem Nights*, a career highlight for me.

Time passes, Richard's disease comes on hard, and he gets increasingly sick. It becomes difficult for him to speak, nearly impossible to move. His body shakes. He speaks in a whisper and a tremor. Doctors confine him to his bed. I call his ex-wife Jennifer, and she arranges with his nurse for me to come to his house a couple times a week. Richard and I watch TV, we talk comedy, and often he asks me about old friends in the business.

"I miss certain people," he says one day. "I miss brother Quincy."

"You want to see him?"

"Yeah."

I call Quincy and arrange for a limo to pick him up and drive to Richard's house. I leave while Richard and Q spend a memorable and emotional afternoon together. Another time, while we watch *The Steve Harvey Show*, Richard pushes himself up in bed and blinks at the TV. "Don't you think that guy looks like me?"

"Steve?"

"Yeah. You know, when I was young."

"He does, a little bit. Same tight afro. I see the resemblance."

"Yeah. Good-looking guy."

I don't tell Richard that Steve and I went to Kent State together and that we've renewed our friendship in Hollywood. I hit Steve up the next day. He's flattered that Richard Pryor thinks they look alike.

"Hey, man, let's surprise him," I say. "I'll pick you up tomorrow and take you to Richard's house."

Fred, Arsenio, and Annie Hall.

My godmother, Idella Branham, with Mom and Dad.

Young Arsenio at a neighborhood store buying a pack of cigarettes.

My dad bought me my first fedora.

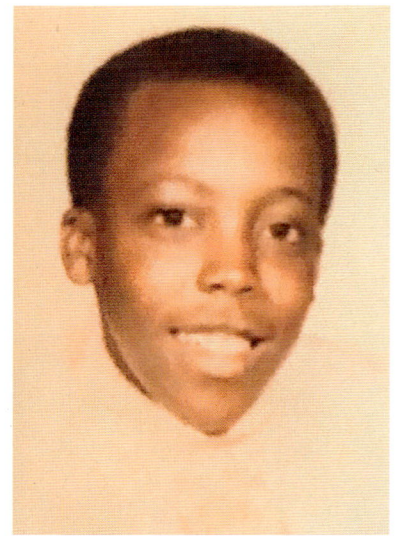

This is where I was born:
2773 East 73rd Street
Cleveland, Ohio
The top window, with the Kenmore
air-conditioning unit, was my bedroom.

Someone could have told me not
to wear a sweater that matches the
background for this year's school picture
(age ten).

My grandma Elizabeth Martin, who taught me to
love God, family, and the Cleveland Indians.

". . . One more thing, Santa,
I want to do stand-up at
Carnegie Hall someday."

In a mirror practicing the Zombie Ball illusion.

I think this photo speaks for itself. I was a weird kid. A magnet to the neighborhood bully looking to whip somebody's ass.

The linking rings look interesting, but even more interesting is the writing on the palm of my hand. I think I had a test that morning.

My last performance as a magician on a local Cleveland TV show called *Rap* with host Barbara Caffie.

Alexander City, Alabama, had an Annie Hall long before Woody Allen did.

Drummer in the Warrensville High Marching Tiger band.

I was no Travis Barker.
Thank goodness I found stand-up.

When I was sixteen, I had a singing
group called Rare Element.

The last photo at Grandma's house
before the fire in 1976: 8214 Dawn Ave.
Cleveland, Ohio.

That basement where I did my first talk shows:
3610 E. 120th St. Cleveland, Ohio.

Manager John Levy (and my mom).

At age thirteen, Johnny Britt and I started our first band as students of R.H. Jamison Junior High School.

Ball 'til you fall, daily. Poinsettia Park, where I first met Roger E. Mosley, Mark Jackson, and Muhammad Ali.

Richard Pryor, Mitzi Shore, and yo' boi.

Sharing my last laugh with Nancy Wilson.

Home of *The Arsenio Hall Show*. A long way from that basement in Cleveland.

Jay Leno and I on the day I got my star on the Hollywood Boulevard Walk of Fame.

Me and my friend Marla Kell Brown. Staff pajama party on stage 29.

Dana (Freedman) Walden and me (1989).

When I walk into Richard's bedroom with Steve Harvey, Richard lights up. I give them time alone, and when I return, Richard seems more animated than he has been in a while.

"Funny guy," he says. "And damn he's handsome."

I take Richard out when he feels up to it. Richard moves around on a motorized cart, which I load into my Range Rover. I take him to the Sherry Lansing Theatre on the Paramount lot for a private screening of Eddie Murphy's latest movie. I teach a summer comedy class for kids, and Richard comes with me and talks to the students. Through it all, even as the disease progresses and his symptoms worsen, Richard never loses his sense of humor.

Don Cornelius calls me and tells me that I'm going to receive the Richard Pryor Award at the Soul Train Comedy Awards. I decide to surprise him and everyone else and bring Richard himself to the taping.

I load Richard's cart in my Range Rover and carry him to the front seat. At the show, I bring him out of the car, situate him on his cart, and guide him toward the stage door. We come onto the stage together, both of us in tuxedos, Richard sliding along the stage on his mobility cart. As soon as he appears, the audience erupts and stands, their ovation booming through the Shrine Auditorium. Tears fill my eyes. Richard weakly waves to the audience. A woman in the balcony shouts, "I love you, Richard!"

"Well, suck my dick then," Richard shouts back.

Toward the end, when the disease becomes more debilitating, Richard's spirits sag, depression sets in, and he asks for favors that he knows the doctors have forbidden.

"I would love a cigar," he says one day.

I call Jennifer, get her permission, and bring Richard a cigar. We watch TV and smoke cigars, neither of us speaking, but I glance at Richard and see him inhale deeply, his eyes closed with pleasure.

Another time, after going to a strip club, I get an idea. Why not bring the strip club to Richard?

I get Jennifer's permission to have a private party with "exotic dancers" and then I tell Richard.

"Richard, I'm bringing over a couple of friends to do a show for you."

By now, Richard's hands shake nearly all the time.

"What kind of show?" he says.

"I'm bringing over some hos. Is that okay?"

"Absolutely," he says.

I make arrangements, set a price, establish a time, and two beautiful young women arrive at Richard's door. I lead them into the bedroom, where I've propped Richard up in bed. They recognize him immediately. I'm not sure who's more excited, Richard or the hos. I put on the music the strippers have requested, and leave Richard alone with his entertainment.

I return in time to find the strippers holding their clothes and a snowstorm of glitter filling the bedroom. I'm not sure what happened in there, but it involved more glitter than I've ever seen in my life.

I follow the two women into the living room, and the taller one, Chantal, the head ho, says, "Money."

"Oh, right, I almost forgot."

I reach for my money clip in my leather clutch bag.

It's not there.

I pat myself frantically, then I realize I left my knot at home.

"This is embarrassing," I say. "I forgot the money."

Chantal screams, "You FORGOT the MONEY?"

"I know. This looks bad. But it's a simple mistake. Can I get it to you tomorrow?"

"Can I use the phone?"

I point to the phone and watch Chantal's fingers fly as she dials a number. "Hello, Tony? Yeah, your friend Arsenio says he FORGOT his WALLET. Uh-huh. I'll tell him." She hangs up. "He's on his way."

"No, no, no. That's not necessary. I made a mistake. I'll get you the money later tonight. You know who I am. I'm not gonna ghost you for some bullshit money. How's this? I'll meet you tomorrow and I'll buy you lunch."

Chantal tilts her head and stares at me for what feels like infinity.

"I'll call Tony back," she says, finally.

When I tell Richard about forgetting my knot and almost getting killed being his talent coordinator, he cracks up. I laugh with him, thinking, *All I wanted to do was bring some hos over for Richard. Man, you try to do something nice for a friend.*

Richard Pryor, five-time Grammy Award winner, Emmy Award winner, the first recipient of the Mark Twain Prize for American Humor from the Kennedy Center in 1998, genius, legend, my mentor, my guru, my friend, dies of a heart attack in 2005. He is sixty-five years old.

I think about him every day.

15

BETTER *LATE*

IN 1986, I SCORE a gig on the long-running syndicated weekly music show *Solid Gold*. The show, which debuted with Dionne Warwick as host, has moved on to Marilyn McCoo, the former lead singer of the pop rock group the 5th Dimension and features the top songs and artists of the week, similar to Casey Kasem's *American Top 40*, but with dancers and my truncated two-minute comedy segment. Still, I'm on TV every week and my visibility increases.

I meet Eddie Murphy for the first time through Keenen Wayans, in front of the Los Angeles Improv. Keenen and I hang on the sidewalk as Eddie pulls up, about to pop onstage and work out some new material. He daps Keenen up, then stares at me.

"What's up?" he says.

"Nothing," I say, extending my hand. "Pleasure to meet you."

We shake hands, then Eddie shakes his head.

"Nah," he says. "You don't look like me. You think you look like me?"

"Not at all. Who thinks we look alike?"

"My mother," Eddie says. "She watches you every week on *Solid Gold*. She thinks we look like each other."

"I don't see it," I say.

"Yeah, me, either. Hey, I heard you were a magician."

"I was, yeah, growing up in Cleveland. That's all I wanted to do. I wanted to be a famous magician."

"Same thing for me," Eddie says. "Except I was a ventriloquist. All I ever wanted to be. Hey, I gotta go on."

That's the beginning.

From there, our relationship accelerates from zero to a hundred, going from meeting at a parking meter in front of the L.A. Improv to close friends, all in the blink of an eye. Just like that.

I become a regular at Carlos 'n Charlie's, a popular show business hangout on the Sunset Strip. One day, while I'm having lunch with a friend, Bernice, one of the owners of the restaurant, stops at our booth to say hello.

"I'm having lunch with Joan Rivers," Bernice says. "Come meet her."

I follow her to Joan's table. I introduce myself, we bond over friends we have in common, and we talk standup comedy. I, of course, try to make her laugh, and I succeed a couple times. I don't want to overstay my welcome—I'm all about leaving on top—so I apologize for interrupting her lunch and return to my table.

A few days later, I get a call from *The Tonight Show*. Joan is subbing for Johnny, a guest has canceled, and Joan has asked for me to replace him. Mitzi Shore, John Levy, and assorted agents and managers have all repeatedly tried to book me on *The Tonight Show* with Johnny, the goal, the *dream* of every comic. The show's booker has always turned me away, saying, "I'm not a Johnny guy." But I guess I'm a Joan guy. So, in March 1986, I appear on *The Tonight Show*, with Joan Rivers.

I love basketball. I'm desperate to see the Lakers play at the Great Western Forum in Inglewood, but I can't afford the insane ticket prices. Finally, I decide to splurge and see my first game. The Chicago Bulls and Michael Jordan have come to town and I'm eager to see Michael and Magic face off against each other. I stand at the box office window primed to plunk down my two hundred hard-earned dollars for one ticket to the game.

"Sorry," the woman framed in the box office window says. "Sold out."

I start to walk away from the window. A guy in an oversize Lakers jersey darts in front of me.

"Yo, I got tickets. You need one?"

"Where is it?"

He flashes me a ticket. "Good seat, man. Behind the Lakers' bench. Few rows up."

"How much?"

"Two fifty."

I don't hesitate. I fish the money out of my pocket, press the bills into the scalper's palm, and snatch my ticket. I instantly feel a rush. I'm *in*. Magic, Michael, Bulls, Lakers. The game's sold out. But not for me.

Once inside the Forum, I hand my ticket to the usher. "Where do I go?"

The usher peers at my ticket and points to some seats at the top of the Forum, then he gestures beyond them toward Heaven. "You see the band?"

I squint into the distance. "You mean those tiny people with those teeny instruments way up there? I'm sitting with the band?"

"No. You're a few rows above them and two sections to the left."

I begin the climb to my seat. I keep going up, until I finally arrive at my seat. I sit, lean back, and my head bangs against a wall. I am seated in literally the last row of the arena.

The players run onto the court for their layup lines and I try to identify them. They're so far away and so small I can barely make them out. There's Magic, I think. And "Big Game" James Worthy, maybe, Michael Cooper, I'm pretty sure. Byron Scott, possibly. And who's that brother with the glasses? Wait, that's Kurt Rambis. I'm so far up I can't tell a Black guy from a white guy.

Then the band starts playing—"Carry On Wayward Son" by Kansas. Brass, horns, drums. *Loud.* I have no idea who wins the game. But I do learn all the lyrics and every note to "Carry On Wayward Son." To this day, if you sing or hum that song, I will hurt you.

I meet a young lady named Tania and we go to dinner a few times. Tania is fine, fun, and loves basketball.

"Me, too," I tell her.

"You go to many Laker games?"

"I've been one time," I say. "I had a bad experience. I bought a ticket in the parking lot. I ended up in the very top row of the Forum."

"I can get us tickets anytime. Earv is a friend of mine."

"Who?"

"Earv. Earvin. Magic. He's a good friend."

"Oh, yeah? You two fucking?"

She swats my arm. "No. He's my friend. My buddy. Really. I'll call him today, right after his nap."

"He takes a nap?"

"Every day before the game."

Tania does call Earvin. "Hey, Earv, how you doing? Hey, can I get two for tonight? I want to bring my friend, Arsenio Hall. That's right. The comedian." She covers the phone. "He knows who you are."

I'm not sure I believe her.

Back into the phone she says, "Sure. Thanks again." She hangs up. "He says he wants to meet you."

Tania and I go to the game, and this time, thanks to Magic, we sit a couple of rows behind the basket. After the game, we go to the Forum Club, a private restaurant and bar reserved for VIPs. After a few minutes, Magic walks in and comes right over to us. He wears a sharp blue suit and a gray tie. He hugs Tania and then he hugs me.

"I saw you at The Comedy Store," he says, and grins. His smile really does hit you like a spotlight. "I go a lot. I don't advertise it, though. I stand in the back and then I leave. I love comedy. When the season is over, we should hang out, grab dinner or something."

Magic leaves Tania and me tickets to the Laker games and we go regularly. One night after my set, the guy working the door at The Comedy Store says, "Hey, man, Magic Johnson's outside. He doesn't want to come in. He wants you to come out."

I find him sitting in his Rolls-Royce, listening to KJLH radio, a soul station. I lean in the passenger window.

"I didn't want to deal with the crowd in there tonight," he says. "I got a game tomorrow. How was your set?"

"Just all right. I tried a lot of new stuff."

I tell him a Larry Bird joke I tried. He laughs, we talk some more, and he invites me to tomorrow's game. "I'll leave you two tickets at Will Call. You're coming, right?"

"Absolutely," I say.

From then on, Magic—whom I call Earv—and I become friends. I go to Laker games and he comes to The Comedy Store, always standing in the back, watching my set, and then heading out to his Rolls in the parking lot.

Once, after the Bulls beat the Lakers for the NBA championship, I walk through the tunnel in the Forum toward the locker rooms, and I pass

Michael Jordan's dad celebrating the Bulls' win, a historic moment, but the last championship James R. Jordan would live to see. He shouts jubilantly, his clothes soaked through with champagne. I keep walking until I find Magic. He sits alone in the Lakers' locker room. He doesn't look up when I come in. I take a seat near him, fold my hands, respect his silence.

We sit that way, silently, until every player, every coach and staffer, every member of the media, every fan, every employee of the Great Western Forum, every single person in the city of Inglewood has gone home. Magic won't leave. He won't talk. I ask him, finally, if he wants to go somewhere and eat.

"Not hungry," he says. "We lost."

He shakes his head. I can feel what he feels, his emotions pulsing across his face.

We lost.

We *lost*.

Unacceptable.

For Earv, there is only winning. Nothing else.

Finally—I don't know how long—we *finally* head to our cars.

Joan Rivers accepts an offer to host her own talk show called *The Late Show*, on the new Fox network. Not only doesn't she inform her mentor, Fox programs the show opposite Johnny. Word floats in the press and tabloids. "Johnny isn't happy." The show looks like a clone of *The Tonight Show*, complete with Joan behind a desk, a *Late Show* band to her left, led by Mark Hudson of the former teen idols, his siblings, the Hudson Brothers, and presenting two or three guests per night. Fox sees Joan as a fresh face, a woman late night talk show host, a rarity, her acerbic comedy the draw, the reason for the show. But nobody tunes in and Fox's late night experiment with Joan fails spectacularly. The network fires her in May 1987.

Fox doesn't know what to do to salvage the months they have left on their *Late Show* contractual commitment. They try a series of guest hosts to replace Joan, an astonishing twenty-seven in all, among them Wally Cox, Buck Henry, Suzanne Somers, Martin Sheen, Robert Townsend—and that's just in one week. One night, Frank Zappa gets sick and *The Late Show* calls me. They want to plug me in as host for that night. They ask me to pinch-hit for the pinch-hitter. I'm ready.

The announcer introduces me, the theme music plays, I burst onto the set, stop dead, look at the band, shake my head in mock shock, and say, "No, no, no, let's try it again. But like this." I request a James Brown type of groove, bobbing my head, slapping my thigh, suggesting a hipper tempo. Mark Hudson grins and catches on. He plays an impromptu guitar intro.

"That's it," I say. "You got it."

Then I run offstage, hold two beats, and race back on. Mark goes into a funky jam, and adds a lyric, "Arsenio, we be having a ball!" The audience goes nuts. At that moment, I feel the soundstage tilt. Energy shoots through me and the audience simultaneously. I'm making this house *my* house. Something's happening. Something new. I begin my monologue and then greet my guests like they've all come over to my place for a party. I play it loose, fun, not so different from how I did my talk show in the basement when I was a kid. Except now, I have LL Cool J, the Red Hot Chili Peppers, and my old Cleveland buddy Gerald Levert performing the R&B hit "Casanova."

Right after the show, the executive producer calls me. He asks me to guest host for the rest of the week. I say yes, trying not to scream.

Each night goes better than the one before. But I'm still a rookie, learning as I go, taking a crash course at talk show college. I find out that I'm a quick study. After I've hosted five shows, a Fox executive contacts me. They want to hire me as the permanent host of the show. Fox wants me to finish out the remaining eleven weeks of their commitment.

I pace at the other end of the phone. I am dripping with excitement. This feels like more than my break. This feels like *it*. What I'm meant to do. What I have planned to do all my life. I have been blessed with energy and imagination. I am not only going to think out of the box, I want to blow the fucking box *up*.

I explain all this in an impassioned speech to the director and a few other people clustered in the hallway on my first afternoon as host of *The Late Show*.

"I want the show to have a different feel," I say, my voice rising. "I want to play with the band, I want to do sketches, I want to go outside the studio and do remotes. I know we're playing catch-up, but let's go for it, really go for it. We got nothing to lose. And I promise you this, I will work my butt off—"

As I speak, I feel someone staring at me.

Eyes burning into me.

I turn and see a petite young woman. Her eyes are wide, laser beamed on me. She looks like she's barely out of high school. She must be someone's assistant, or some studio executive's relative, or the kid you order lunch from. I half-smile at her.

"And you are?"

"Marla," she says.

"Hi, Marla. I'm sorry, but this is a private meeting for the staff of *The Late Show*."

"I know. I'm one of the rotating producers of *The Late Show* and I think you and I would make a good team. I want you to consider giving me a shot at producing the show myself now that you're going to be the permanent host."

Now I'm staring at her. "You're a producer?"

"Yeah, four of us rotate, and it's my turn, so, yeah, it's me this time. I'm your producer."

I start blinking. "Do you have any, you know, experience?"

"Yes. I did a segment on *Hour Magazine*, and before that I did the tickets for Regis."

"Wow. How old are you?"

"Twenty-five."

"You look younger."

"I know."

I wave in the general direction of the soundstage. "What did you think of my—"

"I love it. All of it. It's fresh. Funny. And you're different. In a good way. But we're tight on time. We're shooting our first show today and it feels like we're two weeks behind."

"Marla," I say.

"Marla Kell Brown."

"Where you from?"

"Chicago. The suburbs."

I pat my chest. "Cleveland. The 'hood."

She laughs.

"Brown," I say. "Sounds like a Black name."

"Married name. I'm Jewish."

Now, this next part, I can't explain.

At that instant, standing with Marla Kell Brown, the tiniest, most subtle *force*—I cannot explain it, but I *feel* it—pulls me to her. I take a step toward her, a small involuntary movement that draws us imperceptibly closer. Linked. Like two magnets. I've been told I have a choice of producers, but I know, in my heart, with my entire being, that I don't really have a choice at all. Marla has claimed this space, staked this ground. Her ground. Our ground.

I'm the son of a preacher. I've lived my life either in the house of God, literally, spiritually, or at the very least, in close proximity to God. I know when God brings you someone. I know when God taps you on the shoulder and makes you listen, or see, or feel.

I'm your producer. I'm producing your show.

Marla Kell Brown.

Sent by God.

With all my heart, that is what I believe. What I know. I swear it.

We go eleven weeks.

Fifty-five shows.

A quarter of a year like no other.

A show that the suits at Fox have never seen, or imagined.

The ratings rise.

I interview Gloria Steinem, Don King, Jackie Collins. I interview Elliott Gould while we shoot hoops. I interview a former girlfriend, Emma Samms, from the prime-time soap opera *Dynasty*, flirting outrageously with her. I sing "When the Saints Go Marching In" around a piano with Emma, Magic Johnson, and Mike Tyson. The show blows through everyone's expectations. Then after one show, Marla asks me to dinner. She says she has something very important to discuss with me.

"I'll get right to it," she says.

We're at a corner booth in the Hamburger Hamlet on Sunset. Marla grabs some bread, rips off a piece. "I hate the desk. I hate that you're behind it."

"What are you talking about? Johnny's behind a desk. That desk is legendary, iconic. The desk protects me. Anchors me. Comforts me."

"The desk restricts you. I *hate* it. You're a standup. You're physical. You walk around. You move. The desk confines you. It's like a barrier."

"I'm not getting rid of the desk. I won't do it."

I don't say, *And that's final*, but that's what I imply, what I want Marla to hear. I'm her boss. I can pull rank on her. And I will.

Marla doesn't care.

"Arsenio, I hate the desk. And I'm going to talk you into losing it."

"Marla, it's a talk show tradition. Every talk show host has a desk."

"That's why I want you to ditch it. You're not like anybody else. You're different. I'm asking you. Do me a favor. Try it once. One show. Eddie Murphy's coming on tomorrow. Try it then. Lose the desk."

"No," I say.

"Yes," Marla says.

"It's my show."

"Mine, too. I am your producer. You have no idea how seriously I take that job. I produce the show and I protect you. I want one thing. A good show and what's best for you."

"That's two things."

"It's the same thing."

She's staring at me. She's staring so hard I swear I feel burn marks scalding my face.

It dawns on me then.

"You're doing this for me," I say, quietly.

"You bet I am."

I don't speak for a count of ten.

"All right," I say. "No desk. I'll try it once. *Once*. With Eddie."

Marla is so giddy, she practically bursts out laughing.

"Thank you," she says.

I won, she means.

Eddie comes on the show with no desk as a barrier between us. We sit side by side in cushy armchairs, we kick it and we kill it, causing both of us and the audience to dissolve into hysterics. Marla has made her point. I never again sit behind a desk.

After Eddie's appearance, as we wind down to the end of my eleven-week *Late Show* run, I basically throw everything but the kitchen sink at the show, comedically. I joke about Cleveland, restroom attendants, fashion, sports, culture, and I talk music with my guests, many of whom are Black. I approach every night as a party.

The show ends. Fox completes its commitment with *The Late Show*. I've surprised everyone with a new kind of talk show experience, an experiment really, a rollicking late night party. I've breathed life into a corpse. Fox has to be overjoyed. You would think that Fox would want to continue this hot *Late Show* run with me as its permanent host.

You would be wrong.

Fox apparently considers *The Late Show*, with me as host, as a placeholder. While Marla and I have been producing this fun party every night, Fox has been preparing a different show, a new entry into late night, a variety-comedy-news-hour hybrid hosted by two Seattle DJs, *The Wilton North Report*.

But I have been bitten. I love late night. It's my time. I've gotten a taste of having my own show and I want more. Some say I saved *The Late Show*. I feel that I at least revived the show to the point that I deserve a chance at my own show. Fox doesn't agree. They see the future and I'm not in it. They've gone over the moon about *The Wilton North Report*. The new network makes me a small offer, which my manager turns down. They come back with a second offer, but still no guarantee for my own show. Then Paramount brings me in for a meeting. They promise me that if I want to return to a late night vehicle, they'll gladly develop it. My manager sniffs around Fox again, asks for a more substantial commitment, financially and creatively, than they've made so far. They'll get back to us, they say.

"Sometimes I get the feeling they don't even know who I am," I say to my manager.

"Believe me, they know you," he says.

One afternoon, I have lunch with a friend at The Ivy, a famous industry restaurant and watering hole. I pay the check, and bound down the stairs to the sidewalk. I hand my claim ticket to the valet parking attendant, who runs off to get my car. A car pulls up, fancy, expensive, a Rolls or a Bentley, and the driver climbs out, a man I recognize—Rupert

Murdoch, president and owner of Fox. Technically speaking, my former boss. What are the chances? I nod at him. He nods back, his car keys dangling in his hand.

Wait.

Does he think I'm the valet parking attendant?

I want to say, "I'm Arsenio Hall. I saved *The Late Show* for you."

But I just smile. He smiles back, then turns away.

Yes. He may actually think I'm the valet parking guy. He definitely has no idea that I hosted *The Late Show*.

Awkward describes the next minute of silence that ticks by as the two of us stand together on the sidewalk.

Certain describes what I will do next with my career.

I sign a three-picture deal with Paramount.

I call Marla and tell her that I am going to do a talk show at Paramount and I am taking her with me.

"When?" she says. "Because they put me on this *Wilton North Report*."

"Doing a movie with Eddie first, then we go."

"Good, because I don't see this *Wilton North* turkey lasting thirteen weeks."

"We don't have a start date yet, or an official green light, we have a blinking green light, but it's happening. I know it. I feel it. And you're going to produce my talk show, right after this movie."

"What's the name of the movie?" Marla asks.

"*Coming to America*."

"I like the title. Sounds like a hit."

She's right about both her show and my movie.

Coming to America becomes Paramount's third highest grossing movie of the year.

Fox cancels *The Wilton North Report* after four weeks.

16

COMING TO AMERICA

EDDIE'S IN TOWN, RENTING a house in Beverly Hills. Eddie likes people around him, and one day, while a few of us, comics, friends, family—Keenen Wayans, Ray Ray, Fruity, Sweetwater, and MaBuda—hang out in his dining room, we start a conversation about the pros and cons of dating Hollywood women. At one point, Eddie says, "Did I tell y'all about this movie idea I have?"

He tells us about a "fish out of water" story he's working on in which an African prince and his bodyguard from a country he calls Zamunda come to America to find true love. He calls the movie *The Quest*.

"That idea is dope," Keenen says and we all agree.

Eddie proposes that I play the bodyguard. He continues noodling with the idea, creates a rough outline, and pitches the movie to the suits at Paramount. Ned Tanen, the president of Paramount's movie division, likes Eddie's idea, but wants something more.

"Characters," he says. "People love when you play characters."

Eddie scored big on *Saturday Night Live* playing several memorable characters, among them an adult Buckwheat, based on the kid from the 1950s TV show, old-time movie shorts *The Little Rascals*; Mr. Robinson, a takeoff on Mr. Rogers; and a pissed-off Gumby.

"Will you greenlight the movie if I put in some characters? Me and Arsenio, too?" Eddie asks Tanen.

"Yes."

Eddie and I go to work. We toss ideas back and forth, inventing characters. Eddie is brilliant at improvising characters, and at first I feel intimidated going toe to toe with him, but doing that ups my game. Then Eddie hits me in my sweet spot. "That preacher you do in your act," he says, "we got to come up with a scene in a church where you're a preacher."

Of course, playing that preacher is not a stretch for me because I've based the character on my dad. I picture him so clearly. I hear his cadence in my head, the way he worked the pulpit, shouting, whispering, pausing, holding the rapt audience captive in the palm of his hand. Playing a preacher in this movie inspired by my dad? I'm all in.

Then we talk about the neighborhood barbershops we went to when we were kids. I remember this one Cleveland barber who gave horrible haircuts. When he called, "Next," everyone rushed outside to smoke a cigarette. People who never smoked left the shop to avoid having him cut their hair. I'm not sure the barber ever cut anybody's hair. All he did was eat and talk shit for eight straight hours.

And so we create Morris the barber. Eddie and I begin riffing, spitballing jokes, inventing voices, talking to each other as two barbers, Clarence and Morris.

"Clint Smith should also be a barber," he says. "He can play that funny Sweets character he does."

Eddie keeps going. He improvises another character, an old Jewish man named Saul who hangs around at the barbershop, and then he creates more hilarious characters for insurance. He pitches all of them to

Paramount. Ned Tanen keeps most, and true to his word, greenlights the movie, which has been given a new title, *Coming to America*.

To write the screenplay, the studio hires two writers Eddie knows from *Saturday Night Live*, David Sheffield and Barry Blaustein, and I fly to New York to meet with all of them. One day, Eddie and I drive through midtown in his new white Corvette, his favorite Rick James cassette blasting. With horns blaring, pedestrians cursing, cops on horseback clopping, Eddie goes silent for three stoplights.

"We need a director," he says. "You know anybody?"

"Me? I've only been in one movie. I know one director. John Landis."

Eddie whips toward me. "That's it. Landis. He was good for me on *Trading Places*. Let's get Landis."

A good director and good writer, Landis feels like the perfect choice. He's come off a string of hits, including *National Lampoon's Animal House*, *The Blues Brothers*, *Trading Places*, *An American Werewolf in London*, *Three Amigos!*, and the groundbreaking music video *Thriller* with Michael Jackson. He began his career with *Schlock* and *The Kentucky Fried Movie*, and later directed my motion picture debut, *Amazon Women on the Moon*. The film, a take on the cheesy 1950s science fiction movies you used to see late at night on local TV stations, consists of twenty-one unrelated comedy sketches directed by five rotating directors, among them Landis. I scored an audition for John, reading for one of the skits that required singing. John laughed throughout my audition and called me the next day. "You didn't get the part," he said. "I went with David Alan Grier because I need someone with a Broadway singing voice. But you were so funny that we're writing a new sketch just for you. You're opening the movie."

In the sketch, "Mondo Condo," I play a businessman who comes home after work and discovers that every item in his apartment wants to kill him. The can of beer I open explodes and douses my face. My garbage disposal snags my tie, tears it to shreds, and pulls me into the sink, nearly strangling me. My stereo blows up. I settle on my couch, aim the remote at my TV, and the television blows up. I pick a magazine off a bookshelf and the entire bookcase topples over and buries me. I pull myself through the rubble of the bookcase, stumble around, stick my foot in my wastebasket, trip, and crash through the window, falling to my death on the sidewalk below. The sketch is a five-minute nonstop slapstick workout. Landis choreographed every detail and I loved every second. The day we wrapped Landis said that he wanted to work with me again. When Paramount signs him to direct *Coming to America*, I tell Eddie, "Landis is a fucking genius."

The first time I see Paula Abdul, I'm at a Lakers game, watching Magic going to war with Larry Bird and the Celtics. During the first time-out, as usual, my attention turns to the Laker girls. A moment before their dance routine, I spot one Laker girl in the middle of the group, fixing her hair. Ponytail, short, adorable. After the game, a Lakers' win, I describe the Laker girl to Magic.

"That's Paula Abdul," Earv says. "She has a man."

I let it go. Months later, Paula moves on from the Laker girls and becomes a go-to choreographer. Her career takes off when she lands Janet Jackson's MTV video *What Have You Done for Me Lately*. She goes from being a Laker girl to one of the hottest, most sought-after choreographers, and John Landis hires her for *Coming to America*.

Right before we begin shooting, Landis and I sit in his office, kicking it, getting to know each other better. We talk about different scenes in the movie, one in which he asks me to play another character, a woman Eddie's character, Prince Akeem, meets on a blind date. The script names the character "Ugly Woman."

"You want me to wear a dress and everything?"

"Everything," Landis says.

"We have a thing in my neighborhood about men wearing women's clothes. Kind of a taboo."

"Too bad because it would be hilarious," Landis says.

I take a moment and think about it.

"Don't tell my mother," I say.

"Maybe she won't recognize you," he says.

She does. And she laughs hysterically.

Day one of *Coming to America*. The table read. The entire cast, including Eddie, James Earl Jones, Samuel L. Jackson, John Amos, Shari Headley, Louie Anderson, and me, playing four parts—Semmi, Prince Akeem's valet and best friend; Morris the barber; Reverend Brown; and Ugly Woman—will read the script aloud around a conference table in 30 Rockefeller Plaza high above the city, in front of John Landis, the producers, Ned Tanen, and a sea of suits.

The table read begins in ten minutes.

I may not make it.

I'm four blocks away and I can't move.

I stand in the center of my suite at the Waldorf Astoria, the plush carpeting brushing my ankles. I stare at a piece of paper I hold in my hands.

A check from Paramount Pictures.

A check for one million dollars.

I caress my name and the number with my fingertips.

I bring the check closer to me and I read—

Payable to: Arsenio Hall.

In the amount of $1,000,000.

Monopoly money. Funny money. An advance on my movie deal. For a million dollars.

Is this real?

Can't be real.

I bring the check closer.

It's real. It's so real. And it's mine.

Slowly, gently, I touch the check to my lips and I kiss it.

Nine minutes to the table read.

I slide the check back into its envelope with the official Paramount seal embossed in the corner, walk to the closet, open the safe, place the envelope inside, close the heavy lime-green door, lock the safe, stare at the locked door for thirty seconds, and then I close the closet door. I leave the room and walk down the hallway. I press the "down" button, summoning the elevator and the beginning of my new life.

The table read ends and we—cast, crew, Landis, Tanen, and the suits—burst into applause. *We may have a hit movie here*, we all think, but no one utters that hope aloud. Cast and suits spring from the table and swarm Eddie and John. I want to say something to James Earl Jones, but the younger actors circle him, leaning on his every word. I decide to make a break for it, maybe grab some lunch, alone, which I prefer, then return to the Waldorf and hang out with my check. I leave the conference room and find the bank of elevators. A man I recognize, youthful, glasses, a kind face, intelligent eyes, stands in front of an elevator.

"Hi," he says, offering his hand. "Mark Landesman. Eddie's business manager."

"Right," I say. "Eddie talks about you a lot. Feels like I know you."

"He was my first client," Mark says. "Special for me. Special guy. Hey, would you like to grab coffee? I'd love to talk to you about your financial plans. Do you have a business manager?"

"I don't. I have an accountant. I meet him once a year for my taxes. I bring him all my pay stubs and receipts. I'm very organized. I keep everything in a shoebox. He's got an office above Kmart in a shopping center on Third Street in L.A."

"That all sounds great, but I'm thinking you need someone to look after you day-to-day."

I picture my check stashed in the safe in my hotel room closet. A million dollars. I have no idea what to do with that kind of money. Eddie has that kind of money. Mark is his guy, and as Eddie tells me often, thanks to Mark, his money makes money. Eddie has worries, we all do, but money ain't one of them.

"Sure, let's get that coffee," I say.

Mark and I sit at a table in the coffee shop downstairs. I'm immediately comfortable with his no bullshit manner, his low-key confidence, his sense of humor. He doesn't push, he doesn't sell. We talk business, lifestyle, life goals, my drive to succeed, my desire to host my own talk show. Nothing we talk about feels forced. Mark offers to jump right into my life. I not only agree, I want him to. I tell him about the money from Paramount. "I have a check for a million dollars sitting in the safe in my hotel room."

"Why?"

"I wanted to show it to my mom."

"Your first million," Mark says.

I look at him.

"You'll have more," he says. "If you're comfortable, give me the check. I'll take care of it for you. You're doing well right now, you don't need to dip into that money. Let's have that money start working for you. As for the check itself, I'll make a copy and put it in Lucite for you. You can frame it, put it on the wall in your home, or your office, you can show it to your mom, and eventually, to your kids."

"You're asking me to trust you," I say.

"We have to trust each other."

"Do you want me to sign anything?"

"No."

"That's it? No contract?"

"I ask only one thing. Don't ever surprise me."

"I won't," I say. "I promise."

Mark reaches across the table, and we shake hands, formalizing our "contract."

Our handshake agreement has lasted thirty-six years. Mark takes care of my money, handles every concern, business and personal. He takes care of *me*. Nobody knows me, the real me, better than he does.

And in these thirty-six years, I've never surprised him.

I've shocked him, but never surprised him.

We begin shooting *Coming to America* in the heart of winter in New York. John Landis is a whirlwind—loud, laughing, barking, inducing the best line readings, adding stage business, and when needed, cutting dialogue or rewriting on the spot. In one of my scenes, I see a tiny glimpse of John's genius. In the scene, someone knocks on Semmi's apartment door. I open the door and find myself facing James Earl Jones, Prince Akeem's father. In shock, I stumble through a couple of lines to cover that I'm hiding Prince Akeem inside. John calls "action," we start filming, I say my lines, and magic does not happen. After three takes, we both know the scene's not working. Landis calls "cut."

"You know what?" he says. "Don't say anything. Lose the lines. When the door opens, react like you would if a girlfriend you haven't seen in ten years—and you never want to see again—is at the door. Or react like you open the door and you're facing a hideous alien."

"Hideous alien," I say. "Girlfriend I never want to see again."

"Let's do one," John says.

He calls action, I open the door, step into the hall, see John, picture a hideous alien girlfriend, scream at the top of my lungs, then slam the door.

"Cut!" John yells. "That's the one. Hilarious. Let's get Mr. Jones on set."

* * *

A few days into the shoot, I find myself alone with James Earl Jones, one of the greatest stage actors of our generation and of course, Darth Vader himself.

"I wanted to tell you," I say, "I saw you do *Fences* on Broadway."

"How did you enjoy it?"

That *voice*. Blows me back five feet.

"You were incredible, man. I remember at one point you were crying, sobbing, banging on your chest, and you said, 'I am your father,' and you cried even harder and some snot came out of your nose."

He roars.

"You got so worked up, actual snot shot out your *nose*. That was the night I was there. I know you don't do that every night."

"Yes, I do."

"Excuse me?"

"I plan it. I shoot snot out of my nose at the same point in the play every night, like clockwork. It's called method snotting."

He looks at me so seriously that it takes me a few seconds to realize that he's putting me on—and then we both break up.

"You had me going," I say. "I'm thinking this guy's such a great actor, he can control the inside of his nose. He can snot on cue."

After that, Mr. Jones and I become friends. I'm so comfortable with him that I ask him for acting advice. In particular, I'm trying to figure out how I'll play the "Ugly Woman."

"First of all, play the character," he says. "Who is she? Who are you? Where are you from? What's your background. See the character as a *person*. Then when John calls action, plant your feet, stand firm, and tell the truth."

When I play the scene, back in L.A., I think about a tough, unattractive woman I used to see in my neighborhood, who worked for Sweet Lou. She scared the shit out of me. I picture her, conjure her, feel her. I've just spent serious time sitting in a chair while the greatest makeup artist of all time, Rick Baker, has transformed me into an extremely homely, scary female. Now, wearing a bright red dress and high-top Converse sneakers, I plant my feet, stand firm, and say to Eddie, with every ounce of truth in my being, "I'm going to tear you apart and your friend, too."

John calls "Cut!" and everyone in the vicinity loses it.

When we hold the premiere of *Coming to America* at the Chinese Theatre on Hollywood Boulevard, that line receives the biggest laugh in the entire movie.

To my unpracticed eye, the New York shoot seems to be going well, but when Eddie and I are in a scene together, I sometimes sense an uncomfortable vibe between Eddie and John. The dynamic between them seems fraught, tense. Eddie's personality and John's don't always mesh. John will sometimes offer a suggestion and Eddie will push back. I'm not concerned. The movie combines John Landis's genius and Eddie Murphy's genius together, scene by scene, a powerful combination.

On my day off, I'm feeling strong, I'm feeling adventurous, and a crew member has gifted me some outrageous New York weed. I make plans for the evening. I invite two women to join me for dinner followed by a private party for three in my suite at the Waldorf Astoria. I have long dreamed of having a ménage à trois. Call it high on my bucket list, maybe in the top three, and tonight's the night. I am about to fulfill my dream.

I'm happy, I'm high, I turn the TV on, I turn the music on, my two dates start making out on the couch, and I'm getting turned on, and then the phone rings. I stare at it. *No*, I think. *I'm not getting it. Not tonight. Not now. No way I'm answering that.*

But what if it's important, a family issue, a serious problem, and I find myself reaching for the phone, and I mutter, "Yeah?"

A man's voice bellows through the receiver.

"What the *hell* is going on out there?"

I almost say, "Well, right now two women are making out right in front of me and I'm about to join in," but instead I say, "Who is this?"

"Tanen!"

Instant buzzkill. I drag the phone into the bedroom, sit on the bed, and lower my voice.

"Mr. Tanen? Why are you calling? Is something wrong?"

"A tiny bit, yeah. The movie's *off*."

Now I'm on my feet.

"What? Why?"

"Why? Your buddy choked John Landis."

"No."

"Oh, yeah. On Queens Boulevard, in front of an entire crowd."

"Eddie *choked* John Landis?"

"That's right. And you know what John Landis did? He fucking *quit*. He walked off the movie. He's gone. It's over. Done. No. More. *Movie*. I think you should call your friend and check in on him."

"I definitely will."

I hear giggling from the other room, music playing, I picture the two women in there, making out.

"Would tomorrow work?"

I sigh, massage my suddenly throbbing forehead. "Yeah, no, I'll call you as soon as I can."

We hang up and I call Eddie. I start pacing back and forth across the room like I'm mowing the carpet, my heart thumping with every step. Finally, Eddie's cousin Ray answers the phone. I ask for Eddie, Ray puts me on hold, and never returns to the phone. I call the front desk and order a car. I slouch into the living room of the hotel suite and take in the two nearly naked women entwined on my couch.

"Ladies," I say, sadly. "I'm afraid I have to take a rain check."

* * *

Sitting in the back of a limo, driving to Bubble Hill, Eddie's house in Englewood Cliffs, New Jersey, I don't plan anything. I stare out the window, watching shadowy buildings whoosh by on Madison Avenue, until we crawl through Central Park, merge onto the West Side Highway and the Henry Hudson Parkway, and head across the George Washington Bridge. I watch the river below, shimmering, a barely rippling plate of silver, and try to sort through my emotions. Mainly I feel loss, a sense of what might have been, what should have been.

I can't believe no one will ever see that barbershop scene, I think. *Or have the pleasure of seeing me in a red dress.*

The car ride to Englewood Cliffs takes forty-five minutes. The car pulls up to a guard gate, I announce myself, and the guard waves me on. In front of Eddie's large Tudor house, I unfold myself from the backseat, walk to the front door, and knock. Someone lets me in and I walk into a cluster of Eddie's close friends and family—Ray, Big Fruity, L.A. Larry, Val the singer, and Val the dog. I go into the kitchen and find Eddie laughing and talking with Clint Smith, comedian and childhood friend who's been cast in the movie. Given Eddie's demeanor, you'd think nothing unusual or interesting had happened recently. Everything seems normal. But I know better.

I slide a peach Snapple out of the fridge and join Eddie's and Clint's conversation. After a few minutes, my head still throbbing from stress, I realize I need a drink. I look at Eddie and realize that he needs one, too, even though he doesn't drink. I nab two glasses, grab some orange juice from the fridge, locate a lonely bottle of vodka in the pantry, mix two screwdrivers, and hand one to Eddie.

"What's this?" he says.

"A screwdriver," I say.

"You know I don't drink."

"Yeah. Every other night of your life. Not tonight. We're both drinking tonight."

He looks at me, then takes the drink I hold out to him. For the first time in our relationship, I watch Eddie Murphy drink an alcoholic beverage, starting with the tiniest sip that's humanly possible. He swallows and makes a face like someone nearby farted.

"Tastes like spoiled orange juice."

"That's because it's orange juice. And vodka."

I grab the ingredients and start fixing a screwdriver for Clint. Before I finish, to my shock, Eddie hands me his empty glass. "I'll have another."

"Word," I say. "Right after this."

I reach into my pocket and pull out a plastic bag of joints I'd pre-rolled for the ladies back at the Waldorf.

"You know I don't smoke," he says.

"I know. Except for tonight. We're gonna smoke and drink. That's what we're gonna do."

I give a joint to Clint, then I show Eddie how to light his while I explain the inhaling process. I don't think he's going to do it, because he laughs, shakes his head, and backs away from the joint. He pauses, then he brings the joint to his lips, hesitates, and puffs cautiously as if the joint might explode. A second later, he exhales.

"Don't blow the smoke out. You have to swallow it to allow the weed to work."

He stares at me, and after a moment, he puffs on his joint and holds it in.

Eddie drinks for the first time, smokes for the first time, and I match him, sip for puff. We speak not one word about the day. We never mention Ned Tanen, or John Landis, or choking anybody, or quitting *Coming to America*. We drink and smoke and get high as a motherfucka. That is what we do. That is all we do.

At one point, hours later, all of us in his house shitfaced and stoned,

Eddie gets on the floor and wraps his arms around his dog, Val, a large, indeterminate mix of breeds contained in one live furry bundle.

"Oh, Val," Eddie coos. "I love you. I trust you more than anyone in the world."

Val wriggles out of Eddie's embrace and skitters across the kitchen floor, and we howl. We exchange stories, old and new, for hours. At one point, Eddie and Clint morph into their barber characters and we all lose it. Hysterical, dangerous laughter. That's it. That's all I remember.

I wake up on the black hardwood floor of the guest room, the sun streaming through a window, piercing my eyes. It may be morning. It may be noon. I can't tell. I sit up slowly. I feel as if someone has bashed me over the head with a Louisville Slugger. After a few minutes, I lean on my elbows, force myself up, and weave across the room, to the kitchen, in a desperate search for coffee, or food, something greasy to extinguish this hangover.

"I need aspirin," I say to myself. "I am never drinking again."

Later that day, I find myself back at the Waldorf, entwined in satin, fitfully sleeping off my hangover, when the deafening jangle of the phone slashes into my head. I answer and someone on the other end tells me that the movie is back on, Landis has returned to work, he and Eddie have met, agreed to a truce, or made up, or—I never do find out exactly what happened that afternoon on Queens Boulevard. It doesn't matter. What matters is that after two days of production purgatory, we pick up shooting the movie in New York, then return to Los Angeles and complete principal cinematography for *Coming to America*. We lock into a release date. Buzz builds. I agree to do publicity for the film, and then out of the blue, I get the call I've dreamed about, the call I've waited for my entire life.

The week the movie comes out, I will be a guest on *The Tonight Show*—with Johnny Carson.

* * *

July 21, 1988.

As I've said, I didn't want to do Johnny. I wanted to *be* Johnny. Now here I am, sitting to his right, promoting my new movie, *Coming to America*, the same way scores of other comedians and actors before me have come on to promote their movies. I glance at him, slick in his tailored suit, his posture straight as a soldier's, and I think, *He is even more dapper in person*, and then Johnny says into the camera, "We'll be right back with Arsenio Hall," and he winks his signature wink and I'm so giddy I nearly burst out laughing from sheer joy.

Then Johnny ducks under his desk, and I see a lit cigarette resting in an ashtray on the floor. He crouches impossibly low, snatches the cigarette and puffs on it twice, smoking it out of the audience's sight, our secret. It's like he's smoking heroin. Then he snuffs the cigarette out in the ashtray, straightens up, and says to me, "I heard you did magic as a kid."

"Oh, yeah, back in Cleveland. I actually wrote you a letter. I wanted to come on the show as a magician."

"What kind of stuff did you do?"

"Mostly doves, a few illusions, some sleight of hand."

He smiles. I show him the front and back of my hand and then I produce an English penny. I place the giant penny between my thumb and forefinger, close my hand, open it, and the coin has disappeared. Johnny laughs, reaches under his desk, and grabs a loose cigarette. He shows me the smoke, does a couple of clean, quick moves, making the cigarette disappear and reappear. I clap. Johnny shrugs.

"Nice," I say, and then we're back from the commercial break, the band kicks in, Johnny silences them with a wave of his hand, he mentions *Coming to America*, says good night to America, stands, shakes my hand, and like a ghost, or a magic trick, he's gone, vanished through the curtains.

FLYING HI

* * *

July 21, 1988.

As I've said, I didn't want to do Johnny. I wanted to *be* Johnny. Now here I am, sitting to his right, promoting my new movie, *Coming to America*, the same way scores of other comedians and actors before me have come on to promote their movies. I glance at him, slick in his tailored suit, his posture straight as a soldier's, and I think, *He is even more dapper in person*, and then Johnny says into the camera, "We'll be right back with Arsenio Hall," and he winks his signature wink and I'm so giddy I nearly burst out laughing from sheer joy.

Then Johnny ducks under his desk, and I see a lit cigarette resting in an ashtray on the floor. He crouches impossibly low, snatches the cigarette and puffs on it twice, smoking it out of the audience's sight, our secret. It's like he's smoking heroin. Then he snuffs the cigarette out in the ashtray, straightens up, and says to me, "I heard you did magic as a kid."

"Oh, yeah, back in Cleveland. I actually wrote you a letter. I wanted to come on the show as a magician."

"What kind of stuff did you do?"

"Mostly doves, a few illusions, some sleight of hand."

He smiles. I show him the front and back of my hand and then I produce an English penny. I place the giant penny between my thumb and forefinger, close my hand, open it, and the coin has disappeared. Johnny laughs, reaches under his desk, and grabs a loose cigarette. He shows me the smoke, does a couple of clean, quick moves, making the cigarette disappear and reappear. I clap. Johnny shrugs.

"Nice," I say, and then we're back from the commercial break, the band kicks in, Johnny silences them with a wave of his hand, he mentions *Coming to America*, says good night to America, stands, shakes my hand, and like a ghost, or a magic trick, he's gone, vanished through the curtains.

V
FLYING HIGH

17

WOOF HALL

I HEAR WHISPERS.

"Lucie Salhany, president of Paramount Television, wants to meet you. She wants you to do your talk show at Paramount, in syndication, like *Entertainment Tonight*. She wants to sit down with you as soon as you wrap *Coming to America*."

Previously, I saw spies. Paramount executives appeared in the audience of *The Late Show* at Fox. They came backstage and introduced themselves, gushing, "We'd love to sit down with you and talk about what you want to do next. Maybe grab dinner?" I even received a giant floral bouquet from Lucie herself. Then, the show ended, and I heard—silence. Crickets. Paramount stopped calling. It's like we were dating and suddenly they lost my number, even when the *Late Show* episodes I did received high ratings in reruns.

For now, I've dismissed the idea of doing a talk show at the new Fox network, even though for a while, they kept pressing me to do one there. I have had other suitors. Michael and Roger King, brothers who run King World Productions, pitch me the hardest, recruiting me over dinner at a fancy restaurant. They know syndication better than anyone, they argue, and they can prove it with one word. Oprah. They signed Oprah a few years ago, and her daytime talk show based in Chicago has blown up across America. Now, over dinner, they promise the same thing for me and even offer to have her call me. It's tempting, but I hold off. I have a lot on my plate, especially *Coming to America*. I would prefer to stay at Paramount because I have my movie deal here, and when it comes to my talk show—if I get my talk show—well, I'll do everything and anything to make it happen. I'm not proud. I'll host and executive produce and write and choose the band and call on my friends to be guests. I'll design the set, I'll build the set, I'll paint the set, I'll pick out drapes, I'll take tickets, I'll do *anything*. But right now, there's nothing concrete, nothing real, nothing discussed in detail, nothing put in writing. So, I lower my head and keep shooting *Coming to America*.

A few days after we finish shooting the movie, I drive onto the Paramount lot to visit Eddie in his office. I find a parking spot just beyond the main gate, below the enormous fake blue sky, and get out of my car. A well-dressed woman wearing a suit and heels appears right in front of me. It's as if she's been camping out in the parking lot, waiting for me. She extends her hand.

"Lucie Salhany," she says.

"Oh, nice to meet you," I say, and we shake hands.

"I want to have a meeting with you. Formally. Like now."

Direct, no bullshit. I kind of love Lucie Salhany already. But I play it cool. "What do you want to meet about?"

"Your talk show," she says. "I want you to do it here. I don't want you going to Fox or anywhere else. I'm sure you've heard all this from Mancuso."

Mancuso being Frank Mancuso, Sr., the CEO of Paramount. The head of the studio. The main man. The boss of bosses.

"I haven't heard anything," I say.

"Interesting," Lucie says.

"How did you know I was here?"

"I told the guards to call me as soon as they saw you drive on the lot. I raced right over from my office."

"I'm confused."

"Your manager won't let me talk to you. He's not allowing the meeting to happen. I decided to bypass him. If we're doing a talk show with you, I want to sit down with you, just the two of us. I want to get to know you."

"Why won't my manager—?"

I stop myself. I know that my relationship with my manager not only won't last, it just ended.

"I want to move this forward," Lucie says.

"Well, I wouldn't mind meeting in your office. Probably better than the parking lot."

"Definitely better," Lucie says. "I have a nice office."

"I'm sold."

Lucie and I spend two hours together in her office, drinking tea, discussing late night television, syndication, and my Cleveland upbringing. I learn that she, too, grew up in Cleveland, attended Brush High School, maybe the only school I didn't go to, then enrolled at Kent State for a year before dropping out. Ten minutes into our meeting, I feel like I've known her forever. Two hours later, I feel like she's my long-lost sister.

I never get to Eddie's office.

Instead I get a talk show.

Five months.

Twenty weeks.

One hundred forty days to launch a talk show.

From scratch.

I officially hire Marla. I insist that the two of us produce the show and that our names appear together every night beneath "created by" in the show's credits.

We agree to replicate the show we did at Fox—no desk, a nightly monologue, a hot band. I keep my promise to Michael Wolff and hire him as my musical director. I will do a show that features a ton of music, more music than on any other talk show, a wide range of musical guests, fulfilling my musical fantasies, from Prince to Placido Domingo to Dolly Parton. And in particular, as I did on *The Late Show*, I want every night to be a party.

Marla, our director Sandy Fullerton, and I stand in the vast, empty soundstage, stage 29, where we will shoot the show. Marla, Sandy, and I make an odd-looking trio. Sandy, dark-haired, a devoted equestrian who often wears riding pants and boots, and blond, five-foot-something Marla, who walks around stage 29 gesturing, while she pitches set design possibilities. I move to a section of the empty soundstage where I envision we'll put the band. Then I go to a spot nearby and face the two women. I imagine that's where I'll deliver my opening monologue.

"I'm not a stand-still monologist," I say. "I'm always on the go. I move. I jump up, I run around."

"I get it," Sandy says. "Like Michael."

"Well, a little bit like Michael," I say. "A *little* bit. But I'm glad you know what I'm talking about."

"I know exactly what you're talking about," Sandy says.

Sandy knows better than anyone. Sandy directed Michael Jackson in his early videos. That's how I found her. I remember watching the videos and thinking, *This director really captures Michael.* I identified her, told Marla I wanted her for the talk show, and Marla tracked her down.

As Sandy aims two fingers at me like a camera, she says, "I know what you want."

Then Sandy, Marla, and I bat around design ideas—overstuffed armchair for me, no desk, a couch, a shimmery curtain as the backdrop. I drift toward the spot where we imagine we'll put the band.

"I want the band to be present, visible at all times," I say. "Not many pieces, four, five, all surrounding Mike, who'll be in the center. I don't want them hidden at all."

I point to an area right behind where I picture the band.

"I see a small section there, set off from the rest of the audience, only a few rows, ten seats or so, like groupies for the band."

Sandy understands immediately. "You're from Cleveland. That's your Dog Pound."

"My Dog Pound," I say.

"Woof," Marla says.

"Exactly," I say. "Woof, woof."

I don't know then that making the sound of dogs barking will become my signature.

18

IT'S HALL OR NOTHING

TO MAKE THE SHOW work, I need the best people around me, an all-star team. I run everybody by Marla first, then Lucie, and they always agree. I never have an issue. Except once, with Michael Wolff, my musical director, the head of my posse. I see Michael as the pulse of the show, the heartbeat. I made a promise to him years ago at Carnegie Hall and I intend to keep my promise. But I make a mistake. I tell Marla that he has Tourette's.

"He has *what*?" she says. "You cannot. He's going to be on camera every night, multiple times. What if he goes off and starts randomly swearing?"

"It's not like that. He has a vocal tic. Like a little squeak, that's all. You can't even notice."

"I don't think our musical director should squeak."

"I'm not budging on this," I say. "I have to have him."

"Let's at least run it by Lucie."

"Fine. Let's go to her office."

"He has *Tourette's?*" Lucie says. "What if he says *fuck* on camera?"

"That's what I said," Marla says.

"He won't," I say.

"Are you digging in on this?"

"Yes. Nonnegotiable."

"There are lots of really good musical directors available," Lucie says.

"Not as good as Mike."

Lucie and Marla look at each other. They shake their heads simultaneously.

"Okay," Lucie says. "If he's who you want."

"He's who I need," I say.

Two seconds after I have an office and a deal, even before I hire Marla, I hire Cheryl Bonacci to be my assistant. Cheryl becomes much more—my right hand, my confidante, and eventually, the mother of my son. I met Cheryl on *The Late Show* at Fox. She was Marla's assistant. We remained friends after the show ended. I constantly call up three little words she says to me whenever I display the tiniest shred of doubt about the show.

"Bet on yourself," she says.

"You cool that I stole Cheryl?" I ask Marla now.

Marla rolls her eyes, a gesture she will make at least a thousand more times in the next six years. "Of course I am. I'll get another assistant. No problem. I know you hired Cheryl because she's really good, not because she's cute."

Now I roll my eyes at her.

But she's right, on both counts.

Mark Landesman and I sit at dinner, planning the future. *The Arsenio Hall Show* debuts in less than three months, but the future, including the show and beyond, financially and otherwise, looms over us. Since

Lucie gave the go-ahead, I have been obsessed with forming my all-star team, the team that can't lose, while also doing my job, polishing my standup, working out at The Comedy Store, three, four times a week.

"I'm just a comic on the verge," I say. "I have *nothing*. I also have nothing to lose. I have no children. I am going to bet on myself because if I win, I win big. If I lose, only I get hurt."

"I'm going to make it so you can't lose. At least financially. That's my job."

"How?"

"They won't give you a piece of the show, exactly. No ownership. We have to go in another door. I think we should ask for profit participation, but in a different way. I want you to be attached to the ratings. An incentive, on top of your salary. If the ratings go up, you get more money. They'll go for that."

"You think so?"

"Yes. Because *The Pat Sajak Show* premieres on CBS a week after us, and everybody, even Paramount, believes that's the horse to bet on."

"Not Lucie."

"No. She believes in you. Big-time. It's not personal for the studio. It's more about the challenges of syndication."

"Attached to the ratings," I say. "I like it. I could bust out."

"You'll have to work harder," Mark says. "Sajak has a big advantage. He's likable, he's well known from his years hosting *Wheel of Fortune*. Plus, he has a network behind him. If he has a guest who's starring in a movie, the *CBS Mornings* show will have the same guest, plugging her movie. So, which late night show does her agent, manager, and the movie studio want her to go on? The one with the cross-pollination."

"You know what Robin Williams said to me last night at The Comedy Store? He said syndication is like masturbating with sandpaper. You'll get there, but it's going to hurt."

"Perfect definition," Mark says.

"That's why I'm building this all-pro team to get me there."

"You need to add another player. Someone who can publicize you, protect you, put out fires. A PR crisis manager."

I recall a conversation that *Soul Train*'s Don Cornelius and I had about syndication.

"They're going to send dogs after you," Don said. "Make sure you have dogs of your own. Find the smartest person you can, someone you trust, and pay them. They need to work for you. Don't let Paramount hire them. Pay them yourself."

Paramount has assigned us a PR firm, on their payroll, and I've become increasingly impressed with a young member of their team, Dana Freedman, who often covers our show. I'm so impressed with whip-smart, savvy Dana that I request her permanently. Dana is present, on top of every crisis, and seems to have the answer for everything. One time she says to me, "Anything I don't know, I'll find out." It becomes obvious quickly that I need her on my side to take care of me, and to deal with the suits. She's so good at telling me how to deal with them that I soon refer to her as my "Caucasian whisperer." Finally, the recently formed Arsenio Hall Communications hires Dana Freedman as our own PR person. I pay her out of my own pocket.

I've now filled the roster of my all-star team, led by my three captains, Marla, Lucie, and Dana. I call them Arsenio's Angels.

Quincy Jones is adamant.

"Make sure you write your own theme song. Put it on that tape recorder you have. And when the studio tells you they want to hire somebody to write your theme, tell them you already did it yourself, you got your song, and you play it for them."

"I don't know if I can write any kind of song, Q. Especially a theme song for TV."

"You can, Pip. You absolutely can. Look, you were in the marching band, right?"

"Yeah. I played drums. I played bass in my own band, too."

"Okay, so sit down at the piano and just pick out your melody. You know the notes on the piano?"

"I do."

"Good. You pick out each note and write it down on a piece of paper."

He catches me staring off into space, because he says, "You don't need a violin section, you know? Or harmonies. Nothing like that. Simple. The main melody. That's all you need."

"I don't know," I say.

"Get the melody, the chorus, then back again, melody and chorus. Don't overthink it. Just *feel* it."

"I'll try," I say.

The next day a messenger arrives at the door of my condo with a gift from Quincy, a portable keyboard. I place the keyboard on my dining room table and stare at it for a solid minute. Then I back away from it and start walking. I take a loop around the living room, come back to the dining room table, bend over the keyboard and stare at it again. I pull up a chair and tinker with the keys, playing a note, a chord, jabbing, poking, prodding, trying out the keyboard, getting the feel. Finally, I crane my neck, and ponder the ceiling.

I need a story.

That's what I do. I tell stories.

I consider what many reporters, media critics, and celebrities such as Howard Stern have said and written about me since the press announced my new show. A storm of shit. For no reason.

"Who is this guy?" Howard, the self-proclaimed "King of All Media," asked on his number-one-rated radio show.

Then he and other critics went harder—

"He won't make it. He'll be another Alan Thicke."

"He'll never compete with Pat Sajak."

"Everybody loves Pat."

"Arsenio's in syndication. That will never work."

On and on, adding up to how much I suck.

I'm a human punching bag.

What the fuck?

They haven't seen the show yet.

We haven't *had* the show yet.

Nobody knows me.

They don't know me.

I write to that.

My story pours out of me. A challenge to those critics, reporters, to Howard. A confrontation.

I am in your face. Here I come.

The phrase "all or nothing" jumps into my head. A play on those words follows—"It's *Hall* or nothing."

I scribble those words on a yellow legal pad. I add, "No one else will do." I write furiously, "It's Hall or nothing," then my competitive side raging, I write, "You'll be mine before I'm through."

Simultaneously, my finger finds the keyboard. I plunk a note, then another, and I fall into a kind of trance and a melody flows through me, something slow, jazzy. I'm channeling Quincy Jones, the former trumpet player, and I get up and move to this slow, mournful melody, a luxurious feeling. But the beat feels wrong. It's too sad, too ponderous. I'm writing my theme song. I have to walk out to this song. This music has to *move*. I table the slow jazz tempo and press my eyes closed. I envision Clint Holmes, the announcer on *The Late Show*, introducing me the first night I hosted the show. He asked me if I wanted him to do anything special. I said, "Bring me out the way my mother used to call me to come in before dark when I was a kid in Cleveland—*Arseni*—O—hold the 'O.'"

I hear that now, I hear Clint announcing me, and I hear *funk*, something like Earth, Wind & Fire or Rick James, and the slow jazz persuasion drops away and the tempo picks up. I hear drums blasting an intro, a thumping bass, my fingers fly across the keyboard, and, suddenly, "It's Hall or Nothing" *burns*.

I record the song—the up-tempo version—redline the volume, then I play it back. I strut through my living room, pretending to walk onto the stage. The tempo's so hot I could run out if I wanted. I know then. I got it. I've done it. Written my song. My theme song. And it is *fire*.

I sleep on it, wake up early, tinker with the tune, a note here, a note there, but not much. I call a keyboard player I know and ask him if he'll add some chords, spruce up the song, make it sound professional. He comes over, plays the shit out of my little ditty, and we record his version. I love what I have now, but I need one more opinion. I need validation. Confirmation. So I call the man with the best ear in show business. I call Eddie. I tell him I have something for him to hear. I go to his house and play "It's Hall or Nothing." He goes nuts.

"It's perfect. You did it. You wrote a great theme song."

Only problem is, from that moment on, for the next thirty-five years, he never lets go of the title as a punchline. If I call him and say "Hey, man, have you heard the new Cardi B?" he'll say "Oh, yeah, it's good, but it ain't 'Hall or Nothing.'"

I bring my tape recorder to Lucie and play her the song.

"This rocks," she says. "I love it."

I leave her office on a cloud.

Then Mark gets a call.

"Paramount is going to use your song. But they want ownership."

"Quincy warned me about this," I say. "How much do they want?"

"You'll get sole credit, but they want a significant piece."

I feel my cheeks burn. I don't want to share what I wrote.

"Listen, Mark," I say. "They don't even know the song. How can they own something they don't know? Lucie heard it once. If I take them to court and say, 'Go ahead, hum it. If you own this song, *fucking hum it*, they couldn't do it."

"Arsenio," Mark says, "let it go."

"Let it *go*?"

"It's business. They could say no to the song. They could hire another writer, get John Tesh or somebody to write a song. They're willing to share this with you, give you a piece—"

"It's my song. They're willing to give me a piece of my song?"

"Yes. And that means they'll indemnify it."

"I'm not even going to pretend I know what you're talking about."

"If you go on some other show, and they play you on with this song, they have to pay you for it. If you're the sole owner, good luck chasing that money. But nobody will fuck with Paramount. Every time somebody plays that song, they have suits who track that shit, they have lawyers, and you will get paid. Whatever part you own."

I get it now. "Zero of a hundred percent is zero."

"Right. Ten percent of something is something."

I give it one last shot. "But aren't we in a strong position here?"

"No," Mark says. "You will be. But you have to win first. Once you win, then we have more leverage. But you have to win."

"I get it. I'll share the song."

"You have to pick your fights. This isn't one."

19

THE FIRST SHOW

PARAMOUNT SETS THE DATE.

January 3, 1989.

The countdown begins.

Days flash by, meld into one furious blur.

A week goes by, two. Happy Thanksgiving.

Construction crews build sets.

Teamsters roll in bleachers.

Electricians hang lights.

The design team creates a giant pale blue "A"—the first thing you'll see when you tune into the show. The rest of my signature follows, a thin line shooting off from the "A" like an arrow, the concept borrowed from watching Dinah Shore.

Sandy, Marla, and I discuss how we'll start each show, how I will appear, how I'll be revealed. We talk about Johnny, how he stands behind his curtain, and waits—and *waits*, building the audience's anticipation—

THE FIRST SHOW

the curtain rustles, and finally, Johnny knifes through and the audience and America goes wild.

No curtain, someone says. Something different. Newer, hipper.

A screen.

I'll stand behind a large, opaque screen, in view, but motionless, head bowed, a figure in shadow. A slight hesitation and the screen rises, I come to life, raise my head, and burst onto the stage, "It's Hall or Nothing" playing me on.

"Liberate the bland," I say, my new mantra.

A month to go.

I decorate my office myself. I once hired an interior designer to do my condo, but one day I came home early and found her on the couch, doing the contractor. Since then, I do my own decorating. More efficient and cleaner. Plus, she didn't get me. My place said "older white lady," which is who she was.

I love color. In my office, I go with blue, everything blue, shades of blue. Blue walls. Blue décor in my bathroom. And mirrors. I dig mirrors. I also like neat, clean, minimal. Couch, moon-shaped desk, bookcase, a TV that stays tuned to stage 29 all day. Right now, nothing much to watch except people hammering, painting, plugging in wires, moving cameras around, mopping floors.

Three weeks to go.

Merry Christmas.

The studio and Dana hit publicity hard. They plaster my face on buses, benches, a billboard on Sunset, a sign on the Paramount lot. I do local TV spots, talk about the show, publicize the premiere. I do one commercial with my mother. She's a natural. In the spot, she criticizes my clothes, stepping in front of me, promising America that I'll be wearing suits.

Pat Sajak's face pops up everywhere, too. I get that. We share a time slot, but I don't look at him as my competition.

I'm lying. I do.

But he's not the enemy. He's a nice guy. We're involved in a friendly late night battle.

I'm lying. We're not.

It's war. A death match. I want to kick his ass.

I'm not lying. I really do. I'm certainly the underdog.

He's famous and I'm just a face on a bus.

The week of.

Lucie pops in, slaps a sheet of paper onto my moon-shaped desk.

"A hundred forty," she says.

"My IQ test result came in?"

She cracks a smile. "That's how many stations are carrying *The Arsenio Hall Show*."

"Good number?"

"Good number," she says. "Especially since nobody's seen the show."

"Got to get more," I say.

"We will," she says.

Liberate the bland.

Saturday, January 1, 1989.

Happy New Year.

Don't recall if I go out or stay in. I remember, vaguely, perhaps in a dream, smoking a joint, sipping champagne, watching the ball drop in Times Square, and listening to "My Prerogative" by Bobby Brown.

Great song, I think.

I hear Eddie in my mind, *Oh, yeah, but it ain't no "Hall or Nothing."*

January 1, 1989.

Sunday.

Two days before.

I pray.

I arrive at mid-morning mass at my church, First AME in Watts, my weekly ritual. I slip into the back row, lower my head, close my eyes.

I see myself as that kid in Cleveland, putting on my talk show in the basement. Then I go deeper. I thank God for bringing me here, to this place in my life. I thank Him for looking over me. Then I ask God for help. *Please let me do well.* I pray a lot, I realize. I pray all the time, for everything. I start to worry that God might be getting sick of me. A lot of heavy shit going on in the world and I'm asking Him to help me out with a talk show?

I feel a tap on my shoulder.

A woman I've never seen before stands in the aisle next to me. Older woman. I must be in her seat. I apologize and start to get up, but she presses on my shoulder and whispers, "God told me to tell you it's going to be all right."

Then she's gone.

I come to First AME every Sunday. I've never seen that woman before.

I never see her again.

Tuesday, January 3, 1989.

The premiere.

Game time.

The air I breathe feels electrified. Yet I'm calm, eerily calm. Feels like this thing has its own momentum. It's happening. It's on. I'm just going along for the ride.

I head into the studio around eleven. I walk toward my office, say hi to Pam, the switchboard operator, then a door flies open and Marla bursts in. She holds a clipboard and an armful of folders. They're part of her. She's all business, no bullshit, in go-mode. Her default. On the move, in charge, calm, confident. She escorts me to a room where we meet with the writers. We talk monologue. Concepts fly, jokes hit, miss. Tonight I want to lean on material I've worked on at The Comedy Store. I need to be comfortable this first night. It's basketball season, my sport, so I'll do Lakers, Magic, Jordan, Bird, and then move to music, my passion, segue to James Brown going to jail. Don't want to reinvent the wheel for show one. I know that if I kill in the monologue, momentum will carry the rest of the show, like a snowball rolling downhill. The writers disburse. We'll meet one more time two hours later when I'll finalize the monologue. Marla goes over tonight's guests—Brooke Shields, Leslie Nielsen, and my friend and favorite singer, Luther Vandross. I'll meet Brooke and Leslie for the first time on camera. I never speak to my guests beforehand. I want the audience to feel what I feel, the genuine excitement of meeting someone for the first time.

"Do you ever want to meet someone ahead of time?" Marla asks.

"No," I say, then correct myself. "Well, if Colin Powell's on the show, then, yes, of course, I'll pop into his dressing room. But I'm going to let you decide. When it comes to running the show, I'm going to live by two words—*Ask Marla*."

I check in with audio, walk onto the stage, stroll back to front, side to side. I talk with Sandy, the director, and meet with my brain, Whitney Brown, the cue card guy. I call him my brain because he puts what's inside my head on sheets of cardboard and presents them to me so I can read them aloud. Then I buzz by the dressing room, approve what I'm wearing—a charcoal-gray suit for opening night. A few people track me down and ask for favors—"My auntie from Alabama is here. Could we put her in B section?"

"Ask Marla," I say.

Thirty minutes.

I'm feeling *fire*.

But first, ice.

I shout for one of the production assistants, the iceman, Tom Leonardis. "Tom! It's time. I need my ice!"

A minute later, Tom arrives at my office, hugging a bucket filled with ice. He presents it to me like an offering. I close the door and pour the ice into the sink in my bathroom. I fill the sink with water, take a deep breath, and plunge my face into the ice water. Then again, and again, and again, three, four, five times. The ice shocks my system. Cleans my pores. Exfoliates my skin. The ice plunge heats me up.

I dry my face and head to makeup, where I meet Marla. I sit while a brush dances across my cold face, a puff of powder dabs my cheeks, and Marla goes over her notes for the show. I'm silent, still, a captive in my makeup chair. I take in every word Marla says, assimilate most of it. I know she'll be standing a few feet away from me during the show, in front of the couch, close to a TV monitor, next to Whitney, the cue card guy, and, most important, the phone, the direct line to the control booth. Everyone knows that if Marla picks up that phone, some shit has gone down. Nobody—including me—wants Marla reaching for that phone.

My skin still tingling from the ice water, I leave makeup, head to my dressing room, and put on the charcoal-gray suit. I check myself in the mirror. I look as if I'm dressing for church. That seems right. I'm dressing up for both my mom and dad.

Minutes away.

I walk downstairs to stage 29. I pass the control booth, check in with Sandy and wish her a good show. She lifts her headset, wishes me the same.

I duck backstage and settle in on my spot behind the screen.

I hear the audience. Their chatter. Their laughter. Dailey Pike, the warm-up guy, winds down, the audience cheers, applauds, and then he introduces Burton Richardson, the maestro, our basso profundo announcer.

Behind the screen, I drop to one knee. Shutting out every sound, I slam my eyes closed, and I pray. "Thank you for this, thank you for my life, please go out there with me."

The drums pound. My posse blasts "It's Hall or Nothing," and Burton, his voice profoundly deep and at peak volume, belts, "Live from stage twenty-nine at Paramount Studios on Melrose Avenue in the heart of Hollywood, California, in these United States, on the planet we call Earth—"

I open my eyes. I stand. I spread my legs, lower my head, fold my hands in front of me.

"—It's *The Arsenio Hall Show*, starring Arsenio Hall, with tonight's guests, Brooke Shields, Leslie Nielsen, and Luther Vandross—"

Burton pauses and then bellows, "And now, let the party begin—it's Arseni—OOOOOOOOOOOOOO—"

He extends the "O" for ten seconds, the longest I've ever heard— Burton will eventually shatter that record and stretch the "O" to an astonishing *twenty-one seconds*—"HALL!"

The screen rises.

I bound onto the stage. I'm moving, sprinting, waving, bowing, and then I sprint straight for Michael Wolff, who leaves his keyboard and meets me, standing over me on his raised platform. I extend my index finger to him and he taps his index finger to mine, the audience screaming and clapping over us, and under the crowd's roar, I say to Mike, "We're always going to be number two, but let's think number one. Let's touch these ones every night."

I raise and twirl my fist to the Dog Pound behind the band, return to my spot, ready to begin, bowing, grinning, thanking the audience, and finally, after what feels like a nonstop, one-minute ovation, I exhale. And then I leap. I sail through space without a net, I free-fall into—

Show one.

It begins.

20

PHENOMENON

A FEW WEEKS BEFORE the first show.

I sit next to Janet Jackson in Luther Vandross's family room in the home he's recently purchased from gossip columnist Rona Barrett. Quincy Jones sits across from me, telling us about collaborating with Frank Sinatra back in the day. Elton John plays piano in a far corner of the room. He tinkers with a tune I don't know and then begins playing and singing "Candle in the Wind." Luther joins in. They sing together at first, then Elton defers to Luther, to that voice; he drops away, and Luther lets loose.

I'm stunned. Everyone in the room is stunned.

I think—

Oh. My. God.

Then I think, *You're not in Kansas, anymore, Arsenio. Or Cleveland.*

This feels like a dream, but it's not. It's real. And I'm here. Hanging with Luther, Janet, Q, and Elton—at Luther's house.

As Richard would say, "This is where you are. You earned it. So sit back and fucking enjoy yourself."

* * *

The next day, I call Luther to thank him for inviting me, and I get up the nerve to ask him for two favors.

"I'm doing that talk show," I tell him. "You're my favorite singer and I want you to be my first musical guest."

"I'd love to," Luther says.

"Thank you so much. My second thing. A bigger favor. I need to pick your brain. The studio tells me that I have to come out strong. It's all about my first week. Especially Friday night when most people won't have school or work the next day. Paramount will look at ratings. They'll mail out questionnaires, do focus groups, talk to station managers. My numbers Friday night will be really important. Music is key to my demographic. They're looking at the eighteen- to twenty-five-year-olds. So, who should I have on Friday night?"

"Bobby Brown," he says, no hesitation. "I love me some Bobby Brown."

I expected Diana Ross, or Julio Iglesias, or the Sugar Hill Gang.

"Child," Luther says, "that Bobby Brown checks all the boxes. He can sing, he can move, and he's got a new album coming out. I've heard some of it. It's *fierce*."

"*Two* songs?" Lucie stares at me.

"Yeah. Probably open with 'My Prerogative' and close with 'Don't Be Cruel,' not the Elvis version. Oh, and here's the other thing. I kind of wish you would sit down for this—"

"I'm fine," Lucie says, standing, folding her arms.

"Bobby will do the regular version of 'Cruel,' but I want him to do this five-minute version of 'My Prerogative' that I saw him do live on the Heartbreak Tour."

"Carson does one song and never more than three minutes."

"Johnny's my idol," I say. "But I'm not Johnny. Let me have this Friday. Please. If I'm wrong, and it doesn't work, and it's bad, and we tank, starting Monday, I will do everything your way. I promise. But let me have one chance to try it my way. Lucie, I want to be different."

Lucie circles back behind her desk, dives onto her chair.

"Okay," she says.

The first week, I bring out Quincy Jones, Robert Downey, Jr., Whoopi Goldberg, Ted Danson, Pee-wee Herman, Louie Anderson, and Kareem Abdul-Jabbar. Every guest scores, every show gets better, the heat, energy, the water cooler talk, the momentum building all week. Then, Friday. Bobby Brown. I don't remember my other guest.

I remember only Bobby, his scorching band hotter than fish grease, his fresh, fluid, frenetic backup dancers, Heart and Soul, his insane performance, nearly ten full minutes of blistering R&B.

The weekly ratings come in Monday morning.

Lucie practically screams.

Paramount has never seen such numbers.

We finish second to Johnny.

We dominate our demographic.

We own the under thirty-fives.

We rule the week.

21

YOU'RE GONNA BE AROUND FOR AN AWFUL LONG TIME

1989.

The Arsenio Hall Show explodes.

A shock to the culture, hurtling out of nowhere.

We're *it*—arriving like a late night meteor. New, fresh, funny, and *jammin'* with music you'll never see on Johnny. Indie bands. Alt country. But mainly Black music. R&B. Soul. Jazz. Gospel. Hip-hop. Black artists. *Black* music. We're the place to be and be seen. Managers and agents clamor to book their hottest clients on the show. Crowds converge outside stage 29, people lining up at 7 a.m. for tickets to our 5:15 p.m. show. *The Pat Sajak Show* debuts during our second week and our ratings go *up*. We crush Pat.

In the next weeks, Lucie occasionally pops into stage 29 to watch, standing off to the side. Marla greets her, then loses herself, focusing completely on producing the show. After the show, she tells me that Lucie made an appearance.

"The police came today," she says.

In February, Paramount puts up a large billboard at the front gate, against the sky, showing my smiling face, and in blue script, "Happy Birthday, Arsenio." I stop in at Lucie's office to thank her.

"You're entirely welcome," Lucie says. "We've got a tiger by the tail, Arsenio. We have to hold on to it. We cannot let it go. We're going to take fewer hiatuses than other shows. You cool with that?"

"Absolutely."

"Good. You're young. It's your time. This is your baby."

She's right.

I'm thirty-three. Marla is twenty-eight. This is our time. And as I leave Lucie's office, trekking back to stage 29, I realize, *This is also Lucie's time. No show at Paramount has succeeded like this for her. This is her baby, too.*

I booked Leslie Nielsen on my inaugural night. His movie's a hit and has legs, so I book Elvis's ex-wife Priscilla Presley because they're both stars of the Paramount hit comedy *The Naked Gun*. The film also features O.J. Simpson in a supporting role. The day after Priscilla Presley appears on the show, I get word that O.J. wants to see me. He's on the Paramount lot, waiting for me, sitting in his car outside the elephant door of stage 29. Something tells me that he's pissed and he's not here to talk about USC football. I pop outside and approach his car. He glares at me. He's seething. His car is not as cool as I expected it to be. Maybe that's why he's pissed. I smile at him. "What's up, Juice?"

"What's *up*? Brother, you have Leslie Nielsen on your show, then you have Priscilla Presley on your show. But the Black actor in the film doesn't get so much as a *call*? My publicist tells me you've booked Anna Nicole Smith to come on your show. Seriously? I don't get it, brother. This is supposed to be the Black talk show."

Now, that hits a nerve.

"Woo, pump your brakes," I say. "Juice, don't go there, Bruh."

He starts to speak, but I cut him off. "Look, I apologize for not having you on the show. I got a lot on my plate."

We talk further and he calms down. I promise O.J. that I'll try to get him on the show soon, but for some reason, that never happens.

To be honest, if I'd known that O.J. would be charged with double murder, I might've put him on the first night before I booked Leslie Nielsen, and below the Dog Pound, I would've chyroned, "Convicts who make Heisman candles out of earwax."

One day I meet one of my idols, Sammy Davis, Jr. As a kid in Cleveland, I remember watching him as a guest on all the talk shows and then as the host of his own variety show, *Sammy and Company*. I've always been in awe of his talent, his exuberance, his high energy. Sammy acted in movies, television, and on Broadway, ran with Frank Sinatra and Dean Martin as a member of the Rat Pack, then became a top act in Vegas, the best show in town. He sang, told jokes, played several instruments, did impressions, and *danced*. Man, did he dance. Originally a tap dancer, Sammy had moves as slick and thrilling as Michael Jackson. Then Sammy got political. Originally a Democrat, he switched sides and started hanging out with prominent Republicans. He even hugged Richard Nixon. That didn't sit well with Democrats in Cleveland, which included most people I knew, except for my father. After the hug, everyone in my neighborhood turned on Sammy. My aunts, uncles, my neighbors, my friends and their parents all said, "That's it. We're finished with Sammy." We had no social media back then, but today my community would have canceled him.

Except I couldn't. I loved him. I was too enthralled by him. I let the hug pass. I wrote it off as one of Sammy's moments of exuberance. Watching him on TV, I always got the feeling that he was simply that guy— warm, passionate, over-the-top affectionate, an indiscriminate hugger.

And now he invites Eddie and me to his house for movie night.

Sammy greets us at the door and gives us a tour of his house. He brings us to a room and shows us his collection of six-guns inside a glass case. As part of his act, Sammy would strap on a holster, draw a six-shooter, twirl the gun, throw it in the air, catch it, spin it behind his back. He became a fast-draw artist, entered competitions and won. Now he closes his gun cabinet and brings us to his screening room, where Eddie and I, our dates, and his other guests, Goldie Hawn and Kurt Russell, settle in to watch the movie he's chosen, *Cocoon*.

When I start the show, I hear he wants to come on. I jump at the chance. Sammy's older now, and he's been sick, but he's still working steadily. This time, I make an exception and visit him in his dressing room before the show. I knock softly, then open the door, expecting to see an entourage—his manager, his agent, his wife, a group of people, but Sammy's alone. He sits in front of the mirror. He wears a stocking cap and holds a sponge in his hand. He slowly, meticulously, dabs his face. "Come in, man," he says.

He stands, we hug, and then he slowly sits down. He seems frail.

"I just wanted to say hello and thank you for doing this," I say. "It means a lot to me."

"Are you kidding? I'm doing this for *us*."

He tells me a story about a time—not that long ago—when he worked at a hotel in Vegas and a Black kid went swimming in the hotel pool. The hotel found out and shut the pool down. Then he talks about having to go in a different entrance than the white entertainers. He talks with pain and sadness.

"You broke barriers," I say.

"Got the shit kicked out of me, too." He faces me, still cupping the sponge in his hand. He speaks softly. "I don't think I can sing tonight, man. But if I feel I can, I'll try."

"You don't have to—"

"No, I do. I've always done a little song or something on Johnny and I don't want to give you any less than I give him."

He grabs my arm.

"It's too important."

I put my hand over his. "Thank you."

Sammy turns back to the mirror and continues dabbing his face with the sponge. "I'll see you out there."

I have two guests planned, the second, following Sammy, is a young female comic with shoulder-length blond hair named Ellen DeGeneres. Now I hold up Sammy's new memoir, *Why Me?*, and I say, simply, "I've always wanted to say this. I can now. This man truly needs no introduction—*Sammy Davis, Jr.*" Sammy, to Mike's jazzy take on his biggest hit, "The Candy Man," strolls out. The crowd erupts, Sammy and I hug, and I lead him over to the couch. We begin our conversation with a discussion of the line of barbecue sauce and mustard he's selling, and his devotion to cooking.

"I got into cooking after I got off drugs," he says. "I had to find something to do with my hands."

"You were probably thinking, 'What else can I do with a straw?'"

He—and the audience—crack up. We talk more about his addiction—"I'm still waiting to get high"—and he mentions drinking, fondly. "Now, booze? I *love* booze. If I want a buzz, give me bourbon or vodka. Yeah, I *miss* booze."

"Why did you stop drinking?"

"Because the doctor said, 'You gonna die.'"

He talks about getting sober and setting up an institute for medical research. We break for commercial, during which Sammy lights up a cigarette. When we come back, we talk about Michael Jackson. I'd seen Sammy on HBO performing his own take of Michael's "Bad."

"You were *bad*," I tell him. "You were working it."

"I truly love Michael," Sammy says. "He's like a son to me. I love his moves. And I guess—you know, I started as a dancer, a hoofer—but then I got into instruments, and doing impressions, and dancing fell back into a second position. But I think I might have been the Michael Jackson of the fifties."

Some applause and then I change the subject. I choose my words carefully. "Reading your book, I got sad. I guess I always thought that a man with your talent would have a little easier time living in America. A *little* easier time at least." I indicate my chair, and Sammy sitting on the couch. "Because you did this at one time."

"I did."

"Everybody told me not to do this. They said a Black man couldn't pull this off in America. It scares me when I read that they painted you white, that they poured urine in your beer. Did those things really happen?"

"Yes. They really happened."

Sammy begins talking about his experience in the military in the 1940s, which leads into the most direct conversation I've ever had publicly about racism. As Sammy talks, the audience goes silent. But I know they're riveted, in a state of shock, leaning on Sammy's every word. Those days, in the army, he thought at first that being in show business might insulate him from racism. But he found himself caught in the middle of Blacks and whites. Because he tried to connect in some small way with the whites, the Blacks called him a Tom. At the same time, the whites called him the N-word. This is, I realize, the first time anyone has said that word on my show, or on any show. The emotion flows from Sammy as he talks about trying to fight back physically.

"I was too small," he says. "I got my nose broke three times. And I had no one to back me up. No one. No one there, not the government, not the people, nobody. If I wanted to do anything with somebody white, I had to sneak around. Just to have dinner with someone, or have a good time, or just talk—" He pauses. "I got so tired of sneaking around."

Sammy keeps going, his voice cracking, the emotion raw, the memories brutal, and then I see Marla, behind him, gesturing. We have gone way past our time for the segment. When Sammy pauses to take a breath, I say, gently, "We have to go to a quick commercial—"

When we come back on air, the audience applauds Sammy for his honesty, his courage. Their applause reverberates. I start to speak and Sammy interrupts. "Before we go any further—I know it wasn't planned—can I do a number with the guys?"

I'm completely thrown. "Sure. Of course. Wow. You can work something out with the guys?"

Sammy and I walk toward Mike and someone hands Sammy a hand mic as we go. He steps up to the bandstand. I say, "Mike, all right, you guys work it out."

Sammy whispers "Time After Time" to Mike, and the bass player begins the intro to Cyndi Lauper's hit song. Sammy says, "No, the other one, Sinatra," and sings, "Time after time, I tell myself that I'm so lucky to be loving you—"

The bass player switches gears, and the band jumps into the Sinatra, Jule Styne, Sammy Cahn classic.

"This is truly ad-lib," Sammy says.

Sammy goes into the song, snapping his fingers, his voice clear and strong. I stand to the side of my posse. I close my eyes, taking in every note that Sammy sings. He finishes, shakes hands with Mike, acknowledges each member of the band. I link my arm through his and help him down from the bandstand.

"My man," I say, leading him back to the couch.

The audience's applause builds, then finally ebbs and settles. Sammy nods to them, and to me. "I say this to you, personally, on a one-to-one basis. You ever need me, you got me, for the rest of my life. As a friend, or anything. You ever need me to come on. That's the reason I did the song. I don't want anybody ever saying, 'When he's on Johnny Carson, he always sings a song, how come he didn't sing on Arsenio?'"

His words touch me, and yet they sting. I know what he means. My booker has told me that certain stars are defined as "Johnny guests," and either won't come on my show at all, or will come on weeks or even months after they've appeared on *The Tonight Show*.

"I'll make a deal with you right now," Sammy says. "When I come back—because you're gonna be around for an awful long time—let me come back for the fall season, and let me bring my guys and augment them with your guys, and let me do some stuff one night."

"Oh, man, that would be great."

I catch Marla giving me the "wrap it up" finger twirl. We've run out of time. Sammy waves at the audience while he clutches my forearm. We end the show. We hug. Sammy hustles offstage.

Over the next few months, Sammy's health deteriorates. His doctor orders him to cut back on traveling and performing. He never makes it back to the show for a second appearance. In March 1990, I head to the Shrine Auditorium in L.A. to receive the Soul Train Music Sammy Davis Jr. Award for Entertainer of the Year, won the previous year by Michael Jackson, an honor that humbles me. Two months later, in May 1990, Sammy succumbs to throat cancer. He is sixty-four years old.

22

LARGE AND IN CHARGE

IT'S THE LATE EIGHTIES, I'm young, got some money in my pocket, and I'm making it in Hollywood. Meaning, like a lot of young men my age, I go through a phase. A party phase. A particular phase where young men like me learn that certain women will do anything if you have cocaine. Yes. I admit it. I party, too much. Too many late nights, too many strip clubs, too much cocaine, too many women.

Marla knows me well, doesn't like the company I keep, and she worries. She doesn't want me to play so hard that it will affect the quality of the show. Meanwhile, she can't turn off her work engine. She watches each show several times a night, studying it, analyzing it, taking notes, finding mistakes, searching for improvements, producing the show again, in her mind, long after she's produced the actual show on stage 29.

One day, she comes into my office, holding her clipboard and folders and asks, "Did you go over the notes I gave you?"

I squirm in my chair, press my fingertips into my throbbing forehead. "I'm blanking on exactly which notes—"

"Did you read the Jackie Collins book? She'll be on the show next week."

"I meant to. I did skim the early chapters, well, the early paragraphs, it's a fast read—"

"You didn't read the book. Or look at the notes."

"Not yet."

"What about the tape I gave you? Did you watch that movie?"

"You gave me a tape?"

Massive eyeroll.

"Look, our relationship is not going to work this way."

Those words knock me back.

"I think you may be overreacting slightly," I say.

"This is all so new. I get it. It's crazy. I know you're having a lot of fun. You like to party after the show. Great. I know sometimes that's business. But you can't have hangovers the morning after the night before. You have meetings in the morning and a show every night. There can't be any 'No, Marla, I'm sorry I didn't read the book.' You have to put in the work after the show. At least read the notes."

"Yes, the notes are very helpful. I'm told."

Marla laughs. She can't help it.

"I'll do better, I'll be more disciplined, I promise," I say. "This job goes twenty-four-seven."

"Only if you want to win," Marla says.

I flip a switch. I kick into high gear. I put everything I have into the show, every minute of my time, every ounce of energy. I stop hanging out with certain people. I cut out partying, unless it's related to the show, and Marla and I develop a routine, a rhythm. She watches the show at least three times a night—live, in the moment, as we tape, then we watch it together in her office after the show, and then we watch it together, separately. She watches the nightly broadcast in bed with her husband Steve, while I'm on the phone with her, watching the show in my bed at my house.

"Marla, what was that?" I say one night over the phone. "I think I hear somebody in the audience, shouting *no!*"

"That was just Steve talking in his sleep."

I can be hard on myself, a tough critic. Marla can be brutal. "Look at that shot! That's the second time! I know you and Sandy think it's *artsy*. But we're not making a foreign film here."

The camera cuts from a young, captivating Bobby Brown performing to a reverse shot where the camera is positioned behind Zorro, Bobby's drummer, who fills a quarter of the frame, with Bobby and the audience off in the distance.

"No, no, I would never take the camera off an artist like Bobby," Marla says.

Marla scrutinizes each show, dissects every moment, frantically scribbling notes. The first time we begin our ritual, sitting in her office after the show, she seems so critical, I almost ask her to chill. But as she mutters something about the editor choosing a bad angle on me during the monologue, I realize, *She just wants me to look good. She's protecting me.*

Marla hates surprises, but she accepts that I never practice the monologue. After we set the jokes, I look over the cue cards briefly, usually while I'm sitting in the makeup chair. We do stick to opening the show with the theme song and the monologue, even though I tend to race around the set, tapping fingers with Mike, acknowledging the posse, sprint over to the Dog Pound, sometimes running into the audience, my fist pumping, barking along with the crowd. We shake things up on occasion. When we book Al Green as our musical guest, we prerecord a cold opening. Instead of beginning the show with my monologue, we start with Al Green in the audience, standing at the top of the stairs leading down to the stage. He begins singing, "I'm so in love with you—"

He takes one step, trips, and tumbles thirty steps, landing at the floor leading to the stage. Of course, Al hasn't fallen. We've hired a stunt double. The camera cuts to me, standing over Al as I help him up. Behind us, the audience, half of them laughing, half of them gasping, applauds the stunt.

Another time, I open the show shooting dice with the Olsen twins, Mary-Kate and Ashley, the five-year-old stars of the hit sitcom *Full House*. One of them rolls a seven and loses. I scoop up all their money and grin into the camera. The audience goes crazy. They find me taking a wealthy, famous twin's money funny for some reason.

I always clear the cold openings with Marla and she always goes all in.

"We're doing a groundbreaking show," she says. "We have to take risks."

We blast through 1989, the days ticking off, time a blur. Early on, when it comes to guests, I select people who have been important parts of my life—Nancy Wilson, Franklyn Ajaye, Johnny Gill, Magic Johnson, Dick Clark, Don Cornelius, Carol Burnett, Eric Dickerson, Jesse Jackson, James Earl Jones. In one of my favorite shows, I sit down with Muhammad Ali for an entire segment, go to commercial, and then surprise him by bringing out Sugar Ray Leonard and Mike Tyson. Although Muhammad has begun slurring his speech from Parkinson's disease, Ray and Mike completely engage him. The three boxing legends talk shop, relive some of their memorable fights, and then Ray and Mike offer a heartfelt testimonial to the greatest boxer of all time. Reviewing the show later with Marla, my voice cracks with emotion as I watch these two boxing greats giving flowers to their idol and inspiration.

I showcase a couple of hot, young comedians—Chris Rock, who goes on to become one of the greatest comics of our generation, and George Lopez, who becomes a dear friend and my most frequent guest, appearing seventeen times. Acknowledging my years as a magician, I bring out the best magician I know, David Copperfield. I sit with George Carlin, Ringo Starr, my neighbor Miles Davis, Ernie Banks, Little Richard, Smokey Robinson. I introduce the late night audience to MC Hammer, whom I met a year earlier on Sunset Boulevard when I was coming out of The Comedy Store and he was coming out of the hotel next door.

"Hi, my name is Stanley," he said. "I want to tell you that when you left *The Late Show,* it broke my heart. I'm a rapper and I'm not finished with my album yet. You're hip-hop's best friend. Everybody knows that. There's nobody like you on TV."

"That's very kind. Well, I have good news. I'm finishing this movie called *Coming to America* and then I'm going to have a talk show at Paramount. I'll get you on then."

Stanley Burrell—MC Hammer—and I stay in touch and become friends. In June, I introduce him and his song "Turn This Mutha Out" from his album *Let's Get It Started.* Hammer, who dances at a level of energy and athleticism rivaling Michael or Bobby Brown, comes on the show with a crew of a dozen dancers, some of them shirtless, creating the most elaborate production I've ever witnessed on a talk show. He begins the segment standing in front of a phalanx of dancers, talking about the glories of several cities they have visited and *hit*. I casually walk onto the set. The audience roars, and when they settle, I say to Hammer, with attitude, "Yeah, look. I'm real happy that you're hitting in all those places and everything. But you ain't hitting on *The Arsenio Hall Show*."

"What?" Hammer says, pretending to be offended.

"What you gonna do about that—*Hammer?*"

"I am gonna—*Turn This Mutha Out.*"

The music rises, Hammer raps, and his dancers, singers, and rappers rip the place up.

Hammer will appear again later in the year and I will break his new song "U Can't Touch This" to the world. It will be the second of eight times he'll appear on the show.

Eddie Murphy comes on often, three times in 1989. He's always hilarious and, because he's Eddie and so busy, always has something to sell. Once he comes on to plug his music album, *So Happy*, and the single from the album, "Put Your Mouth on Me." I say, "I've wanted to ask you this. When you need advice, or someone to talk to, who do you go to?"

"Just you," he says, and the two of us and the audience laugh. Later in the conversation, I blurt, "You were a ventriloquist."

I say this because he does a hilarious impression of a puppet using his thumb and forefinger, mimicking the ventriloquist Señor Wences who appeared often on *The Ed Sullivan Show*. He looks at me and I read his eyes—"No way I'm doing that shit right now."

"No, I wasn't." He quickly lies and flips the script. "I was not. But you were a magician. The Great Arsenio."

The audience laughs. Eddie keeps going, making fun of my long fingers. "You would make doves disappear. People would say, 'Where'd that dove go?' The dove would be hiding behind your finger."

Another time, while I'm talking to Eddie on the couch, Michael Jackson suddenly appears, holding a large plaque. The audience loses it. Eddie and I hug Michael, and I say, "Eddie, I believe Michael has something for you."

"Yes," Michael says. "I want to present this to Eddie Murphy, the greatest comedian of our time, the king."

Eddie looks completely taken aback.

"This is an award that MTV put together," I tell him.

"Wow," Eddie says, reading the inscription on the award. "The viewers voted. Thank you." The audience applauds and Eddie turns to Michael. "And thank you for giving me this. Now I got something for you."

Eddie reaches out of camera shot and returns with an award for Michael. "This is the MTV award to Michael Jackson, for the greatest video in the history of all videos—*Thriller*."

I explain both awards to Eddie, to Michael, and to the audience, "I set this up with MTV. They rated the eighties and gave Eddie the award for comedy and Michael the award for videos. I'm so glad you got to present these awards to each other, right here."

The audience roars, and Michael, always uncomfortable when he's not performing, vanishes, almost as mysteriously as he appeared.

"I did not expect that," Eddie says. "I wasn't even sure it was him. I thought, *That can't be him. That must be a lookalike.*"

The audience, in total agreement, applauds.

"Wasn't a lookalike," Eddie says.

On my birthday, in February, I receive another surprise. This one shakes me up. I'm about to perform the monologue, and the audience starts shrieking at someone behind me. I turn and see Whitney Houston, dressed all in white. I practically fall over. I *love* Whitney Houston. Whenever I've seen her across the room at someone's party or in a restaurant, I clam up. I feel that way right now. I introduce her to the audience, and we hug.

"I just came out to wish you a happy birthday," she says.

"Oh, wow, thank you."

Whitney nods at the audience. "And I have to tell them that you've been lying."

"I've been lying?"

She shakes her head. "I don't know why you don't tell them the truth. Tell them that I'm having your baby."

The audience flips out. *I* flip out.

"I'm never, ever, nervous," I say. "But right now, everything on me is shaking."

Whitney roars. "Everything?"

"Everything. Every part of my body. Every single thing."

For the past year or so, since *Coming to America*, Paula Abdul and I have been hanging out whenever we can. Since we're both so busy, that amounts to a couple times a week, a dinner here, an evening there, our times concentrated and filled with laughter. Comic that I am, I'm cursed with trying to make her laugh as hard and as often as I can. Once I make her laugh so hard she pees, the comic's ultimate compliment.

After choreographing the musical numbers in *Coming to America*, Paula's career has skyrocketed, both as a performer and choreographer. She has recently gone into the studio and put together an album called *Forever Your Girl*. She's begun working on a video for a single from the album, "Straight Up."

One day, I drive to the studio to pick her up after work. I sit in the car, waiting for her, listening to the Lakers on the radio. Paula appears at the driver's side window. "This is going to take at least another hour," she says.

"That's okay. I'm good. I got the game on. Take your time."

"No, come on in and hang out."

"I'm cool out here, really—"

She opens the car door and takes my hand. "Come on. Check it out."

Inside the studio, Paula says, "You want to be in the video? A quick cameo. We'll shoot you watching me. It'll be cool."

"Like this? I got no clothes. I'm in a sweatsuit."

"One of the dancers is exactly your size."

"What's her name?"

"Ha. He's got an extra bomber jacket. It's perfect."

I step back. "You and David already worked this out, haven't you?"

David is David Fincher, the director, who's shot videos for the Rolling Stones, Madonna, Jay-Z, Justin Timberlake, and Michael Jackson. He will go on to become the A-list director of films such as *Fight Club*, *Gone Girl*, *Alien 3*, and *The Social Network*. Now, he and Paula are plotting to slide me into her video for "Straight Up."

They find the bomber jacket, which fits like I own it, they slap some powder on me, and I make my appearance in the stunning video, which

David shoots in black and white. The video itself *is* brilliant. "Straight Up" wins four MTV video awards—Best Female Video, Best Editing, Best Choreography, and Best Dance Video—and I celebrate her victories and Paula, on the show, in a flirty interview.

"Are you a page in my history?" Paula whispers in the video. "Or are you just having fun?"

We arrange an interview with a new rapper who's burst onto the scene in a *big* way. I just hope we can pull it off. I sit down with my brother Chunkton Arthur Hall, known as "Chunky A," a three-hundred-pound rapper and former roadie for Barry Manilow. Stuffed into a spandex jumpsuit and wearing a necklace with a giant gold "A," he sprawls next to me on the couch. In fact, you can barely see the couch. I ask Chunky what drives him. He bounces on his humongous butt and says, "Arsenio, you're driven by the need to succeed. I'm driven by the need to feed."

Chunky has come on the show to promote his new single "Owwww!" from his album, *Large and In Charge.* He runs down a few other songs from the album—"Dipstick," "Stank Breath," and "Ho Is Lazy." I ask Chunky another question. He hits me with a raunchy response and an oily smile. He reminds me of another heavyset rapper I know, Heavy D, who gave me the inspiration for this character.

Of course, you know that I am Chunky A, and thanks to Marla, Sandy, and the magic of blue screen, I'm able to interview myself as Chunky A.

A few months ago, I went into a recording studio, and as Chunky A, I recorded a song I wrote called "Stank Breath." I play it for my friend Irving Azoff and I get an MCA comedy/music album deal. What's crazy is the first single from the album—"Owwww!"—gets urban radio airplay. The album *Large and In Charge* doesn't become

Off the Wall, but it goes gold, with chocolate inside, reaching number 71 on the Billboard Top 200 albums. Now Chunky A appears—with me—on *The Arsenio Hall Show*. The interview works. This year, everything seems to work.

Around this time, Eddie has jumped into his passion project, *Harlem Nights*, a spoof of gangster flicks, which he's written, stars in, and directs. Since I'm shooting the show at the same time Eddie is shooting his film, he offers me a small part, only a couple of scenes.

"Hey, man, I can't be in the movie," I tell him.

"Why? It's a great part. You're the Crying Man, my mortal enemy, a gangster who always cries. You cry the entire time you're in the movie. It's hilarious."

"It sounds fantastic. But you shoot at night and I shoot at night."

"So?"

"So? You shoot from seven p.m. to seven a.m. then you want me to be ready to come into work at ten in the morning, after I get maybe three hours of sleep. I can't do that."

"You got to, man. I need you to do this. I can't get anybody else to cry the way you can."

"I can't. Our schedules conflict."

"You'll take catnaps all night."

"Man, I'm sorry."

Later, Eddie's manager calls me. "Seriously? You don't want to do *Harlem Nights*?"

"I never said that. I said I can't. How am I going to shoot all night in downtown L.A. then get back to the lot, ready to shoot my show?"

"Catnaps."

"Shit. You've been talking to Eddie."

"One week. That's all he needs."

I give in. I want to do the movie for Eddie. I also want to do it because it sounds like playing the Crying Man will be hilarious.

I don't remember much about the shoot because I sleep a lot between takes. Occasionally, after I wrap, I hang out with Eddie while he directs, trying to be a supportive friend, but sometimes I doze off, snoozing in my chair when he does his thang. On the final night of an outdoor shoot downtown, dressed in my full costume, I collapse on the bed in my trailer. I wake up at six a.m., when the sun starts to rise, and stumble outside. I find Eddie sitting in his director's chair, talking to members of the crew.

"You still here?" he says to me.

"Yes. You never wrapped me."

"Oh, I'm sorry, man. I could've wrapped you a few hours ago. I don't really need you anymore."

"The fuck you mean?"

I stare at him, then I scream, "I could've gone *home*?"

"Oh, man, I'm *so* sorry—"

Eddie loses it, dissolving into his classic laugh, the laugh we all know so well.

My fucking friend Eddie. Who needs enemies?

I survive the night shoots of *Harlem Nights*. More than that, I love the movie. Eddie and I got to work with our idols, Richard Pryor and Redd Foxx, for a memorable week, and I got to cry like a fucking maniac, playing a larger-than-life gangster. I love my performance as the Crying Man in *Harlem Nights* almost more than any other I've done. It's a role that peeps in the culture dig and mention often.

Simple fact. We don't have an easy time booking big name movie stars. Their agents go to the networks first before agreeing to put them on our little syndicated talk show. Then we hear rumors that if you appear on SNL, you can't come on our show for a certain number of weeks. We also know that certain guests are "Johnny guests," and won't come on our show at all. Sammy Davis, Jr., hinted at that, but refused to follow that unwritten rule and came on our show anyway. We're that small, syndicated talk show, relying on our wits, hard work, and connections.

Like my friend Reggie, the security guard at the Gower gate.

Reggie stands right outside my office and calls me when someone famous drives onto the lot.

"Harrison Ford just pulled in," he says.

I race out of my office, run down to the gate, corner Harrison Ford as he comes out of his car, introduce myself, and ask him, "Any chance you could do a walk-on tonight? Right before the first segment. Five minutes. Two minutes."

"Well, I got this movie coming out. I play a submarine commander. Yeah, sure, why not?"

I chase down Harrison Ford, Andy Garcia, Cher, and a slew of others. I go after Robert De Niro. I somehow lose him, but it turns out he's a fan of the show and a close friend of my friend renowned chef Nobu Matsuhisa. Nobu puts in a good word for me and De Niro agrees to come on the show, making his first appearance on a late night talk show. I chase after so many stars on the Paramount lot, thanks to Reggie, that Dana calls these spontaneous guest shots "security leaks."

Andrew Dice Clay, notorious, infamous, misogynistic, homophobic, filthy, and the biggest comic in the world, has a movie coming out. *Saturday Night Live* books him, and cast member Nora Dunn and musical guest Sinéad O'Connor boycott the show in protest. To our surprise, we get a call soon after asking if we'll have Dice on our show. I don't have to chase him down. He *wants* to do our show. Paramount doesn't want him at all, but defers to me.

I hesitate.

Driving on Sunset Boulevard, on the way to The Comedy Store, I see that someone has defaced a billboard of Dice. Everything's going so well. Do I want to create a shitstorm of negative publicity? Or do I take him on, call him out on the offensive things he says in his act?

I talk it over with Marla, Dana, and talent coordinator Kim Swann. To varying degrees, they all find him offensive. I argue, quietly, that he's one of the guys I started out with at The Comedy Store. They all say they'll support any decision I make.

I decide I don't want to ban him—or anybody else—from the show.

When Starr Parodi, one of the musicians in my posse, learns that I've booked Dice as a guest, she tells me she's uncomfortable and won't perform while he's on. The night of the show, she plays the opening, hangs with the posse while I do my monologue, then leaves.

I bring out Dice to a thunderous standing ovation, many of the audience members women. He wears an eyesore of a red leather jacket. We talk about his feud with Sam Kinison, another brash shock comic. Dice denies the feud, says he and Sam have patched things up. Dice doesn't convince me. I tell Dice I'll have Sam on and get his side of the feud.

Then Dice and I talk about his style of comedy. I tell him that I heard him do a racist joke and it made me uncomfortable. I ask him, "How would you like it if you were in a club and heard somebody do an antisemitic joke?"

"It's been done. It's a *joke*. Look, when I'm onstage, there's no editing, that's all."

He justifies his shock approach to comedy, saying that he only tells jokes about what he observes every day from real people. "It's what I hear. I don't make it up. I just deliver the jokes."

With a couple minutes left in the segment, he says, "Look, people go 'What's the real Andrew Clay Silverstein? Who is that, as opposed to Dice?' I get that. Who is Dice? Who's this Jewish kid who's acting Italian? Well, you want to know who he is? I'll tell you."

He stands, to screaming applause, takes his signature stance—feet wide apart, shoulders thrown back—and like a magic trick, theatrically produces a pack of cigarettes from inside his jacket. He pops a cigarette into his mouth. The audience loses their minds. They think he's about to go into his act. I—and they—expect a torrent of profanity. I imagine this portion of the broadcast as a series of bleeps.

Instead, Andrew Dice Clay starts to cry.

I cannot believe what I'm seeing. Sitting in my armchair, I twist toward Dice to get a better angle, but I can't see his face. I check the monitor behind Marla. I catch her eye. She shrugs. Is he really crying?

"No," Andrew Dice Clay says, tearfully, "let me get this straight."

He pauses. His eyes have welled up. He *is* crying.

Through his tears, he says, "Andrew Clay is a guy who came out here ten years ago and *broke his ass*. You know what I mean?"

The young women in the audience scream, but most of the audience has gone quiet, leaning into his every syllable.

"He believed in himself," he says, tears coming. "And he became the hottest comic in the world and anybody who doesn't like it can *wipe their ass* with whatever they say about me—"

He can't finish his thought. He shakes his head.

"I get choked up," he says. He makes his way back to the couch and sits down.

We end the segment and the entire audience stands. I look over at Andrew Dice Clay. I expect that we'll lock eyes and he'll wink at me, or mutter something to indicate that he was putting on those tears, that he was faking that emotion, but he looks at the floor, and I believe his tears were real.

In mid-November, *Time* magazine profiles me and puts me on the cover. They call the article "Let's Get Busy!!" The writer, Richard Zoglin, hangs around stage 29 for a few days, attends the show, interviews me and members of the staff. I'm happy with the piece. *Time* says, "We are seeing the future of the TV talk show, and it is, well, funky . . . less a talk show than a televised party: hip, hyperkinetic and hot." Later in the piece, Zoglin writes, "Hall's popularity may signal a geologic shift in late night TV . . . Hall is the first to catch on, and he has done it by reaching out to a new group of viewers."

I feel the wave, and the wave translates into numbers. Our ratings continue to rise—we rank first in that coveted under-thirty-five demographic—and we've added more television stations, growing our total from 160 to over 200.

Lucie sums up our show best in an interview.

"It's a phenomenon," she says.

23

FIRST BLURT

I FULFILL A DREAM. I buy my mom a house in L.A. She moves from her place in Cleveland to a crib in the San Fernando Valley. I love that she's here, but I worry that she's moved away from her siblings and lifelong friends. To be honest, I'm also concerned that since I walk, talk, eat, sleep, live, *breathe* the show 24/7, I won't have much time for her. I admit as much to Michael Jackson, who's tight with his mom, Katherine.

I'm hosting the Soul Train Awards at the Shrine Auditorium in downtown L.A. Michael is performing on the show. During a break in rehearsal, Michael and I talk about our moms, and I say, "Mom is living here now. I saw her more when she was back in Cleveland."

"You should bring her to the show," Michael says. "I'd love to meet her."

For most people, *I'd love to meet her* translates as your typical obligatory show business bullshit. But Michael is not most people.

"I will," I say.

I hadn't planned on my mom coming to the show because bringing anyone with me when I'm working always becomes a giant distraction.

But now that's changed. I'm bringing her. I have to. Michael says he wants to meet her.

I arrange for a car to pick her up. We shoot the show, Michael performs, kills, and the show ends. Afterward, a security guy locates my mom and escorts her out of the auditorium's artists entrance and toward the limo. I don't see Michael anywhere. I figure he forgot about meeting my mom and left. I open the limo door for her and Mom slides into the backseat. Suddenly, Michael's bodyguard appears in front of me, imposing as a hit man, silent as a ninja. "Michael is still in his trailer," he whispers. "He says he's not going to leave because he promised to meet your mom."

"He's still in his trailer?"

"Waiting for you. And your mom."

I stick my head through the limo's window. "You can't go yet. Mike wants to meet you."

"Who does?"

"Michael Jackson. He's *waiting* for you."

I hustle her out of the limo, and we walk to Michael's trailer. The whole way I'm anxious and my mom's muttering. She doesn't believe me that we're actually going to see Michael Jackson, but when we step inside Michael's trailer, he comes over to her and gives her a hug.

"It's so nice to meet you," he says.

"It's so nice to meet you, too."

Michael shakes his head. "Arsenio, you look just like your mom." Then he laughs quietly and says, "I can't believe your name is Annie Hall. I'll never forget that. It'll always put a smile on my face."

Michael and my mother start talking familiarly, intimately. It seems so crazy, these two people, the biggest star on the planet talking with my mother, Annie Hall from Cleveland by way of Alexander City, Alabama, engaging like they're close friends or *family*. I'm not sure my mother appreciates the specialness—the uniqueness—of this moment.

My mom and *Michael Jackson*? I'll always love him for giving my mom that moment.

1990.

We roar into the new decade.

Elton John, Tom Cruise, George Burns, Milton Berle, Tom Hanks, and Jerry Seinfeld sit on the couch next to me. Moses—Charlton Heston—whom I met at The Comedy Store with Richard, drops by. I bring out my pal, Patti LaBelle. Magic returns. I honor my dad and book gospel great Shirley Caesar. On my birthday, Whoopi Goldberg comes on and celebrates Earth Day. A really nervous Dolly Parton comes out and, instead of sitting on the couch, sits in my chair. I share a look with the audience, shrug, and plunk down on the couch. I ask Dolly a couple of questions and then I say, "You know you're in my chair, right?"

With total composure, Dolly says, "You're right. I'm supposed to be over there on the couch."

"Well, yeah, but if you're more comfortable in the chair, I'm happy over here on the couch—"

"No, no," Dolly says, springing to her feet. "The couch is not yours. It's mine. You're sitting on my couch."

To screams from the audience, we switch.

Dolly. Cool. And all class. She wrote "I Will Always Love You," a big hit for her in the 1970s, which will become an even bigger hit for Whitney Houston in 1992. After Whitney passes away in 2014, someone asks Dolly if she has any regrets about Whitney singing her song. Dolly says she has one regret—that she and Whitney never got to sing the song together.

Some might consider me standoffish because I don't talk to my guests before they appear on the show. I do that for a reason. I want to preserve what I call the "First Blurt." Too often, I've seen interviews on talk shows that seem stale because I'm sure the host and guest are repeating a conversation they had ten minutes ago. I want my conversations to be fresh, real, new. So I insist on maintaining my First Blurt rule. I break my rule exactly four times—the first for Sammy Davis, Jr., and the second time for Maya Angelou.

"She's really nervous," Marla tells me. "I'm not sure what to do."

"Bring her to my dressing room," I say.

Maya Angelou—brilliant poet, passionate activist, best-selling author of *I Know Why the Caged Bird Sings* and many other books—sits in my dressing room before the show.

"I don't know why I'm so nervous," she says. She looks around the room. I follow her eyes as she takes in the small bar in the corner. She nods at a bottle of liquor in a purple bag.

"Crown Royal," she says. "That might calm my nerves. Do you mind if I have a little taste?"

"I'll join you," I say.

I grab two glasses and pour us each a splash. She swirls the brown liquor in her glass and gives me a look and a smile. I read her smile and pour her a little more. We clink glasses. Maya Angelou sips, swallows, sighs.

"Maybe another drop," she says. "Just to be polite."

She knocks back my pour.

"I feel a lot better," she says. "Now, here's what I want to say to you. Rap is poetry and poetry is rap. These rappers are poets, without a doubt."

"Tell me more."

"That's all I'm going to say. Saving the rest for out there."

Later, I bring out Maya Angelou, who seems calm and chill and sits demurely on the couch. When she begins to speak, she talks with a resonating power. But first, she compliments me.

"You work so well," she says. "You really do. You work *so* well."

She brings up the similarity she sees between poetry and rap, and when I ask her to explain, she says she'll show me. She goes into the poem, "A Negro Love Song," written by Paul Laurence Dunbar in 1895, delivering it with a beat and a rhythm that almost lifts me out of my chair.

"Seeing my lady home last night, jump back, honey, jump back," Maya Angelou recites, bobbing her head, throwing her shoulders back. "Held her hand and squeezed her tight, jump back, honey, jump back."

"Yeah," I say, my eyes closed.

"Heard her sigh that little sigh, saw that light gleam in her eye—" Maya lifts her voice, "saw a smile go flitting by, I say jump back, honey, jump back. *Woo!* Raised her lips and took a taste. I said love me honey, do you love me true? Love me as well as I love you."

Maya Angelou leans forward and whispers, "And then she answered, of course I do." She finishes the poem. "Jump back, honey, jump *back*."

Now I do jump out of my chair.

The audience explodes.

Maya Angelou, *poet*, rocks the house.

She will return six or seven more times. We take a taste of Crown Royal each time.

Corey Haim, heartthrob, heartbreaker, drug addict.

I first met Corey six months ago.

He had just turned seventeen years old. Corey burst into the public's attention as one of the stars of the 1987 cult film classic *The Lost Boys*. Since then, he'd blown up, especially with teenage girls. He was coming on that night to plug his new movie, and in preparation for his interview, the writers gave me copies of four current teen magazines. Each one had Corey on the cover.

Rushing toward my dressing room, I met Judy Haim, Corey's mom, in the hallway near the Green Room. She apologized for tracking me down before the show and taking up my time. "It's just—" She fought back tears. I saw that her hands were shaking. "Drugs," she said.

We both went silent. She and Corey reminded me of the relationship I had with my mom. Best friends. Judy and Corey against the world. Same as me and my mom.

"Corey really admires you," Judy said.

She looked at me with such desperation, such worry, and then such hope.

"It's so hard. He's going to open up to you. He really is. He's going to open up to you *on the show*. But it's not about the show. It's about you."

I took her hands. "I want to help. But I'm not a doctor. I'm not sure what I can do—"

"Call him once in a while. Check in on him."

"I can do that."

"Please," Judy Haim said, squeezing my hands. "Please."

After Corey's appearance on the show, I called him a few days later.

"How did you get my number?" he said.

"Your mom gave it to me. I'm gonna be calling you once a week, just to check in."

He didn't say no, so I called him. I called him every week. We talked about sports, mostly, and sometimes girls, or show business, anything that came to mind. Other times, he vented. He sometimes talked about drugs. One time, I bumped into him in a club. I saw the look in his eyes and I began to worry. Then, in one of our phone conversations, we talked about his relationship with his mom. They'd hit a rough patch. They'd stopped talking. I listened. I didn't judge. I let him vent, and when he finished, I wished him well, and told him I'd call him again the next week. I did. I didn't miss a week.

Since that first appearance, Corey has gone through several rough patches. He's been dealing with his parents' recent divorce and battling his drug addiction. Tonight—his second time on the show—he will be making his first public appearance since returning from rehab.

After the monologue, I bring Corey out to a chorus of screams from young girls who've packed the audience. I hug Corey and lead him to the couch. He seems jittery. He sits down, crosses his legs, continually scratches his face.

"How you doing?" I ask him. "You doing all right?"

"I'm doing good. Hey, I brought you something."

He reaches behind the couch and produces an Elvis pop-up book that depicts scenes from Elvis's movies. Corey has superimposed my face over Elvis's on every page. Instead of Elvis in *Blue Hawaii*, this book has Arsenio in *Blue Hawaii*. I find his gift funny and flattering. Then I bring up his addiction. He reveals that he's just gotten out of rehab.

"I've been messed up for a while," he says. "I've been clean now for two weeks. It's a start."

The audience, stunned at his admission, applauds quietly.

"It's not much, but you have to go second by second."

"I believe that," I say. "Isn't it true what they say, a lot has to do with the crowd you hang out with?"

"It's definitely true. You have to change who you hang with, your whole environment. I stay home, watch TV, I started playing hockey again. So, I'm back in school again. Now all I do is go to school and play hockey. I have to focus on living, not on drugs."

"What made you stop?"

Corey pumps his legs, rakes his hand through his hair, rubs his face. "One day, I got undressed to take a shower and I looked at myself in the mirror. I didn't look good. My face had deteriorated. I was so thin. I lost a lot of weight, like fifteen pounds. I looked terrible. I knew I had to do something."

We talk more about how he started facing his addiction and I bring up his relationship with his mom. From our talks, I know they have been estranged, but have since reconnected.

"Tell me how it's going with your mom," I say. "I hear you two got close again."

"Yeah, we're close again. Actually, it's better than that. Me and my mom are best friends again."

"That's good. That's good to know. Hey, what would you tell somebody who was in your position?"

"I don't know," Corey says. "It's hard. You have to talk to somebody. You have to find a way out."

He struggles to give advice because he doesn't have any to give. His biggest suggestion is to learn from his mistakes—to look at yourself, the way he did, and act, before it's too late.

"I'm glad we talked about this," I say. "A lot of people look up to you."

We finish the interview, we hug, and that week, as usual, I call him. I continue to call, week after a week, but life intrudes, his and mine, and after a while, our calls go from once a week to every other week, to less frequently. I try to stay as close to him as I can.

Corey's battles with substance abuse and addiction plague him for the rest of his life. He will check in and out of rehab at least fifteen times. He will get better from time to time, but he will never get well. In 2010, he will die from pneumonia. I cherish his memory and hold it close.

Paula and I hang out off and on for a year or so, seeing each other when we can. She comes on the talk show, and when her Under My Spell tour hits L.A., I drop in on her sold-out show at the Great Western Forum, seventeen thousand screaming fans on their feet, dancing nonstop for two solid hours. At one point, my face flashes on the Jumbotron. The crowd goes wild. What a rush. Fans love the idea of the two of us being together, an item, I, hosting the MTV Awards, while introducing my girl, MTV's hottest diva. In some fans' eyes, we're the Taylor and Travis of the moment. Absolutely magical.

But I, of all people, know that magic is an illusion. I also know that I have an ability to see the future, or at least around corners. I can tell when it's time to go. I want to leave early and on top. With Paula, I know our schedules will always interfere, our careers will always conflict with the time we need to spend together. So, rather than commit to something we both know can never be, we decide to slow down, pump the brakes. We stay close—we remain friends to this day—but we allow our dating life, our intimacy, to taper off gradually, until we identify as best friends and no more. My timing and innate ability to end things before they're finished may be my superpower.

24

LIKE A VIRGIN

WALK DOWN THE HALLWAY next to stage 29, open the nondescript door, and you step into a fuzzy, dim light. Feels like you're walking into a dream. But you know at once where you are. You have found it. The Green Room. Where guests gather, mingle, gossip, waiting until someone summons them to the show. Every TV show has a green room. But not like ours.

Our green room is a vibe. A scene. The place to be. You walk in and face a large mirror behind a long bar stocked with non-alcoholic drinks, sodas, juices, teas, tended by a professional bartender. The Green Room features cushy carpeting, two oversize plush couches, a table laden with food that's *beyond*—appetizers, entrees, and desserts—as good as any high-end restaurant. Mood lighting encircles you, comforts you, seduces you. Music murmurs, then right before the band strikes up "It's Hall or Nothing" on stage 29, we switch off the tunes and pipe in the show, live. The show tapes at five-fifteen, finishes at six-fifteen, and the Green Room goes ghost town by six-thirty. Supposedly. Sometimes guests stay in the Green Room way past closing. After George Lopez's first appearance on the show, I join him in the Green Room and we camp the fuck *out*.

"Man, everybody is hanging out, eating, drinking," George says. "We're in there for three hours after the show."

People who aren't even booked on the show come to the Green Room. I'm not sure how some of them get in. People *know*, I guess. Talent producers. Bookers. Managers. The guards at the gate. Somebody calls somebody. I don't really know. I don't really want to know. They just arrive. The Green Room becomes a clubhouse, *the* celebrity hang, the place to be seen.

Magic Johnson leaves the privacy of his dressing room and hangs out here. He says, "Being in the Green Room is as much fun as sitting out in the audience."

Comedian David Spade says, "Hey, man, the first time I came to the show, I brought Chris Farley, who wasn't even booked on the show. We just hung out. It was unbelievable. Everybody was there."

Athletes hang out. Lakers and Clippers and ballers on teams in town playing the Lakers and Clippers show up. Clyde Drexler of the Portland Trail Blazers, Charles Barkley of the Phoenix Suns, dozens of others. Comedians I know and have never met arrive to perform and to eat because that's what comedians do. Musicians, singers, and rappers show up. Everyone from Cher to Chappelle comes to the Green Room just to hang out. A young kid with a luxurious Jheri curl shoots out of the Green Room before a show one day and catches up to me in the hallway. "Yo, my name's Ice Cube. Would you listen to this when you get a chance?"

He hands me a cassette tape. I read the label. "'Fuck Tha Police.' Interesting. You in a group?"

"Yeah. We called N.W.A. Niggas With Attitudes."

"Man, I can't even say your name on TV. But I'm intrigued." I hold up the tape. "I'll listen to it."

I do. The song is fire and it addresses an attitude and problem in the neighborhood that America needs to hear about. The rap, the beats, the rhymes blow me away. Recently, Paramount has gifted me a golf cart so I can drop in on Lucie for a quick conference if I need to. I decide it'll be worth it to play her "Fuck Tha Police," just to see her reaction. I introduce the tape to her by saying this is tonight's musical guest, a new band I've discovered.

Lucie gets into the beat, cringes only slightly at the curses in the beginning, but when Ice Cube starts rapping, "Fuck the police comin' straight from the underground . . . ," Lucie loses it. *"Seriously?"*

"Nah. I just wanted to watch your head explode."

Eventually, after the group breaks up, I have Ice Cube, Eazy-E, and Dr. Dre on separately, performing and in conversation with me on the couch.

MC Hammer hangs out in the Green Room and performs. He does a couple of numbers with his dancers. He finishes and says, "We'll do one more thing."

"You know we're off the air, right?" I say.

"Yeah, nah, I know, I'm fine," and he goes into his next song.

New stars are born in the Green Room. Before one show, my music producer Sharon Olson tells me that Suge Knight has brought in a very young rapper named Lil' Bow Wow, an adorable six-year-old who freestyles for Marla and me. We put Bow Wow on that night, rapping and setting stage 29 on fire until the credits roll. Afterward, our switchboard lights up, with people loving him and at least one person expressing parental outrage—"Why is he even up that late?" But someone in postproduction or broadcast practices and standards misses the real outrage. If you listen now on YouTube, you can clearly hear six-year-old Bow Wow saying the N-word and possibly saying *shit.* Nobody catches it. Nobody bleeps it. Man, you can get away with anything if you're cute.

People make connections, pitch shows, propose deals in the Green Room. Will Smith and Quincy Jones discuss doing a sitcom about a Black teenager from a poor neighborhood who moves in with a wealthy Beverly Hills family. While I'm working on *The Arsenio Hall Show* on stage 29, they're working on *The Fresh Prince of Bel-Air* in the Green Room.

Maybe I should paint our Green Room red. It's the hottest hang in town.

On May 1, 1990, the show officially blows up. We hit our highest ratings ever while landing comfortably in first place among those coveted eighteen- to thirty-five-year-olds. It's fueled by one show, one notorious night. Madonna makes her first late night talk show appearance on our show, staying almost the entire hour.

Born in Michigan, Madonna left the University of Michigan and moved to New York to hone her dancing and singing skills. Flash forward to now. International superstardom. Madonna, dancer, singer, recording superstar, actor, outspoken and scandalous pop icon who lives to shock, chooses our show to publicize her new movie *Dick Tracy* and tease the world about her affair with costar Warren Beatty. The show starts with a jolt.

Burton Richardson, our announcer, belts his usual high-volume introduction, elongating "Arseni-OOOOO" for a solid fifteen seconds, the posse cranks the theme, the audience roars, the screen rises, and instead of me, Madonna, dressed in a white suit, appears. She strides onto the stage and impersonates me—strutting into the audience, shaking hands, slapping palms, pumping her fist, howling, "Woof! Woof!" She makes a full circle, returns to the stage, tapping index fingers with Mike, and then I step out from the wings, wearing a black suit. Over the screams of the crowd, I say, "That was Madonna! If you're gonna be chumped, might as well be chumped by the best." After a tentative hug—we're meeting for the first time—I escort her to the couch for our conversation. The audience roars over us, shrieking ecstatically until they scream themselves out, finally quieting enough to hear Madonna speak.

Over the next forty minutes, in a funny, steamy, sometimes confrontational interview, Madonna heats our set *up*. She talks about "giving good face." I ask what that is. She says, "It's not exactly like giving good ****___"

Bleep.

We talk about her breasts. I mention them because she'd recently posed for a *Vanity Fair* cover with one breast hanging out. I ask her why she made that decision. Madonna says, "If you've got it, flaunt it, right?"

Then we talk S&M. She has recently released a song called "Hanky Panky," which Madonna says is about a young woman who likes a "good spanky."

"I'm not talking about the spanky you get when you're bad," she coos. "I'm talking about the spanky you get when you're *good*."

She defines an acceptable S&M spanking—"not too hard, stings a little, you know, it hurts so good."

We show her in a flirtatious clip from *Dick Tracy*, playing opposite Warren Beatty. She talks about Warren. I ask her, on behalf of men worldwide, what he has that the rest of us don't. Madonna elicits a huge laugh by pretending to think about the answer and smiling salaciously. I press her, ask her, seriously, what does she like most about Mr. Beatty. She says, "He's not threatened. He's very sure of himself."

"Joan Collins once called him sexually insatiable."

"Well, when he dated her, he was twenty at the time. Aren't all twenty-year-olds insatiable?"

"That's a good point. How is he now?"

"I would say he's satiable."

"Are you satiable?"

"Yes."

"So, it's a match made in heaven."

"Or hell."

The audience combusts. It feels as if they are eavesdropping on an intimate conversation, kids listening outside their parents' bedroom.

"Is Warren a jealous kind of guy?"

"No."

"Are you?"

"Definitely."

"What kinds of things make you jealous?"

Madona scrunches her forehead, looks up into the lights, thinks. I decide to coax her. "Does the name Joan Collins make you jealous?"

"No. Have you seen her lately?"

The crowd goes bananas, erupting into the loudest laugh and applause of the night.

"Dammmn," I say. "That was ice cold. That was a cube."

"*I* want to know," Madonna says. "Are you jealous of John Stamos?"

I lose it. I throw myself back into my chair. In this moment, I wish I could disappear. But I glance at Marla and she is laughing, loving this.

"I want to know how it feels to be dumped for John Stamos," Madonna says.

After the applause and shrieking dies down and I compose myself, I look into the camera and say, "For those of you who don't know what we're talking about, there was a rumor that Paula Abdul and I were dating—"

"A rumor," Madonna says. "Right."

"Then Paula showed up at the Grammys with John Stamos—"

"You said you wanted to be with someone who was home more often—" Madonna says.

I practically fall out of the chair. "Oh, Ma, you're telling all of my business."

The audience goes pin-drop quiet. I grab on to that vibe. I go with it. "Look, the audience is going, 'Are they gonna fight?'"

The audience roars, hitting a level of hysteria I've rarely heard on our show, on any show.

"I know you were heading in the direction of getting into my shit, so I thought I'd turn it around," Madonna says, the word "shit" coming out as a *bleep* on air, our second bleep of the interview.

"I heard you got some good shit, so I ain't turning it around," I say, causing our third bleep of the show.

We'll have at least two more bleeps as we talk more sex, more Paula, more Warren, and then, of all things, Madonna disrespects my haircut. "If any of my dancers got their hair cut like that, they couldn't be in the show."

"Why not? Too much fade, or this part, or—why?"

"It's tired," Madonna says.

"What should I have, hair like Warren Beatty's? Talk about tired."

The audience laughs. Then Madonna and I somehow segue into mentioning her bedroom and Paula's bedroom, and Madonna asks what kind of bed Paula has, a king or *queen*. I glance at Marla and see we have less than thirty seconds to go. I say, "You are coldblooded. Anything else you want to talk about?"

"These couches," Madonna says, randomly, slamming her hand on the arm of her sofa. "These couches have to go."

"You don't like the couches?"

"No. You know when you drive down the street and they have those bargain furniture stores? And you see those couches in the window and it says, 'Half off'? Is that where you got these?"

"See? She's dogging me at every turn. I ain't said nothing about her Run-DMC necklace."

Time's up. We're done. I applaud and shout over the audience's applause, "Give it up for Madonna, give it up!"

The segment ends, Madonna hustles out, and I bring out the unique and weird comedian Emo Philips. After the show, Marla and I huddle in her office. I feel both breathless and shaken.

"Wow," Marla says. "Just wow."

"She had that stuff prepared, she was ready," I say. "Man. She dogged me, she dogged Paula and me, she insulted my haircut, she insulted the fucking *couches*. What the hell was that?"

"Great TV," Marla says. "We got to have her back."

Madonna returns, a few months later, with Rosie O'Donnell, both starring in the hit film *A League of Their Own*. Our show becomes Madonna's go-to TV home. Every time she appears, the ratings rise.

During a commercial, Madonna says to me, "I saw your interview with Charles Barkley."

I say, "Yeah, Charles is crazy. I love Charles."

"I *love* Charles," she says.

"Oh, really?"

Madonna and Rosie laugh.

"You want to meet him?"

"Yes," Madonna says.

"The Lakers are playing the Suns soon. Let's go to the game."

I call Charles at home that night. "Dawg, it's Arsenio."

"Hey, man, how you doing?"

"Apparently not as good as you. I had Madonna on tonight. She thinks you're cute."

"Really?" Charles says. "Bring her to the game."

We go, the three of us, Madonna, Rosie, and I, and after the game, we go to the locker room and I introduce Madonna to Charles. Cupid leaves it there. The playoffs begin and next thing I know rumors start flying that Charles and Madonna have become an item, which Charles adamantly denies. I don't know anything about their relationship, but Charles scores more in the playoffs than in the regular season. Now that's something that makes you go hmmmm.

By year's end, I'm flying so high, I want to pinch myself. The entire year feels like a dream. *TV Guide* names me "Television Personality of the Year." I'm honored with the Sammy Davis Jr. Award at the annual Soul Train Awards. I win the People's Choice Award as Favorite Late Night Talk Show Host. Then the big one.

I earn a star on the Hollywood Walk of Fame, right next to Marilyn Monroe. Entertainment outlets everywhere cover the award ceremony. I bring two guests—my mom and Jay Leno. I kneel on the sidewalk, rest my hand on my star in cement, and smile into a bank of cameras.

I'm soaring, can't get any higher.

VI
LOSING GROUND

25

ARE YOU GONNA BE BLACK EVERY NIGHT?

WE POWER INTO 1991. I bring out Mayim Bialik, the precocious fifteen-year-old star of the hit sitcom *Blossom*, whom I get to sing. I meet comedy royalty, Mel Brooks. The "King of Soul," James Brown, performs two songs and blows the roof off stage 29. I laugh my ass off with Billy Crystal, Redd Foxx, and Will Smith. Arnold Schwarzenegger gifts me his black leather jacket from *The Terminator*. I talk sex with Dr. Ruth Westheimer. I ask her if she's ever faked an orgasm and she replies, "Of course." In a spoof of *Star Search*, I introduce a six-year-old Elvis impersonator who brings down the house, a Hawaiian kid named Bruno Mars. We continue to do an occasional crazy cold opening, and I add a bit I take from my standup called, "Things that make you go hmmmm"—

When Black women breastfeed, how come they don't give chocolate milk? Hmmm.

And I create a group of guest stars who become regulars because they're reliable and always *on*, which takes the pressure off me—George Lopez, Sinbad, Howie Mandel, George Wallace, and Steven Seagal.

Seagal, martial arts expert, star of *Above the Law*, *Hard to Kill*, and a string of other successful action movies, and a world-class conspiracy theorist, makes the first of many appearances. The first time Steven comes out, I dap him up the way I do most guests. But unlike most guests, under his sport coat, I feel a gun. The guy is packing. Most of my guests leave their guns in the dressing room. Steven sits on the couch, we start talking, and I bring up his recent appearance as the guest host on *SNL*. Nearly thirty-five years later, everyone agrees—cast, writers, TV critics, the audience, *everyone*—that Seagal was the worst host in the history of the show. On our show, he tries a joke. At least I think it's a joke. I can't really follow what he's saying. The audience reacts with a long and disturbing silence. Steven adjusts his sport coat, pats his gun, and says, "I guess maybe I'm not good at comedy."

I like Steven Seagal and his films. He intrigues me. Even though we have very little in common, we go to dinner after the show once and Marla invites him to my birthday party, held in a hangar at the Santa Monica airport. As I mingle with invited guests, I hear a loud *whirr* outside. Marla instructs all the guests to go to the open doors just as a helicopter lands. Steven Seagal and his wife, actress and model Kelly LeBrock, climb down. He rushes over to me shouting "Happy Birthday, young man!" and throws his arms around me. I hug him back and—yup—there it is. Under his sport coat. His gun. Dude's always packing.

Keenen Wayans is an old friend. I met him in New York while I was working with Nancy Wilson and Michael Wolff at Carnegie Hall. One night, I went over to the Improv and Keenen was the doorman. We started talking, we hit it off, and we reconnected when we both moved to Los Angeles. Keenen hits comedy gold when he creates *In Living Color*, the groundbreaking sketch comedy show on the new Fox network. The show is known for its parodies of successful TV shows and movies. I'm not bothered when Keenen decides to take on me and my show.

They go full-on spoof. Keenen, playing me, comes out to an announcer's voice-over elongating the "O" in Arsenio, then Keenen introduces the Dog Pound, which is made up of real dogs, live Golden Retrievers, and he taps fingers with his bandleader who wears a cowboy hat and fronts his band who all wear cowboy hats. His *posse*. To imitate me, Keenen wears a suit with a hilarious oversize padded bottom. Keenen sits down with a "guest," disgraced Washington, DC, mayor Marion Barry, played by David Alan Grier. In real life, Barry has been convicted of several counts of drug possession and perjury. Keenen conducts a clueless interview, asking off-the-wall and irrelevant questions, presenting me as an over-the-top caricature.

"I hear you've written a book," he says to Marion Barry.

"I didn't write a book. I *was* booked."

Keenen asks several inane questions, and before Barry responds to one, Keenen stomps his feet and throws himself on the floor. He ends by telling Marion Barry that he has a clip of Barry's new film.

"What film? I didn't do a film."

"Roll it," Keenen says.

The film clip shows grainy footage from a hidden camera, part of a sting operation on Marion Barry and a prostitute, actually an undercover cop, taken from inside Barry's hotel room. As the cops drag Barry—David Alan Grier—out of the hotel room in handcuffs, he shouts into the camera, "I'm ruined!"

But if "imitation is the sincerest form of flattery" as Oscar Wilde wrote, then I'm flattered beyond words by another parody—comedian Dana Carvey doing "Carsenio" on *Saturday Night Live*. Carvey, who does a killer impression of Johnny Carson, appears in this sketch with a shock of Carson-like white hair moussed high and tight and wearing a bright red suit, which I wanted to own, but that's the only color suit I don't have.

"Carsenio" bounds onstage pumping his fist and barking. He shows us his prosthetic, elongated forefinger—a reference to my long fingers—as he tries to morph into me, but constantly lapses into "Johnny" talk, repeating throughout the sketch, "I did not know that," and "This is wild, weird stuff," while Phil Hartman, playing Ed McMahon, loudly ho-ho-hos in response. "Carsenio" refers to rumors that Johnny needs to appeal to a younger, hipper audience—my audience—and insists that "I'm not going anywhere." He will, of course, leave *The Tonight Show* a year later. "Carsenio" confiscates a few of my other tropes, calling himself a "party maestro," and saying that he'll "see us again in twenty-three hours."

The *SNL* sketch impacts me harder than Keenen's parody. I spent my younger years wanting to be Johnny, and now on *SNL*, the show that many consider the barometer of popular culture, Carvey's "Carsenio" is telling the world that Johnny wants to be *me*.

Stunning.

Humbling.

I play Cupid exactly twice, with Madonna and Chuck, and with my musical director, Michael Wolff.

Both of us being single, Mike and I often talk about women. Recently, he's been on a cold streak, dating a few women, with nothing developing beyond a few weeks. One night, while I look over our guest list, my eye fixes on a name. "Mike, you know who's on the show tonight? That chick from *Thirtysomething*. Polly Draper."

"She's kind of cute."

"Cute? She's hot."

Mike shrugs, but I can tell he's interested. I walk out for the monologue, then after the commercial I introduce Polly. She comes out wearing a red sequined dress cut to mid-thigh. She is *smoking*. I look over at Mike as she sits on the couch, and I can see he's smiling. Polly and I begin our conversation, and I point out that she's known as a sex symbol on the show. "So, in real life, are you single?"

She blushes. "Yes."

The audience howls. They think I'm coming on to Polly, but I'm getting information for Mike. During the next break, I say to Polly, "You know my musical conductor, Michael Wolff? Hey, Mike, come say hello to Polly, man."

He's so wound up he practically dives off the bandstand. He says hello—I don't hear a trace of Tourette's—then he sits on the couch next to her. They talk. They laugh. They flirt. We get the prompt that we're about to come back from the break and Mike returns to his keyboards. But he and Polly have connected. From that moment, during the commercial break, until this day, they have been together—married, practically inseparable, parents of two fantastic kids, music and screen stars Nat and Alex Wolff.

It begins as a low, relentless hum, an insistent nonstop undercurrent. I more than hear it, I live it. It ebbs, sometimes, but mostly the intensity spikes. I've felt it my entire life. I feel it more now.

Racism.

In the middle of the third year of the show, Lucie beckons me. She wants to talk. I announce myself to her assistant, who sends me into Lucie's office immediately without an offer of a beverage. I greet Lucie and settle on the sofa in front of her as she paces, then she sits next to me.

"We're seeing a dip in the ratings," she says. "Nothing too concerning. But noticeable."

"I'm aware," I say. "What can we do about it?"

She takes a beat. She looks pained. "Well, okay, this isn't coming from me. I'm the messenger. But I'm being besieged by advertisers, focus group feedback, station managers, my 'bosses.'"

She pauses again.

"Lucie, what are you trying to say?

"The show is very . . . Black."

"Well, as I think you're aware, I am, and always have been, Black."

"Yes, but are you gonna be Black every night?"

"Am I going to be—?"

"That sounded terrible. Let me try again. Do you have to be *so* Black? I mean, can you be less Black? I'm really digging myself into a hole, aren't I?"

"Very deep hole. But I'm lost. Can you give me an example?"

"Last night. Do you have to call a guest 'brother'?"

"I called someone 'brother'? There was nobody Black on the show."

"I heard you call somebody 'brother.'"

I rack my brain. I remember.

"Mark Wahlberg," I say. "I did call him 'brother.' He's white. I call everybody 'brother.'"

"Okay, here's another example. From the feedback. You go into the audience and everybody's Black. The whole audience. It feels like a Black show. So, if you're at home, watching the show, and you're *white*—"

She doesn't finish. She doesn't have to. I don't say anything. I'm annoyed and deeply hurt.

Finally, I say, "They want me to change my audience?"

"Maybe not go into the audience so much."

I rub my forehead, trying to massage away the migraine that I feel firing up. "What are you trying to say?"

Lucie sighs loud enough to shatter a window. "Don't let the show get too Black," she says.

"It's *Black*, it's going to be Black, because that's who doesn't have a talk show."

"You know what I mean."

The conversation meanders after that, winding into a dead end. We come to no conclusion, don't arrive at a direction. But Lucie's made the studio's point. The show's ratings have started dipping because the show and I are too Black.

I drive back to my office in a daze. I pull into my parking space and sit in the golf cart for a solid minute, still annoyed, hurt. I look straight ahead at stage 29, a gray concrete structure shimmering in the early summer sun. I feel a sudden chill and I shiver. Then I feel something else. Something I don't recognize. I can't identify it. Can't put my finger on it. Then I recall another meeting a while ago in my office, before the show started, the opening salvo of a battle that still rages.

Back before the show even aired, Willis Edwards, the president of the Beverly Hills–Hollywood chapter of the NAACP, sent me a letter in care of Marla. He claimed he had received numerous complaints about my hiring practices. According to his letter, I hadn't hired enough Black people to work on the show. He requested a meeting. I invited him to my office. Before the meeting, I called a few friends, all of whom were white. Jay said, "I feel sorry for you, man. You have to deal with stuff I'll never have to deal with."

"Unbelievable," I said. "You'll never have to answer these questions, 'Are you giving back to your people? Are you hiring enough Italians?'"

Another guy I know, a well-known executive producer and creator of a hit sitcom starring a Black comedian, said, "He just wants money. I wrote him a check, a donation, and he went away."

I started to tell him that's extortion, but I held my tongue. While that may be extortion or even blackmail, it may also be business as usual. I get it. But it's bullshit. And I was not writing a check to anybody. Especially when I knew how diverse my staff was.

What rankles me most is that I keep finding myself caught in the middle position between being too Black and not being Black enough. Spike Lee, after appearing on the show, calls me an "Uncle Tom" in an interview. We've since buried that hatchet. But I keep fighting battles with Black entertainers. A famous singer calls me and says, "Why did you put Ted Danson on first, before me? I thought late night would be different now that you have a show."

I try to reason with her. "You got to understand. I have to walk a line. I can't stumble. Sometimes I have to make business and ratings decisions so there will continue to *be* a Black show."

Meanwhile, I constantly push the envelope, introducing my audience to rap music, a mainstay on my show. I put on the culture's finest—Ice-T, LL Cool J, Salt-N-Pepa, A Tribe Called Quest, 2Pac, Heavy D & the Boyz, and Snoop, who freestyles on my show when he makes his television debut. I spend every waking second working on the show, going over the show with Marla, trying to improve, tweaking this, changing that, going out to clubs, looking for new musicians and comedians, sleeping less and less, operating on fumes. People ask me about my social life. Am I seeing anyone, do I have a woman in my life?

Yeah, I do.

The woman in my life is the *show*.

Willis Edwards arrives with a cluster of people, mostly from his NAACP chapter. Marla and I and my manager represent our side. Edwards, serious, measured, accusatory, wastes no time. He tells me that I have a responsibility to find Black people to work on my show. I lock my lips, fight back the temptation to say, "What you talkin' about, Willis?" I gotta be serious, especially since he seems outraged that Marla, my producing partner, and Sandy, the director, aren't Black.

"Well, they are women, which is unusual, practically unheard of," I say. "And Marla is one of only two executive producers. The other executive producer *is* Black. That would be *me*."

I hear my voice rise. I tell myself to breathe. I have to avoid getting angry. Me and Willis moving furniture around up in here would be horrible press. Then he says, "Still, the director should be Black—"

"Yo, I looked at a ton of directors' reels and résumés. I wish more of the choices I had were Black. I hired Sandy Fullerton. I actually didn't know what color she was when I requested to meet with her." I attempt a little joke. "Maybe Sandy *is* Black, but she's real, real light-skinned."

Willis is not entertained. "What about Black writers?" he says.

I say, "I found two Black writers that I've asked Paramount to put on staff, and I'm trying to find more. If you know any funny Black union writers, send them my way. I'm not totally staffed up. By the way—" I can't keep the sarcasm out of my voice. "I wonder if there are any experienced Black writers on *The Tonight Show* right now. Maybe I can steal a few from Carson. Has there ever been one Black writer in the history of that show? How about Letterman?"

"I haven't really looked—"

"You should look."

I'm beyond ready for this meeting to end. My pulse is racing, my breath is coming fast and hard. I calm myself.

"I have also created a minority intern program, with Paramount's blessing. I want to leave late night better than I found it. And as far as Black camera operators, lighting, finance executives, props, talent coordinators, security, heads of costuming and wardrobe, I got 'em! I will bet you that I have more Black people working on my show than on most Hollywood shows, period."

Edwards doesn't seem satisfied. So, here I am, once again stuck in that vicious middle, but this time, I feel trapped, squeezed. I feel the sides closing in.

Somehow, the meeting ends cordially. Marla, I notice, has been uncharacteristically quiet all this time. I move toward her, and as I huddle with her, I notice Edwards whispering to my manager. They shake hands and Edwards leaves.

Later, my manager tells me that Edwards asked if I'll donate forty thousand dollars to his chapter's annual Image Awards ceremony.

This really pisses me off.

I tell the NAACP that I refuse to attend the ceremony.

Edwards writes me a letter, apologizing for any misunderstanding. Pressured by the studio and my publicist, I go to the ceremony, reluctantly. I receive an award, along with Michael Jackson, Eddie, Whoopi Goldberg, and Jesse Jackson.

The week the show premieres, Edwards sends a press release to the *Los Angeles Sentinel,* a local Black newspaper, accusing me of discriminating against Blacks in my hiring practices.

I totally crash out.

I sit down with two reporters from the *Sentinel* to set the record straight. I call Edwards an extortionist, and forget to say "allegedly."

Edwards sues me for libel.

I'm so livid I sit for another interview for a magazine cover story and I call Edwards a pimp. The exact words I use are "phony motherfucking black tennis shoe pimp."

Willis sues me again.

I fight back. I engage lawyers, sit for depositions, hear arguments, endure aggravation, frustration, anger, and exorbitant legal fees—all while trying to do my talk show.

The legal back-and-forth never stops. It persists throughout my six years on the show. At one point, the Beverly Hills–Hollywood chapter of the NAACAP fires Willis Edwards, the court throws out his lawsuits, he appeals, the court throws out his appeal. Eventually, the whole ugly muddy mess fades away, after costing hours—*days*—of my life that I wish I had back.

26

DOWN THE WAY

ONE DAY, MARLA BOUNCES into my office, and Marla never shouts, but this one time I can see that she's bursting. She wants to let loose.

"Prince wants to do the show," she says.

"Get the fuck out of here."

"I'm serious. He loves the show, he's a big fan. But."

"Here it comes."

"He wants to do the whole hour."

"*Hell* yeah, it's Prince," I say.

"Hell *yeah*, it's Prince," Marla says.

Marla shuffles through a bunch of manila folders, finds the one she's looking for. She points to a date, first week of September. "Will this date work?"

"Hell, yeah, anything works," I say.

"It's Prince," she says.

"We should get a cohost that night. Somebody has to talk to me if Prince doesn't come to the couch. Who loves to talk? Prince and I both love Patti LaBelle," I say. "Other than my mom, nobody loves to talk more than Patti. Let's pitch Patti to Prince's camp."

Marla gets word to Prince's manager that we're thrilled to give Prince the whole hour, and Prince loves the idea of Patti as the designated talker that night. Prince has written and produced songs for Patti and adores her. She loves him, considers him an adopted son. We book Patti.

The Prince show will go down as one of the most electrifying hours I've ever experienced, not just in television, but in my life.

Burton Richardson introduces the show with Mike and my posse performing my theme song, then the screen lifts, I step out, and the band pumps up a Prince signature song, "1999." The audience, every single person on their feet, goes crazy, shouting, singing, applauding. I bring out Patti, the audience roars louder, and I introduce her.

"I'm so excited," Patti says to me. "This is real fun. I love it."

"Oh, yeah. Now, since this is a major event, I needed a date." I grin at Patti and squeeze her hand. She smiles, but I can feel the tension. I know her. She's nervous.

"Hey, Patti, you know the Dog Pound, right?"

As rehearsed, she looks at the few rows behind the band and says, "Yes. They're people whose Prince has finally come."

Laughter, applause, and Patti, still a little nervous, talks about her kids. "I have five kids, four sons, and I have another one, and his name is Prince."

The audience roars. I look at Patti, who smiles. Gripping my hand hard like she's holding me for the police, I nod into the camera. "Why don't you bust that card?"

"I'm gonna bust that card," Patti says. "Here to perform 'Let's Go Crazy' and 'Kiss'—PRINCE!"

The stage goes dark for a moment, then the lights come up on Prince standing at a floor microphone. He says, "We gather here today to get through this thing called *life*—"

Then he starts singing "Let's Go Crazy," his band, the New Power Generation, thundering behind him, with Prince's backup dancers, flying, tumbling, hurtling through the air. Prince, singing, dancing, doing the splits, again and again, in a jaw-dropping display of gymnastics, ballet, and virtuoso guitar playing, absolutely shreds stage 29.

Prince performs five songs, including a mesmerizing and frenetic version of "Purple Rain." The audience never sits. After his first two songs, we go to commercial, and then Patti and I sit for a segment while Prince changes for his next number.

"I'm so nervous," Patti says. "Prince wore me out."

"He's wearing everybody out tonight."

Patti talks about Prince with familiarity and kindness. Prince is unmistakably different. In every space he enters, he arrives surrounded by an aura, a pulsing light. But Patti insists that he's approachable, engaging, funny. He's not cold, or judgmental, or silent.

"He does speak," she says.

"He's actually quite talkative," I say.

"Yes, he's very down-to-earth."

I switch it up and tell her that I'm always fighting to keep my weight down. I wonder if I could ever look like Prince.

"Well," Patti says. "He doesn't eat."

"He doesn't eat? You mean, not at all?"

"No. Just bread. He likes bread."

She pauses.

"He lives on the spirit," she says.

The show connects Prince and me, we become friends, and we hang out sometimes when he comes to Los Angeles. He'll make several more appearances on the show and he surprises me every time. On one show, he places some copies of nasty reviews inside his piano, pours on lighter fluid, and drops in a match. Flames shoot up. Marla sprints toward the fire marshal, but he's already on his way, running toward the burning piano, brandishing a fire extinguisher. He sprays the flaming stack of reviews and douses the fire to wild applause from the audience, who must think this was all planned.

In 1991, I host the MTV Awards. Prince appears and stops the show when he performs his rocking dance tune "Gett Off." Prince fronts a wild production number that he designs as a mock orgy, featuring a dozen half-naked male and female dancers, simulating a variety of sex acts while he sings. Prince wears a striking yellow mesh suit as he wails on his electric guitar. He suddenly spins around. The backside of his suit has been cut out and we see his butt cheeks. Shocking. Audacious. Hilarious.

As host of the show, I can't let that go.

I ad-lib a couple of Prince naked ass jokes.

After the show, the next day, and the day after that, everybody seems to be talking about Prince's MTV appearance. *I* certainly can't stop talking about it. I continue to joke about his ass during my monologue on the show. Then Prince sends me a fax, saying, "You know what I love about you? You mess with me, but you never hurt me. You do jokes about my ass and I laugh at them."

I'm thankful for his fax because he's right. I would never intentionally hurt him.

The next day a long box arrives at my office. Cheryl brings it to me. I see the Prince emblem on the box. Cheryl clears her throat, trying to stifle a laugh. The woman knows something. I open the box and find a beautiful black suit. I hold it up.

"This is so thoughtful," I say.

"Turn it around," Cheryl says.

The suit has no back.

Nothing. No fabric. No back at all.

And no ass.

"Gett off," Cheryl says.

Simply, Prince is one of the funniest, smartest, savviest people I've ever met. One night, sitting in the private VIP rooms at the House of Blues on Sunset, he predicts the future. He envisions a music industry that will abandon the current model of records and CDs and move into something that will become Napster, a peer-to-peer sharing service, detrimental to the financial future of artists. I can't imagine the future the way he does. His vision becomes prophetic.

Another time, I visit him in a recording studio. I walk in and see that he's draped colorful silk scarfs over the lamps and a wall sconce in the studio, giving the room an amorphous, moody, mellow personal Prince ambience. The vibe you get is the polar opposite of late night or early morning in the studio with Snoop. With Prince it's quiet as a church at midnight. Nobody else around except me and the engineer. No entourage. And absolutely no smoke. Not even nag champa. You dare not light up a blunt in the presence of Prince Rogers Nelson.

I settle in and watch him and the engineer work, Prince tinkering with new songs, experimenting with new sounds. I close my eyes and listen, just listen, realizing, *This is beyond amazing. Me, Prince, hearing this music for the first time.* I'm in awe and I feel privileged.

Around one in the morning, Prince says, "L.A. shuts down so early. Not much happening after one or two, is there?"

"Oh, there's stuff happening. You just have to know how to find it."

"Like what? Any place with music? I want to hear what people on the West Coast are listening to and dancing to."

"We can always go to an after-hours joint."

"An after-hours joint?"

"Yeah. They have them down the way."

Down the way.

Rashon Khan told me and Richard about a place in the 'hood, an illegal club way south of Wilshire Boulevard.

"Tell me about those," Prince says.

"It's where people go to dance after they finish working. Strippers, pimps, you know, night folks."

Prince goes silent, nods as he considers this. I'm sure he's about to say, "Negro, you must be out yo' damn mind," but instead he says, "I want to go to the after-hours joint."

After the show Friday night, I go home and take a nap. At two a.m. my driver and I pick Prince up in my new custom-built stretch limo—leather seats and upholstery, a drawer filled with my personal creams and lotions, my Arsenio signature stretching elaborately across the outside of the entire vehicle.

My driver opens the door, the new car smell eases out, and Prince, snacking on a lollipop, settles into the cabin. He wears a white suit and matching white boots, all made from the same fabric. He carries a clear acrylic cane, which he places across the seat.

"After-hours joint," he says.

"Going to Miss Mary's," I say.

We drive through the Mid-Wilshire district, down La Brea Avenue, heading south, passing the Parisian Room, where I opened not too many years ago for Joe Williams. We pull up in front of a nondescript house surrounded by a high chain-link fence guarded by two growling, barking pit bulls. A man in a suit appears at the fence. He gestures and the pit bulls back up and sit at attention. The suit opens the gate, and Prince and I follow the guard toward the rear door of the house. He leads us inside.

We enter a living room illuminated by floor lamps with red and blue bulbs. We keep walking, into a dining room with a bar. Several people, mostly women, congregate in corners or sit on a plush red sofa. I notice only one or two guys. Smoke fills the air. Music plays through a sound system. The women in the corners sway, one or two dance alone, a couple dance together.

"Here's how it works," I say to Prince. "You put some money on the bar—I'm taking care of it—and you tell the woman behind the bar what you want."

"Okay," Prince says.

"What you want?"

"Nothing. I don't drink."

"You want some water?"

"Not here."

We take our seats. I place a large bill on the bar. I say my drink order and thirty seconds later the beverage appears in a paper cup. Prince straddles his barstool, leaning on his cane for balance, for protection, for security. He scans the room, taking everything in. I try to sense what he feels—shock, discomfort, but mostly fascination. He studies the surroundings clinically, like a scientist.

I sip my drink. "I can't believe you let me bring you here."

"I can't stay relevant if I don't roll with you down here. I'm looking at what these girls dance to at three in the morning. What moves them. What makes them put down their drink and dance."

The music goes from something slow to something funky. A woman sitting on the sofa springs to her feet, claps her hands, and says, "Oh, that's my song." She starts dancing by herself in the middle of the room. Prince watches her intently. He says nothing until the song ends and she sits back down.

"Did you see that? What was it in the first bar of that song that made her have to get up and dance?"

We stay at Miss Mary's for two hours. We never move from our seats at the bar. I sip my drink, keeping an eye on Prince, respecting and protecting his boundaries. He sits with erect posture, nearly motionless for the whole two hours, leaning on his clear acrylic cane between his legs, his eyes on the strippers filtered through the red and blue lights, watching how they move, how they grind, how they dance. Occasionally, a woman edges toward him and whispers, "Hi, Prince," and lightly brushes his forearm, or his shoulder, or his back. Drunk or high or simply disoriented by the surprise guest, they seem to want to know that he's real, that they're not dreaming, that he's not a vision in the smoke. For those hours, his fascination with the strippers never lessens, and their interest in him, their awe of him, never fades. We leave close to dawn, heading from the dining room through the living room, out the front door, past the guard, the suspicious pit bulls, and into the backseat of my limo, where Prince, energized by his research trip into the field, launches into another vision of the future, again imagining Napster, or Spotify, the end of albums, the reconfiguration of the music business as it currently exists, seeing the end of the world as we know it.

I stay close with Prince through the end of my show, through the years afterward, until his death, twenty-five years after he sang "Let's Go Crazy" and "Kiss" on stage 29, the first week of September, 1991.

His death shocks me. I can't get my head around it, can't grasp the reality of it. Prince, overdosed on fentanyl, or painkillers, or painkillers laced with fentanyl, found dead in an elevator, alone? Impossible. I never once saw him drink, or smoke, or take a single drug. I always respected his boundaries. I never did drugs around him, never even ate an edible. I had no idea he'd gotten hooked on drugs. The shock of finding that out, of not knowing anything about his drug addiction, obliterates me. I wonder if I really knew him. But I did. We knew each other. I think of that first time on the show, spending the entire hour, with Patti, then later, his subsequent appearances, remembering—the smoldering piano, receiving his joke gift, the backless suit, our two a.m. excursion to Miss Mary's down the way, private parties in L.A. clubs in the middle of the night, every laugh we shared, every astonishing moment. His death shattered me. His death broke my heart. I lost my brother.

27

YOU'RE GOING TO HELP ME LIVE FOREVER

ON A SCORCHING HOT September day, I drive to work, listening to a new rapper on a cassette tape, grooving to it, digging it, and I think—*I love music. I live for music. I breathe music.*

I think about my musical trajectory, beginning with Al Green, Aretha Franklin, and the Temptations, my main Motown attraction, "Get Ready" my basement show theme song. Then in college came War; Earth, Wind & Fire; and the Ohio Players' "Fire" and "Skin Tight." It all changes when I get to Hollywood. A new addition arrives like a "grandmaster" flash of lightning, my music veers into a different universe, and I hear *it*, the first rap song that got me, that really got *into* me, the Sugar Hill Gang's "Rapper's Delight."

I search out this music. I listen for hours, inhale it, absorb it, and when I hear that Don Cornelius doesn't feel it and Oprah doesn't like it, and I know Johnny Carson hates it and will never get it, I realize that I've found my lane. I've found my *meal*.

Once I create that safe place for rappers to perform regularly, word spreads. I invite them in and rappers find more than their comfort spot. They find their home. The first solo rapper I bring on is a young man named James who goes by LL Cool J. Other rappers quickly follow—A Tribe Called Quest, Leaders of the New School, MC Lyte, Whodini, Yo-Yo. When I meet Tupac, he doesn't rap. He dances with Humpty, a guy who wears a fake nose, in the group Digital Underground as they perform their hit, "The Humpty Dance." After the show, Tupac approaches me shyly and says, "One day, I hope to rap here."

"You're a rapper?"

"Yeah, I'm a rapper."

I look at this kid. He's nineteen, maybe. "Okay, when you got an album, call me."

He does. His first album, *2Pacalypse Now*, establishes Tupac as a generational star, rapper, activist, poet. He sits with me a year or so later, his first interview on any talk show. He gets personal, revealing his brutal run-ins with the police, his motivation for his music. A year later, he makes another appearance on the show. Two years later, he's assassinated in a drive-by shooting in Las Vegas.

Not surprisingly, rappers talk to each other. Dr. Dre tells me about this guy, Calvin. "Hey, man, I'm gonna hook you up. His album's not ready yet, but if you could just throw him on, it'd be nice to introduce him to the world."

"But if the album's not ready, what's he gonna do? Does he have a single from it?"

"Nah, he's gonna do this thing called freestyle. All you got to do is have your posse give him a beat."

I bring on Calvin, a young man wearing a Toronto Maple Leafs jersey, his hair braided on both sides in dog ears, and I introduce him not as Calvin, but the way Dre told me to, "From Long Beach, this is Snoop Dogg."

The rest, well, you know.

Nobody embraces hip-hop the way I do. No other talk show host engages rappers the way I do. I offer them a forum to express themselves and to interpret their music. Ice-T sits on the couch and explains the lyrics on his album *Cop Killer*. He insists that he's not promoting violence against the police. He's writing songs protesting police brutality.

"I'm playing a character," he says. "You know how you watch the Terminator kill people? You would never be afraid of Schwarzenegger if you saw him in a mall. Same with me. I'm not a cop killer. I'm a guy. I'm a parent. I'm a husband. I'm just trying to show you what we're experiencing every day in the neighborhood."

The Arsenio Hall Show becomes synonymous with hip-hop. I break more rappers than any other show. Fans line up for hours to see the biggest rap stars of the day. We are the home of hip-hop. The audiences packing stage 29 love every performance, exploding with raucous cheering, screaming, stomping from my introduction of the artist to each song's final note.

America, though, at least the small sample that makes up the Nielsen ratings, doesn't seem to love hip-hop as much as our audiences do. Our ratings continue to slide. A few affiliates jump ship. The ratings dip and the affiliates' exodus create a strange new vibe in our offices, something I haven't felt before. Paramount hires an outside research company to conduct focus groups to get a sense of what our TV audiences like and what they may object to about the show. The focus groups' findings annoy me. Their research disparages my wardrobe. The focus groups overwhelmingly feel that I shouldn't wear jeans, and they really hate the ripped jeans I wear. But who are these people? Are they white or Black? Young or old? I want to scream that the torn jeans are designer jeans and cost more than most of the fifty faceless people in these focus groups make in a month. But I'd be screaming into an abyss.

Now, nearly three years into the show, I feel a shift. The earth beneath my feet trembles. The sudden swirl of negatives dizzies me. Ratings peaking, then falling. Focus groups hating my jeans. Rumors flying, about who will replace Johnny Carson. Letterman, Johnny's guy, currently on NBC after Johnny, is the clear front-runner. But other names come up, Jay's most prominently. I notice that nobody floats my name. I can only imagine that conversation, "If you were to replace Johnny, you'd have to change your look, lose the leather jackets, the wild outfits, and wear suits exclusively. You'd be inheriting a much more conservative audience. You can't be so Black."

I love Johnny. Always have. As a kid, I wanted to be Johnny. But I have my own show now and I don't want to be Johnny anymore. I want to be me.

"You heard?" Marla says one afternoon. "You know what's going on?"

I have no idea what she's talking about. But her face is flushed. Her breathing seems ragged. She looks kind of sick.

"No, what?"

"Sit down."

"I'm fine. I don't need to sit down."

"You really do."

"I'm not going to sit—"

"Lucie's leaving."

A gut punch. A blow out of nowhere that knocks the wind out of me. I drag myself to my chair. "When?"

"Effective immediately. She may be here another day or two, but she's already out the door."

"Where's she going?"

"Fox. Diller hired her to be chair of Fox TV."

"What a power move," I say. "She'll put her imprint on the network."

I want to bury my head on the desk.

"This is so fucked. Lucie has been my biggest supporter, my biggest fan, the creative force behind the show. It's her show, too. She called it 'her baby.'"

"She was the police, but she was a good cop."

"Why didn't she tell me?"

"I guess because it's happening so fast."

I sit up straight in my chair, try to get to my feet, but I can't move. I'm stuck to my chair. Frozen. Marla goes quiet.

"Who's taking over?" I ask.

"Brandon Tartikoff."

"Really? Former head of NBC. Johnny's guy."

"You know him?"

"No. But he wasn't very complimentary about me in the *Time* magazine article."

I've actually memorized what Brandon said—"The race is not a sprint, it's a marathon. Whatever burns the brightest, fades the fastest."

That was more than two years ago. I'm still burning bright. I make a mental note to remind Brandon of that.

"Well," Marla says, "I'm sure he's—"

Her voice drops off.

"I'm sure he is," I say. "But I know what he's not."

"Lucie," Marla says.

"I'm sorry I didn't tell you myself."

Lucie has offered me a chair, a beverage, and an apology, but I can't sit or drink, and I'm having the hardest time accepting her apology. I stand and pace. I look longingly at her couch where Lucie and I have sat and discussed the problems of the world, meaning our world, *our fucking show*.

"You really caught me off guard," I say.

"I'm sorry. It happened so fast, practically overnight. Barry Diller calls and asks me to run Fox TV, the first woman to run a television network. How can I say no?"

"No, no, you can't, you absolutely can't. By the way, not sure I said it before, but congratulations."

"You didn't. Thank you."

She stares at me, hard, her eyes fixed on mine. "Okay, listen. *In Living Color.*"

"Yeah, Keenen's show. He does a funny impression of me. I'm not angry about it. Maybe a little. What about it?"

"It's—"

She clamps her mouth shut, searches for a word.

"Struggling," she says.

I flash on the weekly sketch show that features a bunch of comics, some of them my friends, most of whom have been on my show—Keenen, his brother Damon, Jamie Foxx, Jim Carrey, Tommy Davidson, David Alan Grier.

"My first order of business," Lucie says. "Orders from Diller. Figure out why the show's struggling, what the show needs, and fix it. Well, I know what the show needs."

"What?"

"You."

I take about five steps back, practically slam into the wall.

"What?"

"I want to bring you to Fox. Come with me."

"I have a show here."

"You did three years. Leave on top. Everything's going to change next year. Johnny's gone, you don't know who's coming in, what kind of competition they will be. Come with me to Fox. Take over *In Living Color.*"

"Are you serious?"

"Dead serious. We'll shake up the show business world. Again."

"I couldn't. Keenen's my friend."

Lucie shrugs. "Think about it. I can make it happen in a second. Rupert loves you."

I spit out a laugh. "Rupert Murdoch doesn't know me from any other Black guy. I'm pretty sure he thought I was the valet parking attendant at the Ivy."

"That was then. Before the show. Believe me, he knows you now."

I look down, press my shoe into the floor like I'm crushing a cigarette. "Lucie, I can't. I have to stay here. Ride it out."

"Sleep on it."

"I don't have to. I'm staying here. But thanks."

We don't speak for thirty endless seconds. Lucie looks down at her desk and absently moves stuff around on her blotter.

"You'll be in good hands," she says. "Brandon is great. He's a legend."

"Excited to meet him."

I'm lying. I'm not excited to meet him. At this moment, I couldn't care less about meeting Brandon. He doesn't know me. Doesn't know the show, what we need, how the show ticks. He is not Lucie.

"I know you're not excited to meet him," Lucie says. "But give him a chance. If you're staying, you got no other choice."

We don't say much after that, but I'm feeling everything—loss, shock, abandonment, fear. Lucie's leaving. A best friend—my sister, my champion—moving away, leaving me to fight the daily battles with a stranger. I feel like a star player on a winning team in New York or L.A. who's been traded to Toronto. I won't even be playing in the same *country*.

We end by mouthing those meaningless, generic phrases you say to people when you know you'll never see them again—"We'll stay in touch," "We're more than just business friends," "We can't let too much time go by"—and other bullshit.

Lucie's star rises even higher when she leaves Paramount for Fox. After four months, Barry Diller leaves as Fox Broadcast CEO and Rupert Murdoch gives Lucie Diller's job. Lucie remakes Fox TV, increasing programming from four nights a week to all seven nights. She has her hand in the creation of several huge hits, including *The X-Files*, and with uncanny foresight, she brings the NFL to the network. You can count her misfires on one hand, key among them her new baby *The Chevy Chase Show* that she airs opposite me, kind of shoving Chevy in my face. At least it feels that way. The show fails spectacularly. It lasts six weeks and costs Fox a fortune. I don't gloat, but I'm glad. Lucie herself lasts only three years at Fox. She constantly butts heads with Murdoch, challenging his management style. Their partnership seems like an untenable collision of ideals—she a strong woman who likes to take charge, he not a fan of strong women. Lucie flees Fox and returns to Paramount, where she starts a brand-new television network, UPN. I have nothing to do with that. I'm long gone.

Lucie's leaving Paramount in 1991, three years into our show's run, more than shakes me up. It blindsides me and nearly ends me. I call an urgent lunch meeting with Mark. I ask him if we can move the show to another studio.

"Universal keeps calling me," I say. "Can we go there?"

"Can't happen," Mark says. "You have a contract with Paramount."

"The thing is, Mark." I lean across the table and whisper urgently. "I'm exhausted. All I do—every single thing I do—is for the show, to promote the show, to sell the show, to make people aware of the show. I love hosting the MTV Awards, it's fun, it's a night out, one of few I get to have, but I do it to sell the show. I have to. I don't have a network behind me. I don't have a team. It's not like I'm the *network* late night show and I can book top-line guests because they get to pimp their movie next morning on *Today* or *Good Morning America* or the *CBS Mornings* show. We don't have that syndicated family. I'm on an island. I'm alone. It's not unusual for musical artists to be given an ultimatum that they can't do my show if they want to appear on *Saturday Night Live*. Standup comics I know apologize to me. 'I want to do your show, but the network told my agent that if I do, I'll pay a price.' The networks have leverage and power. It's hard out there for a syndication pimp. So, we improvise. When stars come onto the Paramount lot to shoot a movie, either I literally chase them down, or Lucie starts blowing up phones all over the Paramount lot and suddenly Harrison Ford comes walking onto the show. Lucie called us the little engine that could. We have to work harder to get up the same hill. So we do. We bust ass. Billboards, buses, commercials on local TV, going on the road, doing the show from other cities. Lucie does all that. *Did* all that."

I'm ranted out. I go quiet until Mark finally says, "She left and you're pissed."

"I am pissed. But I'm mostly worried. We're starting to lose affiliates, and in other markets we're starting to get moved around. Lucie came into my office last week. She said, 'The good news is you're killing in Denver. The bad news is they want to put you on at three in the afternoon.' Three in the afternoon? I'm the *late night party*. What the *fuck*?"

"What do you want to do?"

"I know how this movie ends. I want to get ahead of it. I want to leave before the ratings drop even more and the studio blames me. I want to leave on top. I don't want to be on at three o'clock in Denver, and noon in Milwaukee, and two in the morning in Sioux Falls. Mark, it's time. The show's a hit. I want to follow Lucie out the door."

"You can't leave yet," Mark says. "Well, you can. But don't."

"If I stay without Lucie, and by the way, unrelated, Dana's leaving, too, I will be miserable."

"So, let's plan your escape."

For some reason, those words calm me.

"My exit strategy," I say.

"Yes. I promise you that I will set you up so you can leave on your own terms and not have to worry about money. I hear you. But I need time."

"How much time?"

"Three years."

"Well," I say. "Let's talk about the house. Let's put a clock on that, too."

"Because that's what you really want," Mark says. "That's a big part of it. I know you."

Nobody knows me the way Mark does.

Yes. The house.

My dream house.

I've started sketching it, doodling designs on an art pad, envisioning it—*dreaming* it—my ultimate getaway. My escape.

"I'm ready to do it," I say. "I'm ready to go all in."

"Build your dream, then leave the show and move into your house."

"And how long will that take?"

"Possibly two years, but count on three."

Ultimately, Mark's guess will be nearly exact. Cheryl's dad, Albert, finds the perfect site for my dream house—fifty acres in the Santa Monica Mountains, 2,750 feet above sea level, a panoramic view, one side facing the mountains, the other the ocean and Catalina Island. Breathtaking. Majestic views in every direction. A dream parcel of land. Albert locates the architect, Edward Grenzbach, famous designer of stars' homes, among them Johnny Carson's house in Malibu. I immediately hire him. As a kid, I dreamed of doing a show like Johnny Carson's. Now I'm having his architect design my house. So strange, so surreal. A dream come true. Meanwhile, my three-year clock starts ticking.

"Three years, and you'll be set," Mark says.

"Three and out," I say.

Lucie. A force. My champion.

Damn it, Lucie, we shook them up. We made a show that nobody had seen before, and we did it every night. I went all out, pedal to the metal, creating a late night party, night after night after night. I almost never took a break. We never had a guest host. We showed reruns instead.

Eddie Murphy and me as "Shaman Baba"
(*Coming 2 America*).

My dear cousin, Diane Carter. The book she gave me sparked a dream. Changed my life. Give someone in your life a book!

The one and only Patti LaBelle (Patz and Hall).

Sandy Fullerton, Gordon "Gordy" Klimuck, Marla Kell Brown.

Michael Wolff, music director for *The Arsenio Hall Show*. I call him Mike, and he calls me "Cupid"!

My business manager and friend, Mark E. Landesman.

I produced a film called *Bopha!* that Nelson Mandela was kind enough to view and critique for me.

Daddy, A. Cheron Hall, Cheryl Bonacci.

Of course my son was raised to be a Browns fan from day one.

Cheron and I love Dodger Stadium.

My son heading into the Kenny Smith basketball camp.

That day your baby gets his first car.

Jammin' in the basement with my son is surreal. The ultimate joy.

Big A, Little A, and Natalie at our Malibu happy place. #Nobu

My girl, Natalie Watkins-Hall.

Me and Natalie grabbing our morning coffee.

Johnny Gill with "big brother" giving him advice on how he should sing "My My My."

Opening Day: George Lopez, Magic Johnson, and yours truly at Dodger Stadium.

Mom!

I hope I sent this newspaper cartoonist a bottle of Dom Pérignon.
STAHLER © Jeff Stahler. Reprinted by permission of
ANDREWS MCMEEL SYNDICATION for UFS. All rights reserved.

"You're the engine," she told me.

The little engine that could.

We could, we did, and we rocked it.

Yeah, Lucie, we rocked it.

Pam Hyatt, our receptionist, switchboard operator, and gatekeeper, buzzes me from her office right outside my door. "Mr. Tartikoff is here to see you."

I cross my office in two strides and swing open my door. Brandon Tartikoff, the newly installed chairman of Paramount Pictures, formerly the president of NBC Entertainment, where he developed and launched *Hill Street Blues, The Cosby Show, Seinfeld, Cheers, Law & Order, Family Ties, The Fresh Prince of Bel-Air, Miami Vice,* and many other hit shows, propelling the previously last-place network to first place ahead of the other networks by a wide margin, stands outside my office, laughing with Pam. A couple of his lieutenants, stiff-looking guys in suits, stand behind him.

"Brandon," I say, extending my hand.

"There he is."

I gesture toward my office. "Come in, come in."

"The mothership," he says. "Where it all happens."

"Mostly where all the naps happen," I say.

He laughs, thankfully. He heads into my office, leaving the lieutenants behind, at attention.

I close the door behind him. He walks quickly, a man on the move, settles on the couch. I pull my desk chair next to him. Brandon wears a suit and tie, but he appears rumpled, his hair mussed, his eyes flickering beneath heavy lids. He looks as if he'd be more comfortable in a T-shirt and sweatpants. Everybody knows Brandon's reputation—boy genius, named the head of programming for NBC at age thirty-two, turning out hit after hit, the wonder kid with the golden touch, climbing the corporate ladder, assuming the head of the network, and then, out of the blue, his life changes, literally upends. While he's driving with his eight-year-old daughter near Lake Tahoe, the car spins out of control and crashes. He escapes with a few bruises, but his daughter suffers a severe brain injury. He quits NBC to be with her, spending each day by her side, helping her learn how to walk and talk again. Now, several months later, with his daughter improved, Brandon, feeling itchy to get back in the game, has jumped back into show business, landing right on the top rung of the Paramount entertainment division.

"I wanted to say hello," he says. "I felt we should meet, since I'm now your guy."

"I'm glad you did. Can I offer you something, a beverage—"

"No, thank you. This is a quick drop-in."

He looks around the room, takes in the office's two most prominent features—first, the mirrors that give you the sense that you're staring into the end of time and space.

"Wow," Brandon says. "That mirror. Wild optical illusion."

"Yeah, kind of feels like you're staring into infinity."

Brandon looks in a different direction and sees something else unusual—my collection of stuffed animals, fifty at least, maybe more.

"What's the significance of all those stuffed animals?" he says.

I drop my voice. "When my mom separated from my dad, we were really struggling and for my birthday she bought me this little nine-dollar stuffed dog. It was the only thing she could afford. It was really special to me. I kept it as a symbol of my life during the lean years. It was on my bed at my grandmother's house when the house burned down. I told that story in a magazine interview and people started sending me all kinds of stuffed animals. I have at least fifty more at home. Look at that one." I point at a stuffed bear wearing a tiny dominatrix teddy. "It even has a little whip."

"Nice," Brandon says.

Then his eyes lock on something else, something I've created especially for him—a framed copy of what he said in the *Time* magazine article about the race not being a sprint, but a marathon, a sentiment spoken directly about me. He sees the framed quote, leaning against the wall right in front of him. I put it there in anticipation of this meeting. I look at Brandon and paste on a smile. I can't tell if he's amused or embarrassed, but he speaks quickly. "I had to say that. I was at NBC. I was Johnny's partner."

I don't let him off the hook. I keep smiling and let him keep talking.

"I mean, come on, what else could I say?" Brandon scoots to the edge of the sofa. "The truth is, Johnny likes you. He doesn't see you as a competitor. You book guests that he wouldn't. He's cool with you."

"I heard that," I say.

"You hear anything else?"

"You mean the rumors that he's leaving the show next year?"

"So, you have heard."

"Is it true?"

Brandon smiles, then shrugs.

"I'll take that as a yes," I say.

"He's been doing the show for thirty years. He deserves—"

"Anything he wants," I say. "He deserves everything. I'm a fan."

"As for your show, I have no notes." Brandon stands. "It's going great. My plan is for you to keep doing what you're doing and for me to stay out of your way."

We shake hands again, and as he starts for the door, he sneaks a last glance at the framed quote leaning against the wall.

After that meeting, I see Brandon a few times on the lot, all unplanned. We meet officially exactly one more time before he leaves Paramount to form his own production company a little over a year later. Tragically, only six years after that, at the age of forty-eight, he will pass away from Hodgkin lymphoma.

I'm hesitant about sitting down with Brandon's replacement, Kerry McCluggage, but I bound into his office enthusiastically. I act excited, even a little over the top, but he seems—

I can't tell what he seems. He shows little emotion, or enthusiasm, or vitality. I'm tempted to put a mirror in front of his mouth to see if he's alive.

Kerry's an Ivy League preppy type, around my age, great posture, good hair, not a strand out of place. He's formal, soft-spoken, with no discernible sense of humor. He reminds me of an accountant or insurance agent or mortician. And he's white. Very white.

He greets me with a borderline fishy handshake. He smiles, we talk, and then he starts rolling out the clichés—"Here for whatever you need," "Not going to get in your way," "Really important part of the Paramount family," "Keep doing what you're doing, why fix what's not broken?"

Sounds generic, sounds vague, sounds like Brandon. Yup. Marla had it right.

He's not Lucie, either.

Thursday morning, November 7, 1991.

I'm home, running late, rushing to get to Paramount for my morning meeting. I shower quickly, start to get dressed. The black phone, the landline on my lacquered black nightstand, rings. I grab it, cradle it as I tuck in my shirt.

"Talk to me," I say.

"Arsenio, it's Lon."

Lon Rosen. Magic's agent, partner, Magic's *guy*. I've known Lon for years. Lon likes to joke. Lon likes to play. But at this moment I hear a different Lon. He speaks quietly, his voice heavy, carrying a kind of weight I've not heard before.

"What are you doing?" Lon says.

"Getting dressed. About to head to Paramount to start my day."

"Stay where you are. Earvin's going to call you."

"Hey, Lon, can he call me at Paramount? I'm late. I've got to get out of here. Tell him to call me at the office."

"Arsenio," Lon says. "Stay right there. Earvin needs to talk to you. Now."

Lon hangs up and I wait. And I wait. I sit on the bed to get my bearings. I know something's wrong. Magic hasn't played for a week, maybe more. Rumors have been flying, the most common is that he has shingles. A mishmash of garbage has spattered the tabloids. None of it true. I would know. I, of all people, would know.

Finally, the phone rings. I answer immediately. I hear Magic's breath before he speaks.

"Hey, Arsenio, I told Lon to find you because I have to tell you something—"

My throat catches. I swallow. Magic never calls me "Arsenio." He always greets me by saying, "Hey, Dog, what's up?" But he's calling me by my given name. Something feels terribly off.

"You know we've been going through some things, trying to figure out what's going on."

"Yeah," I say.

"We wanted to double and triple check, you know, to confirm—"

He stops. Two seconds pass, five seconds. I don't know how long we stay silent, then Magic says, "I am HIV positive."

I gasp. I can't breathe.

He starts explaining the virus to me. He uses medical terms, but I can't focus, I don't hear him. Nothing registers beyond "I am HIV positive." Earv keeps talking, keeps explaining. I realize now that I'm on my feet and I'm pacing. Terrifying images stab me—sick, emaciated men, lying in hospital beds, their deathbeds, and I picture Earv as one of them. He's going to die, nobody gets through this, and then I can't help myself and I start to sob. Magic lets me cry and then after a few moments, quietly, kindly, he takes over, the point guard who makes everyone around him better, and he says, "Dog, listen to me, it's going to be all right," and then insistently, with the strength of a leader and the will of a champion, he repeats, "*It's going to be all right.* That's why I'm calling you because you and the people who love me are going to help me live forever. I need you. I need my family and friends."

I can't find my voice. Magic keeps going, taking over, as he always does when the game is on the line.

"Listen, I want to tell everyone. I want to tell the world. Later this afternoon I'm going to do a press conference at the Great Western Forum. I'm going to announce my retirement."

Magic speaks over my tears.

"I'm going to explain why I'm retiring, I'm going to say that I have the virus, and I'm going to answer every question the press asks. And then—"

He pauses long enough for my sobbing to let up and for me to catch my breath. I exhale.

"And *then*," Magic says, "I want to come on your show and tell everyone what I'm going through, explain that I'm dealing with it, and *how* I'm dealing with it."

"You know, do you think," I stammer, "maybe you should go on *Nightline* or *Larry King* or some show that's more serious?"

"No, I have to go where I'm comfortable."

"Man, I don't know if I can do this."

"Arsenio, you've *got* to do this. You have to."

"I'm not saying I won't. I'm saying I don't know if I can."

"I'll get you through it."

I almost laugh at the absurdity of that statement, at the enormity of his kindness, dwarfed by the sheer strength of his character. The man has HIV and he's saying that *he'll* take care of *me*.

"We'll do it together," he says.

I nod into the phone. I latch onto Magic's strength until gradually I feel my strength returning. I stop crying. I gather myself. *This is why I have the show*, I think. *This is why people need the show. And this is why I have to stay. For now.*

"Yes, we'll do it together," I say. "Absolutely. Anything you need, I'm here."

"I'm not going anywhere," Magic says. "I'm retiring. I'm not dying."

We hang up, and I call Marla and tell her that I'm running late. I tell her that Magic has contracted HIV and is retiring. We discuss how we should approach tomorrow's show. I cancel the morning meeting and head south, driving past the Paramount exit on the freeway. I continue downtown to First AME Church, where I search out my pastor, Reverend Cecil Murray, the first time I've gone to church in mid-afternoon since I was a kid, when I would go with my father. I talk to Reverend Murray, I fight back tears, rambling about Earvin and the life-changing morning I have just experienced. At one point, Reverend Murray says, "Let us pray." He grabs my hands and closes his eyes.

"Heavenly Father," he says, "we come to you this morning asking for a miracle, dear God."

I don't remember the exact words Reverend Murray says in that prayer, but I remember his conclusion.

"This is not the end," he says. "This is the beginning."

I leave First AME and drive to Paramount. I meet with Marla and talk about the guests we've booked for the Friday show—Roseanne Barr and Tom Arnold. I call Roseanne and explain that I need to reschedule them because Magic will be coming on to talk about something extremely personal, that he will be breaking national news, and I don't know how long he'll stay. Roseanne, not a quiet woman, says quietly, and kindly, "I've heard the rumors. We're coming anyway. If he needs the whole hour, I understand. But we'll sit in the Green Room and wait and come on if and when you need us."

I thank Roseanne for understanding. Later, I learn that Magic plans to stay for two segments.

The rest of those twenty-four hours dissolves into a haze.

*   *   *

Friday, November 8, 1991.

Earv and I walk out together.

The audience erupts, standing, cheering, howling, and barking for an eternity, three minutes nonstop. Magic waves, bows, and taps index fingers with Michael Wolff. I stand back and join the applause, the seemingly nonending standing ovation. I point to the Dog Pound as the words, "People Who Believe In Magic" appear on the screen.

The applause still peaking, I steer Magic toward the couch, where we sit and wait until the audience finally settles. I get right to it.

"Let's talk for a minute," I say. "You called and said you wanted to come on. Why?"

Magic speaks without a second of hesitation. "Having the HIV virus, I wanted to tell everyone to practice safe sex. I want people to use condoms. That's why I made the announcement yesterday. I want to educate the public."

Then Earv lowers his voice and speaks with passion. "This disease—we don't have to run from it. We don't have to be afraid of it. We have to make people aware of it and we especially have to educate Black people. This is not a homosexual disease. Don't think it can only happen to gay people. That's wrong."

Then Magic attacks another myth.

"I want to ruin the myth that athletes are dumb jocks. I want to disprove that. I have invested in many businesses. I'm set for life after basketball. And I want to say, that if I die tomorrow, I've had the greatest life that anyone could ever imagine."

He praises his friends, his family, and most of all, his wife Cookie, who has been tested and does not have the virus. He says that he told her he would understand if she decided to leave. She dug in instead and vowed to stand by him, saying they were in this fight together. I nudge him to talk about his future.

"I want to own a team," Magic says. "That's my big goal. Look, I've accepted God's way and I'm going to carry on." Then Magic says into camera, "Now I'm going to tell you what I told him when I called him yesterday. I got HIV. I got it. I'm going to live with it. And I need you to be you. That's all I need. You don't have to feel sorry for me. You're my boy." Then he says, "What a great man this is."

I stare at my shoes because I have choked up and I am about to lose it, live, on national television.

"He cried when I called him yesterday and told him," Magic says. "We both did."

I sigh heavily, pull myself together, and say, "I went to church yesterday, in the middle of the day, and I prayed, and I spoke to my reverend, and he said, 'There's going to be a miracle.' I believe that. I truly do."

We finish the second segment—seventeen minutes in all—with Magic issuing a warning, "You remember to put a cap on your head when it's cold, well, put a cap on down there, too."

The audience screams. Earv stands, waves, and we hug. We hold on to each other, gripping each other, and again I feel the tears running down my cheeks. Finally, we separate. Earv again waves to the audience, everybody standing, clapping, shouting, barking, and then he leaves. He returns for several more appearances on the show.

Today, Magic Johnson has more than fulfilled his dream to own a professional sports team. He owns or is part owner of *four* teams—the Los Angeles Dodgers, the Los Angeles Sparks of the WNBA, the Los Angeles FC of MLS, and the Washington Commanders. He remains one of my closest friends as he continues to live with HIV, nearly thirty-five years after appearing on the show in November 1991.

As Reverend Murray said, a miracle.

28

WELL-KNOWN BALLADEER AND HOMOSEXUAL

THE MAGIC JOHNSON EPISODE destroys the Nielsen ratings, bringing in the biggest numbers we've ever had, practically lapping our second-highest-rated episode, my controversial conversation with Madonna. Spurred on by the show's overall success, I charge into the holiday season, feeling a powerful wind at my back. That wind also takes human form—Marla—who pushes me to make every show better than the one before. She is a force, my guided missile, my coproducer, my protector. I do miss Lucie, her knowledge, her drive, her commitment, and her investment in me and in the show. Lucie has a relationship to my show that no executive will ever have. Other than Cheryl and Marla, I don't discuss my exit plan with anyone. Mark Landesmen and I agree that I should do the show for three more years. Then, dead stop. So, I put my head down and go to *work*.

In January, we celebrate the third anniversary of the show with guests Paula Abdul, Kirstie Alley, Earth, Wind & Fire, and a surprise drop-in from Arnold Schwarzenegger. After that, I slide into the year cautiously, and thanks to Marla, surround myself with guests who make me comfortable. I sit down again with Maya Angelou, Charles Barkley, Sandra Bernhard, and Mayim Bialik. I want to entertain, continue to host the late night show that keeps you up instead of putting you to sleep, so I bring out all the big guns, movie stars Elizabeth Taylor, Michael Caine, Tom Cruise, and Sean Connery. I kibbitz with a parade of comedians, most of them my pals—Jim Carrey, twice, George Lopez, Howie Mandel, Steve Martin, Louie Anderson, Sinbad, Elayne Boosler, Ellen DeGeneres, Paul Reiser, Chris Rock, Garry Shandling, David Spade, Bobcat Goldthwait, Gilbert Gottfried, George Wallace, Bill Maher, Martin Lawrence, Bill Cosby, Eddie, of course, and in December, Robin Williams storms onto the set and I let him riff. I love athletes, too, especially basketball players and boxers, so I bring on Patrick Ewing, Isiah Thomas, Kareem and Julius "Dr. J" Erving together, Evander Holyfield, and Mike Tyson. One time I bring on a massive manchild, a twenty-year-old giant, who raps with the chart-topping hip-hop group Fu-Schnickens. This kid plays for LSU and will be the number one draft pick in the NBA, a guy named Shaquille O'Neal. Wide infectious smile. Excellent rapper. The next day he sends me a gift, one of his shoes, size 18. Years later he sends me another one, size 22.

I never shy away from controversy. I sit with Gloria Steinem and Vanessa Redgrave, though not together. And my pulse, music, keeps thrumming through me, as I bring on Babyface, James Brown, the B-52s, Boyz II Men, Jimmy Cliff, Harry Connick, Jr. (I sing a duet with him), Chick Corea, Lou Reed, my brother Johnny Gill, Public Enemy, Heavy D & the Boyz, MC Hammer, gospel icons Everette Harp and Shirley Caesar, Whitney Houston, Elton John, and Ice-T. The whole time I keep an eye on Johnny, circling May 22, his last show, on my calendar. We keep pace with him, maintaining a strong second place in the ratings.

Then, in late April, Los Angeles burns down.

* * *

In the now famous videotape taken by a civilian bystander, four white LAPD officers repeatedly taser and brutally beat Rodney King, a Black man, whom they've pulled from the car he's been driving after a high-speed chase. The Los Angeles district attorney charges the officers with assault and the use of excessive force. The case goes to trial and the twelve-person, all-white jury acquits the officers. The verdict horrifies and enrages the residents of the Black communities of Los Angeles, many of whom routinely feel disrespected and ignored, some victims of police brutality themselves. Then the people in the Black communities lose their shit. After dark, they pour onto the streets, shouting, marching, rioting. They burn, loot, and trash stores in their neighborhoods, then they get in cars and drive north to the mostly white neighborhoods, even to the outskirts of Beverly Hills, and they burn and loot stores there. They keep going, to parts of Hollywood, near Paramount Studios, where we shoot *The Arsenio Hall Show*. Mayor Tom Bradley calls for the LAPD to quell the riots—I see the irony there—and when the LAPD fails to stop the rioting, Mayor Bradley brings in the National Guard. On the second day of the riots, Kerry calls me. "You can't do the show tonight. It's not safe. Not to mention that if anyone gets hurt coming or going to the show, we could get sued."

"I understand what you're saying, but I'm doing the show."

"Arsenio—"

"Hear me out. Doing the show will be a good thing. It's exactly what this city—what the country—needs. I'll get Tom Bradley to come on. Sean Penn already said he'll come. I called Edward James Olmos. He's in. He says, 'Let's do it. Black, white, brown, everybody coming together.' It's not only a good idea to do the show, it's important. We'll be showing that we can exist together."

Kerry wavers. "We can't bring in an audience. We pay a company to do that. What if they bring in people and somebody gets hurt? We won't be protected legally."

"What if I get the audience?"

"Where are you going to get four hundred people?"

"My church."

Kerry relents. He gives me his reluctant—and nervous—approval.

We do the show while smoke billows from burned out buildings less than a mile away. We begin with footage of Martin Luther King, Jr., speaking over images of rioting and looting. We then go to the show. No monologue, no jokes, no barking, no Dog Pound. The show opens with Mayor Tom Bradley and me sitting next to each other on two chairs, centerstage.

"I'm missing some of my audience tonight," I say. "And I'm missing some of my guests, but we're going to do a show."

After a brief back and forth, Mayor Bradley says, "These have been two of the most difficult days of my life. Sad days. Days of horror and disbelief."

The mayor talks about how shocked he felt when the jury verdict came down. "Where were these people? In outer space? On the moon? They couldn't have seen that videotape and come to the conclusion that those officers had done no wrong. Yet that was their verdict."

We talk about the overwhelming and pervasive feelings of outrage and anger. The mayor says that in response to the verdict, he invited the people of Los Angeles to express themselves, peacefully, but some people chose to take the law into their own hands. Rioters burned and looted stores, causing millions of dollars of damage. Nine people died, a number that will rise tragically to sixty-three.

"What do you do to stop the violence?" I ask the mayor.

Mayor Bradley grimaces. "I appeal to everyone. Please. I'm asking you. Stop the violence. I've had no choice but to call in the National Guard."

We get into a discussion of our judicial system, which, in my opinion and his, has failed by acquitting the four police officers. Mayor Bradley says that he has spoken to President George Bush, asking him to reopen the case and bring new civil rights violations against the four police officers. The mayor says the president has agreed to do that and he is working on providing small business loans to help rebuild the three hundred buildings that have been destroyed by the fires.

Our conversation leads to the even larger issue of conditions in the poor Black communities in Los Angeles and other cities, people living a life of inadequate education, violence, drugs, no jobs, and no hope. After speaking for fifteen minutes with Mayor Bradley, I spend the rest of the hour with my other guests, including Sinbad and actors Meshach Taylor and Edward James Olmos. I bring out my musical guest, Lou Reed, who sings a stripped-down, emotional version of his signature song, "Walk on the Wild Side," accompanied by jazz singer Jimmy Scott. I offer a plea to America, "Let's not burn down our neighborhoods. Let's burn down our ballot boxes. We got to change."

I end the show with my pastor, Reverend Cecil Murray, who offers a prayer.

"Tonight we are shamed," he says. "Let us commit to each other, to hold each other's hands. Thank you for tomorrow—which must be better than today."

After the show, I drift into my office and collapse on my couch. A wave of sadness rushes over me. Marla comes in, and after a few moments, we begin our usual show postmortem, but my heart's not in it. I suddenly feel exhausted. Wasted. An empty shell. Then the anger returns and builds. I can't locate the source of it, but I feel it, first a throbbing, then a stinging near my heart. I find myself biting my lip to keep the anger from gushing out and exploding and shocking Marla. I suppress it, but I can't stop feeling it. I hold it in. Throttle it. Keep it at bay. I am so deeply *angry*.

After a week, the rioting stops, the burning subsides, the city smolders, and life crawls back to a version of normal, whatever the hell that means. Still, I feel a piece of my soul has been scooped out. A few days after our L.A. riots show, Michael Wolff comes into my office. He's pissed. Someone has stolen his keyboard, some other instruments, a couple of amps. I report the theft to the studio.

That night, I ask one of my assistants, J Dub, to ride with me to The Comedy Store. We approach the Melrose Gate, the main gate at Paramount, and a security guard holds up his hand.

"I'm sorry, Mr. Hall," the guard—a white guy—says. "We have to search your car."

"What?" I'm so angry that I struggle not to scream. I spit the words out. "Search *my* car? Somebody stole equipment from *my* show. I'm an owner of the show so that means *they stole my shit*. You think I stole my own stuff?"

"We just got to search—"

I didn't think it could be possible, but my anger actually rises. I'm so hot I feel my forehead pulsing.

"Let me ask you something. Did you search Ted Danson's car when he left?"

Ted stars in the hit sitcom *Cheers*, which shoots on the Paramount lot. I like Ted. We're friendly. But Ted Danson, unlike me, is white.

I ask the guard again, "Did you search Ted Danson's car?"

The guard stares at me, confused. "I'm not sure I—"

"This is insulting to me. I feel violated."

"I'm sorry, but you can't leave until I look inside your trunk."

Time stops. I'm so furious that my eyes glaze over. J Dub looks at me, feels me, sees me seething. He gets out of the car and walks to the wooden gate barring us from leaving the lot. He steps behind it, puts his shoulder into the wooden gate and bends it back until it snaps off. He walks back to the car, gets behind the wheel and says, "Let's go, Chief. We got to be at The Comedy Store by nine."

I'm not proud that we broke the Paramount gate. I'm less proud of the anger I feel constantly, coiled inside me like a live electrical wire. I fight to keep it in check. I have to, for my mental and professional health. But it's building, beginning when Lucie left, rising slowly, upticking ever since.

I'm sure I'm the only talk show host who regularly deals with outpourings of hate—both blatant and thinly disguised racism. I know Johnny has never been accused of stealing Doc Severinsen's equipment and held hostage on the NBC lot, or stopped constantly by the LAPD for driving while Black. I know he doesn't receive daily stacks of hate mail. Not a few scattered letters from lunatics. *Piles* of hate mail, every day. One time a guy tosses a firebomb at me during the monologue. David Hurwitz, "Dub Boy," chases him, loses him, then calls the police who find him hiding in a restroom stall. And recently, Pam Hyatt, our receptionist, warns me that I've been receiving death threats.

This not only unsettles me, it confuses the hell out of me. People want to kill me for hosting a talk show?

Then, I lose it in the middle of a show. In the middle of my monologue, the Cleveland ghetto in me comes out. A guy standing in the last row of the audience heckles me like he's in a club and shouts, "Why don't you ever have any gay guests on your show?"

I'm stunned. I repeat his question. "Why don't I have any gay guests on my show? Well, I have a lot of gay guests who don't want to talk about their sexual preference, so you don't know if they're gay or not."

The audience applauds nervously and I picture several of my guests, all of them my friends, who are gay and haven't come out—Louie, Rosie, Ellen, Luther, and I think, "What do you expect me to say? Put your hands together for that well-known balladeer and homosexual, Luther Vandross?"

The applause builds. I've made my point. I should move on to tonight's guest, Paul Hogan. But I don't.

I walk toward the heckler. He's wearing a "Queer Nation" T-shirt.

"Now, this ain't Merv Griffin," I say. "You didn't think I'd run from this, did you? This ain't Johnny. I ain't going to run from it. I'm going to deal with it."

The audience cheers.

"Who would you like me to have on my show?" I ask.

"Gus Van Sant," the guy in the T-shirt says.

"I don't know him, but I know Elton John. He's been here and he's rocked the house."

Here it comes. Coming in hot. Rising into my throat.

Anger.

That coiled electrical wire about to ignite the fuck *up*.

I launch myself toward the heckler. I get right into his face. I glare at him.

"Okay?" I say. "This is my show. Okay? This is *my* show!"

The audience is with me. *They* start rocking the house. I glance behind me and I catch Marla waving frantically. She desperately wants me to go to commercial. I spin away from her and get back into the guy's grill. This time I let loose. "You think I haven't had somebody on the show because they're *gay*? What's wrong with you, man? I'm Black! I'm *Black*, man! I'm the biggest minority you know about. I don't want to hear that gay trash. I've got gay friends I've had on the show."

I'm way past angry. I'm raging. I charge down the aisle, away from the Queer Nation guy, and I start shouting, "I apologize to you sitting out there, and you sitting here, it's rude and it's out of order. But the one thing I would not do is discriminate against a guest because of his or her sexual preference."

I whirl back toward the Queer Nation guy and I scream, "But it ain't none of your damned business that they're gay!"

I'm too livid to remember exactly what happens next. I know we go to commercial and I'm suddenly backstage, facing Marla. She cranes her neck toward me, her eyes steely, strong, a coach under pressure in the playoffs. I feel like a Laker absorbing quiet wisdom from a stoical Phil Jackson.

"You okay?" she asks.

Marla's composure calms me down.

"Absolutely," I say.

She hands me three or four blue cards. "Take a look at these questions for Hogan."

"Paul Hogan. *Crocodile Dundee*. He's next?"

Conversation filler. I know he's next, but I ask anyway. I need this moment, a second to breathe before I go back out there.

"Sandy stopped tape," Marla says. "Take as much time as you need. We'll start whenever you're ready."

"I'm ready."

Then I lean down to her, and in a whisper, I sing the first line of "Best Friend" the Harry Nilsson song, the theme from the old sitcom *The Courtship of Eddie's Father*—"People let me tell you about my best friend—"

Marla swats my arm. "Stop it. You know I hate that."

"*You're my best friend,*" I sing.

Marla punches my shoulder.

But she's smiling.

I buy a crack house.

Several friends tell me that I have to find a "church home." My dad would not only agree, I can feel him pushing me from heaven to find a church home. Sinbad, Byron Scott, and other Lakers go to First AME. I feel welcome there and declare it my place, too. I'm moved by Reverend Murray's insightful sermons and his melodic voice.

One day, while meeting with Reverend Murray in his office, I look out the window at a dilapidated house across the street. Even though the house seems abandoned, young men, some of them teenagers, walk to the front door all day long.

"What is going on over there?"

"You don't know, son?"

"I don't."

"That's a crack house." He looks at me when I don't respond. "You never heard of a crack house?"

"I know what crack is."

"That's where they sell it. You knock on the door. The mail slot opens, you put in your money, somebody inside takes the money, then the flap opens again and your bag of crack appears in the metal slot."

"Across the street from a church," I say.

I call Mark Landesman and tell him I want to buy the crack house. He doesn't think it's a wise investment. "Why buy that?"

"It shouldn't be there."

"What are you going to do with it?"

"Give it to Reverend Murray."

Mark arranges for the funds while I think about what to do with the crack house. I come up with an idea, which I share with Reverend Murray. This is 1992 and computers have yet to become omnipresent, especially in poor neighborhoods. The kids here can't learn about computers because they can't afford them. I want to change that. So, I buy the crack house, gut it, paint it, fix it up, furnish it with desks and chairs, and then I contact IBM—Apple hasn't become a player yet—and get them to donate a bunch of computers. We turn the crack house into a computer center where kids can go after school. I don't publicize it, don't want to draw attention to myself, but of course the media hears about it. Articles appear with headlines that make it sound as if I need crack so bad that I bought my own crack house.

On May 22, 1992, like most of America, I watch the last episode of *The Tonight Show* with Johnny Carson. The night before, Bette Midler, his last guest ever, serenaded Johnny with three songs, including a torchy version of "One for My Baby (And One More for the Road)," that brought the usually unflappable Johnny to tears. I watch the final show—Johnny sitting with Ed and Doc as he introduces clips from his thirty years on the show—and I feel a sense of nostalgia and finality. Johnny seems at peace with his parting. "It was great," he says, his words resounding, "but everything—all good things—comes to an end."

29

HEARTBREAK HOTEL

TO EVERYONE'S SURPRISE, INCLUDING, apparently, Johnny's, my friend Jay Leno takes over *The Tonight Show*. Some media outlets try to stir up a rivalry between us. I've loved professional wrestling since I was five years old, so I go full-on WWE character when a reporter asks me how I feel about Jay and me fighting it out for ratings.

"I'm going to kick his ass," I say.

I say it as a joke, talking shit to a writer, but that's how I approach syndication, and every show—to win. In a comedian's terminology, to kill. That's the only way I can come out every night and even *do* a show. I want to be the best. I strive for that. But the cover of a magazine screams: "Arsenio Says He's Going to Kick Leno's Ass."

Jay calls my show, talks to Marla, and tells her to "get Hall on the phone." We speak and Jay gives me a hard time.

"You really got them going, big mouth," Jay says, always there, my big brother, and we laugh as Jay mimics me, "Hall's going to kick my ass."

We also laugh when Jay reminds me that I said, "My show is a party, the home of hip-hop, the young alternative," and then I booked Barry Manilow for sweeps. Bottom line, a fake feud breaks out in the press, but Jay and I remain cool when the smoke I created clears.

We both know the reality. Jay is replacing the king, hosting *The Tonight Show* on the NBC network. I'm still and will always be in syndication, scrambling for affiliates and time slots, forever destined for second place, at best.

At first, Jay struggles in the ratings. He changes the look of the show—no sketches, no Ed, no Doc, a longer monologue, a laid-back interview style. He's not at all quirky like Letterman, Johnny's choice as his replacement. The audience needs time to get used to Jay and I have no doubt they will. This transition period keeps us surprisingly close in the ratings, and a couple of weeks after Jay's debut, I score big, tightening the ratings race even more.

I book presidential candidate Bill Clinton.

We also tried to book Clinton's opponent, the current president, George H. W. Bush. We contacted his press secretary, Marlin Fitzwater. Marla relayed their conversation to me. "We asked, would Bush do the show?"

"What did he say?"

"Absolutely not."

She paused. I could tell she was deciding whether to tell me something else.

"What else did he say?"

"It's not important."

"Tell me. I'm sure I've heard worse."

"Fitzwater said he and Bush are not fans of the show. Fitzwater said, 'They don't even understand the success of Arsenio Hall and Bush would never do a show like ours.'"

"So, he said everything but Arsenio's an asshole. Wow. I wanted to have them both on, in the interest of fairness, but fuck that. Make sure you get Clinton."

"How do we do that?"

"Tell them Bush said no."

After Bush passes, I'm honestly shocked when Clinton accepts. I decide to go for broke. I tell Marla, "See if you can push him further. Ask him if he'll do a sketch. See if he'll bring Hillary. Let's do something special."

Hours later, a talent coordinator, Claudia Cagan, bursts into the conference room where we're having a meeting. "Clinton's in. He's bringing Hillary, and guess what? He used to play the saxophone."

"Can he still play?" I say. "Will he play on the show?"

"He said he would. He wants to sit in with the band."

"YES!" I say. I realize then that I'm standing.

Bill Clinton's staff books a hotel suite the night before the show, and he practices his saxophone outdoors, on the balcony. He requests sheet music for the song he's chosen to play, "Heartbreak Hotel." We decide to open the show with the governor of Arkansas playing saxophone with the posse.

The show starts. Burton Richardson bellows the introduction, outdoing himself, holding an extra-long, possibly record-breaking "Arsenioooooooo." The curtain rises and I pop out onstage as usual to "It's Hall or Nothing," but Mike immediately segues into "Heartbreak Hotel" with Bill Clinton, wearing a suit and my sunglasses, front and center, playing the sax. He plays for a solid minute and a half, adding a tasty jazz riff in the middle of the song and at the finish. The audience goes insane. I applaud, point to him, and say, "The Big Man . . . and the Posse!"

Then I pop off a joke I wrote earlier, for the occasion. I turn to Mr. Clinton and say, "Finally a Democrat blowing something other than an election."

Clinton and the secret service agents laugh along with the audience, thankfully. Nothing more gratifying than writing a joke in the morning and getting a laugh from it on national television that night, no testing, no trying it out at The Comedy Store.

With the crowd cheering us all the way, I lead Mr. Clinton to the couch. No small talk tonight, I've decided. I'm going straight for it. "Let me ask you. A lot of kids say they won't vote because all politicians are the same. Why are you not the same?"

Clinton seems thrown, for a second. I think he expected some small talk, not a direct, serious question. He answers thoughtfully. "I was in South L.A. three years before the riots. I could see how terrible things were and how they could get out of hand. I met with a group of sixth graders who told me their biggest fear in life was getting shot going to and from school."

He edges forward on the couch.

"The reason kids should vote is that we're in trouble now. We've got a lot of problems. We *can* deal with those problems head-on. We're in the driver's seat. But if you don't get in the car, you can't drive."

The audience applauds. I push him further. "I believe the L.A. riot was a spark. Do you understand why it happened?"

"I think I understand some of why it happened. A teacher said to me, 'After we clean up the mess that the riots caused, let's clean up the mess that caused the riots.'"

Loud applause.

He talks about conditions in South L.A. and reminds everyone that most of the people in South L.A. did not riot. He says that this election is about reconnecting those people to the American dream. "We have to make folks feel like tomorrow can be better than today."

We then go into a frank discussion about racism. I tell him, straight-out, "Racism in America is getting out of hand. How do we fix that?"

Clinton admits that the issue is extraordinarily complicated and that there is no easy fix. "We first have to get people talking to each other on a regular, consistent basis, not just across racial lines, but across income lines." Then he says, sadly, "People feel that they don't even exist. They live in substandard housing, unsafe streets, they work their guts out just to make ends meet, but nobody knows they're there. They're invisible. Until there's a riot."

He shakes his head. "You can't run a country that way."

Then, his voice rising, he says, "We live in the most diverse country on Earth. We need everybody. I want to include people. I don't want to exclude anybody."

I ask him if he has any shortcomings. He laughs and says, "We don't have enough time." Then I ask him about his claim that he smoked a joint once, back in college, but he didn't inhale.

"I tried to inhale," he says. "I did. I gave it my best shot. I just couldn't do it."

I don't know if I believe him or not, but I don't care. The audience laughs. More than that, I can tell the audience loves him. He's smooth and skilled, a gifted politician. We pivot to more serious issues—the economy and his promise to raise taxes on people making more than two hundred thousand dollars a year.

"You'll have to pay more," he says to me.

"Yeah, I'm mad about that," I say, but I laugh and the audience laughs with me.

"Only a little more," he says.

He explains how he will use the revenue from income taxes to pay for education and jobs and vows to "put a computer in every classroom in America." He references the crack house I bought that I turned into a computer center.

After we go to commercial, we come back with Bill Clinton and Hillary. I ask a couple of other questions, including how to end Black on Black violence.

"We have to get guns off the street," he says, to tumultuous applause from the audience.

As the interview winds down, Hillary jumps in, "I want to say something to you, Arsenio. I think what you did the night after the L.A. riots was what television ought to be. I was so impressed."

"It was a wonderful show," Bill says.

"It was not only a great show," Hillary says. "It was honest and gave people a chance to connect with each other. It used television in a positive way, involving people, bringing them together."

Still feeling some kind of way with Paramount, I want to say, "Yeah, funny thing. Paramount didn't want me to do that show. I had to kiss their ass and talk them into it. They reluctantly agreed, but they wouldn't pay for an audience, the way they always do, every night. I had to get buses and bring in an audience myself, people from my church."

But I don't say any of that. I smile, nod, and thank them.

Bill Clinton wins the election and asks me to attend the inauguration. I'm grateful for the invitation, but not being a big fan of parties of eight hundred thousand people, I decline.

Political pundits and media talking heads agree that Bill Clinton's appearance on our show is one of the most important moments not only of the 1992 presidential election, but also of his political career. His appearance strengthens his hold on his base of young voters and minority voters, a constituency that carries him to victory. An article in *Time* magazine says that our show "exploited his sax appeal." Another publication wrote that his appearance "broke the mold of traditional politics and changed the way politicians will run for the highest office in the land."

Years later, Bill takes me to a soccer game in the Rose Bowl, USA versus China, ending with that memorable Brandi Chastain surprise celebration when she pulls her shirt off. Another time, I sit chilling with him and James Carville on Air Force One at LAX. Bill thanks me personally.

"I will never forget how your show turned the tide of the election," he says. "Without your help, I might not have become the forty-second president of the United States."

Don't know about that. Probably hyperbole. But it feels good to hear it.

Fuck Marlin Fitzwater.

VII
LETTING GO

30

WE HAVE TO GET A GREEN LIGHT FOR THAT

1993.

    I'm restless. Anxious. On edge. Every night, I feel that I'm walking a tightrope between maintaining my identity, my integrity, my *Blackness*, and trying to be a responsible professional, executive producer, creator, boss, and my job to keep our show on the air, clinging to our tenuous hold on second place in the ratings. I'm also on television every night, hosting a late night party full of fun, laughs, music. But sometimes I don't feel like hosting a party. I don't feel like talking at all. I just want to go home and crash. But I know how to act the part, and I do, acting my ass off, every night. If you didn't know about my feelings of being split in half—if you're not Mark Landesman—you would never know that beneath all my smiling and laughing and energy, I am fucking stressed twenty-three hours a day.

    I book artists whom I respect and enjoy to make that one hour on air entertaining for me—George Lopez, Howie Mandel, Louie Anderson, Roseanne and Tom, Dave Chappelle, Margaret Cho, Bobcat

Goldthwait, Sandra Bernhard, Mayim Bialik, Will Smith, Johnny Gill, George Wallace, Whoopi, and Eddie.

Sometimes Paramount doesn't enjoy the same comics I do. Like Eddie Griffin. So, I don't book him. I sneak him on. I bring him out of the audience during my monologue to do a few spontaneous minutes of standup. Lucie and the Paramount lawyers have a fit, especially after Griffin does a bit about Michael Jackson snorting cocaine.

I bring on Alan Thicke, one of my day one mentors. I bring on Maya Angelou to make me smarter. I bring on movie stars because Nielsen households love movie stars—Tom Cruise, Tony Curtis, Lauren Bacall, Ossie Davis, Louis Gossett, Jr. I introduce Lea DeLaria, the only openly lesbian comedian I know, and I sit with playwright Harvey Fierstein. I cram the couch with boxers and ballers. I interview Oscar De La Hoya, Evander Holyfield, Sugar Ray Leonard, and one night Ali walks out during my monologue. I have on Steve Young and Jerry Rice, Barry Bonds, Eric Dickerson, Deion Sanders, Charles Barkley, and Muggsy Bogues, who's only a couple inches taller than Marla, but unlike her, can dunk a basketball.

And I go heavy with music, bringing on Babyface, James Brown, Peabo Bryson, Mariah Carey, Jimmy Cliff, Lenny Kravitz, Aaron Neville, Teddy Pendergrass, Roberta Flack. The show remains the home of hip-hop—Digable Planets, DJ Jazzy Jeff, Rude Boys, and my new friend, Queen Latifah. Then Dr. Dre tells me about a guy he's producing, Calvin Broadus, a young rapper from Long Beach.

"You have to see him," Dre says. "He's special."

Marla and I drive from L.A. to a recording studio deep in the 'hood in Long Beach to see this Broadus kid, who calls himself Snoop Dogg. When I walk in the studio, Snoop and several other young men stop what they're doing, come over to me, and one by one, hug me.

"Yo, brother," they say, "we appreciate you. You're our man."

Marla and I settle in and listen to Snoop Dogg fine-tune a couple of tracks, and I soon notice that Marla's acting differently. Kind of swaggy. I think she's gotten a contact high from all the smoke in the room. We get back into the music, songs that will make it onto his first album, a massive hit he calls *Doggystyle*.

Snoop feels apprehensive about doing my show. He doesn't trust or like TV. He's concerned about losing his street cred. Of course, nobody knows then that this Dogg will become more popular to television viewers than Lassie. I sell him hard on coming on the show. I practically beg him. I argue that my show is different.

"My audience is your audience," I tell him. "I promise to take care of you."

Finally, he agrees.

I bring him on the show to sit and talk about his music, and then I get him a hand mic and he starts to freestyle, taking us to commercial. He brings the house down.

After our night in Long Beach, as we drive back to L.A., Marla says, "I never heard music like that until I met you."

"Do you like it?"

"Some of it. But people need to hear it. These artists depend on you. You give them a home."

She looks out the window, a landscape of department stores, chain restaurants, and car dealerships flitting by, and she says, "You're so important to them. You have no idea."

On May 13, 1993, we celebrate our one thousandth show, a concert we hold at the Hollywood Bowl. We don't plan a typical show. We sell tickets and give all the proceeds to charity. The show headlines Madonna singing with Anthony Kiedis from Red Hot Chili Peppers. I want to add more music, wall-to-wall music, but *my* music. Paramount has already delivered that memo—the show has too much Black music. But they're not talking about Black music like Whitney Houston's, whose music transcends color. They want me to put on less hip-hop, less Tribe

Called Quest, less 2Pac, and less Black music that white people don't know, such as Toni Braxton, Johnny Gill, TLC, and After 7.

Finally, we go the Paramount way. We book Duran Duran. British, extremely popular, extremely white. By now, I get a clear sense that Paramount is running scared. They're worried about *Dave*.

Dave.

David Letterman.

He will debut his new show, *Late Show with David Letterman*, in three months, on CBS. For the past ten years, Letterman has hosted *Late Night with David Letterman*, which has been airing after Johnny. Letterman's irreverent, biting humor and his quirky show appeal to a younger audience than Jay Leno's. A hipper audience. A portion of my audience. The consummate ratings watcher and numbers analyst, I can't help predicting that Letterman will siphon off some of my viewers. Pulling ratings in syndication and competing with the networks has been a constant blood match. Letterman's a new challenge. A few comics and musicians have already warned me, "We've been told if we do your show, we won't be booked on *Letterman*."

"It's out of our control," Marla says.

"You're right. Just have to keep doing what we do."

"Which is do a good show."

"Which is to have a party. Every night. A nonstop party. Which is exhausting."

But I don't let up. A few months before Dave debuts, I bring back Prince for the hour. But not without a fight.

Prince plans to play all new songs and he brings me a special request.

He wants a purple piano.

I bring Prince's request to Paramount.

"He wants a what?"

The Paramount executive in charge of production, Frank, stares at me.

"How much could it cost?" I say. "Can't be that much. And it's *Prince*. For the hour. He only does my show. It's an event."

A silence descends. It feels like God has turned the sound off.

"We're trying to be conscious of the numbers, the audience," Frank says. "Prince, yeah, but maybe do a little less of other musical acts, more comedians."

I shift position in my chair. I am very conscious of the numbers. I know the numbers better than he does, better than anyone.

He's right. Prince pulls great numbers, but when I bring on hip-hop acts, they don't do as well as some of the comedians I book. I think of the time Howie Mandel walked out with a duffel bag slung over his shoulder. He dropped the duffel on the floor, unzipped it, and a female contortionist wriggled out of the bag. Huge laugh. Huge numbers.

"We've been meaning to talk to you," Frank says.

"About?"

"Budget," Frank says.

I feel my forehead scorching hot. "Yes?"

"We need to cut where we can," Frank says.

"Are you saying no to the piano?"

"Kerry wants to meet with you, so this is a heads-up. The research is showing—"

"You mean, focus groups."

"Well, yeah, that's how we—"

Fucking focus groups.

Frank drones on. His monotone is like a drill into my brain. "The research indicates that we might want to cut down on the amount of music—"

I don't hear anything more.

I'm on my feet and I'm walking toward the door.

Frank keeps talking. "If you watch Leno, he does what Carson did, one musical number, three minutes, tops, at the end—"

"I know," I say. "He'll have on Babyface. Babyface performs, Jay walks over to him and says, 'Thank you, Mr. Face! Good night!'—and roll credits."

"You do twice as much music—"

"At least," I say, hissing the words at him, shutting him down.

Another excruciating silence.

Outside, a car alarm bleats.

My hand circles the doorknob.

"The show *is* music," I say. "That's what the show is, who I am. I'm *all about music*."

I open the door, start to leave, and then I come back into the office, closing the door behind me. I'm careful now. Controlled. I don't want to raise my voice. I speak calmly. Too calmly.

"I know the focus groups also show that *white people* want more *talk*. Black people, my audience, want to hear Bobby Brown, Luther, Mariah. They wouldn't mind ten minutes of music, or more. And when white people are saying too much music, they're not saying too much Streisand. They're saying too much *Hammer*."

Frank pyramids his hands on his desk. Presses his fingertips. He seems to be silently rehearsing what he's about to say. "It comes down to the two issues, trying to be more cost-effective, and appealing to a wider audience—"

Meaning more white people.

I don't say that.

"I'm not Jay," I say. "He's my friend. But we're different people. We do different shows. I got this far being who I am. I'm not going to change. I can't. I love the show I'm doing. And we're winning with it."

"I invite you to think bigger," Frank says. "Be broader. This is an opportunity. Look at what Jay's doing. You can peel off some of that audience—"

I don't let him finish. I leave.

Across the studio lot, back in my building as I walk past reception, Pam Hyatt holds up a finger. "You got a call."

"About the purple piano?"

"Yes. It's a go."

I bring on Prince for the hour and he turns the place *out*. I study the ratings as soon as we get them. The numbers tick up as predicted. Then I stick to my guns and bring on my music. Busta Rhymes sits in with the posse and on another show Digable Planets turns it out. A few weeks later, Howie Mandel comes on with a sheep. Those ratings pulverize the Planets.

Letterman's show debuts August 30, 1993, opening his show with a clearly inebriated Bill Murray, closing the show with Billy Joel. Over the next six months, the media will anoint the Letterman show as the home for new, undiscovered, and major musical artists who rarely, if ever, appear on television. He counters Prince by bringing on Bruce Springsteen.

A precipitous ratings drop doesn't hit us all at once. Instead, the numbers begin to trend downward slowly, gradually, and then the slide intensifies, plummeting, crashing like an avalanche. By the fall of 1993, twenty of our 184 affiliates, some of them CBS stations, drop our show. Others move our time slot. One CBS station puts us on at eleven in the morning. In terms of actual numbers—eyeballs, the executives call it—we lose 24 percent of our audience.

I feel gutted.

Physically, emotionally, financially.

"Make the break."

My words or Mark's, I can't be sure. I am sure that I've vowed to get out before the profit participation checks attached to the ratings go away. They're still coming, but they're starting to get smaller, starting to dwindle. Noticeably.

At the same time the studio's complaints and criticisms swirl in my head.

Don't go in the audience.

Don't show the audience.

Don't call your guests *brother*.

Don't wear ripped jeans.

Don't show this, don't show that, don't do this, don't say that.

Do more talk.

Do less music.

Way less music.

And mainstream music.

Less gospel.

Way less hip-hop.

A voice inside my head screams, *Hip-hop? I've had on Dolly Parton, and she sat in my chair,* but that's drowned out by another voice, *Yeah, but Eazy-E came out picking his teeth with a knife, wearing the bathrobe you gave him. He sat on the couch, put down the knife, and put on a hockey mask. Can't see him doing that on Leno.*

I want to scream to the heavens, *I'm trying, Lord, I really am.*

But in one ear I got Spike Lee saying I'm an Uncle Tom, in the other I got the studio saying I'm too Black. And that's every day, every hour. Black people saying I'm too white, white people saying I'm too Black. Who the hell am I? I'm just trying to focus on the show, trying to please Paramount while staying true to myself. I'm constantly walking the Black-white high wire. I'm walking that high wire so much I'm like the Wallenda of late night, teetering, losing my balance. I start to fall. I catch myself. Walking this tightrope is a bitch. It's impossible. I'm doing my best. Maybe I'm trying too hard to have it both ways. I can't do that. I got to let that go. It's not working, anyway. Turns out I can't change who I am. It's not in me. I can't help it. I am insatiably Black.

* * *

I don't ask Mark to fly out from New Jersey, but he must hear the anger, desperation, and misery in my voice because here he is, making a house call, sitting on a folding chair in my dressing room.

"I got asked to do a movie," I say, rummaging through a row of suits hanging in the closet.

"Yeah? By who?"

"Martin Lawrence. He wants me to costar with him in this action comedy called *Bad Boys*. We play detectives. Michael Bay's shooting it."

"Great director," Mark says. "Tempting, right?"

"I told him no. I can't do it. If I'm going to quit the show, I'm getting out of the business, at least for a while. I want to go home. And I'm going to leave on top. Like Jim Brown. He was the best player in the NFL when he walked away. I want to leave the same way, as a winner."

I stand and inspect a suit Noel, the wardrobe assistant, has selected for tomorrow night's show. Noel has displayed the suit on a wooden valet stand.

"I love this," I say. "Joint is dope. I gotta tell Noel to use it for next week's magazine shoot, too." Below the suit, Noel has placed a pair of custom-made matching blue shoes.

"This works," I say. "This is nice."

A rustle by the door and Noel steps in. He grins. "Don't you love that blue?"

"Oh yeah, nice," I say. "But why a black belt? I thought we were getting a blue belt to go with the suit. I need a blue belt. That would set this shit off."

Noel goes silent.

"What?" I say.

"We have to get a green light from Paramount for that," Noel says. "They said no to having the belt made."

I don't think I've heard him correctly. I feel my mouth open, close, and then I manage to eke out a sentence.

"Did you say you need to get a *green light* to get me a new *belt*?"

"Yes. Their comment was, your belt can't be seen with double-breasted jackets." Then he whispers, "I believe I also heard. 'Get the fuck out of here.'"

"Wait, so, Paramount is micro-analyzing wardrobe requests now? Down to the belt? For my *pants*?"

Noel looks longingly at the door. I read his eyes—"Please, let me out of here." I start to prowl the circumference of the dressing room, like a caged animal. I stop suddenly and glare at Mark. "I'm trying to get my head around this. A green light for a belt to *hold up my pants*? Mark, this is not an extravagance. This is not a luxury. I'm not asking for a walk-in shower. I'm asking for a *belt*. You understand that, right?" My voice rises and goes deeper, and I say, "By the way, this is a belt to wear with the kind of suit Paramount and their stupid focus groups prefer that I wear every night."

I pause, bite my lip to keep myself from screaming. Noel takes this moment to slide out the door. I turn sharply and kick over the director's chair at my dressing table.

"Everything I've done," I say to Mark. "I am so angry." I look at myself in the full-length dressing room mirror. Objects in the room behind me seem out of focus.

"Every fucking thing I've *done*." I shake my head. "Everything I do is for this show. Twenty-four hours a day."

Mark rises from his chair, puts his hand on my shoulder. "Arsenio."

"We're talking about a BELT? Greenlighting a BELT?"

I hold for a second, and then I say, "You know this is not about the belt at all. It's about what it symbolizes. A sign of the times."

My breath comes fast. I retreat, begin to pace. Then Marla shoots into the room, a jolt of energy, oblivious to what's just happened. "Hi, guys. We just lost our musical guest for tomorrow." She peers at an ink scribble on the top folder of the stack she cradles in her arms. "Here are your choices. Of course, it doesn't have to be a musical guest—"

Back to business.

Business as usual.

Except that everything—every single thing—has changed.

Mark goes back to New Jersey the next day. Twenty-four hours later I call Marla into my office. I tell her to close the door. I ask her to sit down. She refuses. Instead, she stands as straight as a soldier, clutching her ever-present folders.

"I'm quitting," I say.

She crash-lands onto a chair.

"I'm going to stop doing the show."

"I figured that's what you meant by 'I'm quitting.'"

"I haven't told anybody else. Just you."

"What about Mark?"

I shake my head. "I wasn't sure until this morning. I'm going to call him. He has to figure out some things. Legally. Financially. Whatever."

Marla stays quiet but the silence screams. She knows what I'm going through, what I've been going through.

"I just." I stop.

I start again.

"I see the handwriting on the wall. The ratings are dropping and my money, my profit participation, is attached to the ratings. The ratings going down hurts me, personally. Things have been heading in the wrong direction for a while—the studio micro-analyzing my wardrobe, hating hip-hop, stacking the audience, *casting* the audience, trying not to make it look so Black, *that* really pissed me off. All those things. Everything. I've gone as far as I can go. Strong number two. But never gonna get to number one. I can't. A Black talk show host cannot. The world's changing. But not fast enough. Certainly not quick enough for me to keep doing the show."

More silence, then Marla says, "Now what? Do you have a plan?"

"Yes. I'm gonna move into my dream house. But first, I'm going to write a letter to Paramount."

"A letter of resignation," Marla says.

"I've been composing it in my head." I look at Marla. "I admit it. I'm nervous. I'm a little—honestly, I'm scared."

"Me, too," Marla says.

"You'll be fine. People will line up to hire you. You'll get a million job offers."

"I don't want another job," Marla says. "I have a kid to raise. When this ends, I'm going home to Chicago."

"You wouldn't work on another show?"

"There is no other show," Marla says.

31

I GOTTA DO WHAT I GOTTA DO

MY CONVERSATION WITH MARK lasts about ten seconds.

"I'm done, Mark. I need to end it."

"I'm shocked, but I'm not surprised. You've given me about a hundred hints."

"I want to leave the show before the show leaves me."

"You have a way of seeing the future," he says.

"I'm writing a letter of resignation."

"Happy New Year," Mark says.

"Maybe that's how I'll start it," I say.

I write a couple of bad drafts of the letter, toss them, then bat some ideas around with Cheryl, who takes notes as I spitball thoughts, sentences, key words.

"Can't rush this," she says.

"Harder than I thought," I say.

"We'll get it done," she says.

I thank her and head out to dinner.

Cheryl, Marla, and Mark.

The only three people who know.

Three people I trust with my life.

I escape in the company of two gorgeous friends, supermodel Tyra Banks and Miss USA, Kenya Moore. We sit at a table in the inside garden of Georgia, a soul food restaurant and celebrity hangout in Hollywood owned by Eddie, Denzel, Kareem, former L.A. Laker Norm Nixon, and his wife Debbie Allen. I can usually clear my head at this place, obscured by the shrubbery of exotic potted plants and surrounded by friends, but tonight I poke at my food while Tyra and Kenya talk to each other. At one point, I consider excusing myself, grabbing a ride home, and taking another stab at the letter. I'm so zoned out that I don't even see the three men wearing pin-striped suits and bowties approach our table.

"Excuse me," one of them says. "I'm sorry to interrupt."

He offers me his hand. I recognize him immediately. I laugh, stand, shake his hand, and give him a hug. "Mustafa," I say, although I used to call him Wallace.

He looks behind him. "My dad's here, sitting in the back, and he wants to meet you. Would you mind coming over for a minute to say hello?"

Mustafa's dad.

Minister Louis Farrakhan.

The leader of the Nation of Islam, the notorious, divisive figure who's currently blowing up all over the media. A fervent, riveting speaker, Mr. Farrakhan holds views that have shaken up the establishment's stance on religion and race. He's also been accused of spewing angry, homophobic, antisemitic, and racist venom in his speeches, causing a firestorm of controversy while building a huge following in the Black community. *Time* magazine has recently written a cover story about Farrakhan and the Nation of Islam called "Ministry of Rage." Farrakhan caught my attention when he began talking about a "Million Man March" that he plans to organize next year in Washington, DC. The mainstream media loathes and fears Louis Farrakhan.

I find myself on my feet, flanked by Mustafa and his three bodyguards, heading into a back area of the restaurant. His dad, also wearing a pin-striped suit and a bowtie, sits at a table, studying the menu. As I approach him, I say, "I hear their bean soup is amazing."

Louis Farrakhan smiles, puts down his menu, and stands.

"My brother," he says, shaking my hand. "I've never met you, but I feel like I know you. I want to tell you how much I appreciate what you're doing, what you do every night. I love your show. You are so entertaining and so important."

I almost say, "Well, thanks, I'm glad somebody likes the damn show. Too bad I'm about to give that shit up," but I just smile.

Maybe I need to hear this compliment right now. Maybe I need the validation, even from someone as controversial as Louis Farrakhan.

He gestures toward an empty chair and I sit across from him. For the next few minutes, he talks about his ministry, his mission, and his vision for the Million Man March. He gets specific, fiery, talks about the desperate need for Black people, especially Black men, to get their *shit* together, my word, not his. He hits me with a stunning statistic—*95 percent* of Black people are killed by *Black people*.

"Sometimes you can't blame the white man," he says. "We do a lot of damage to each other. We burn our own neighborhoods down. When you walk down our streets, who do you fear?"

Before I can answer, he says, "Not white men. Young Black men."

He talks about the poetry and urgency of hip-hop, but decries the violence against women depicted in rap lyrics. He talks about Black empowerment, insisting, "We have to lift *ourselves* up, treat each other with respect," and then he quotes the former leader of the Nation of Islam, Elijah Muhammad, "Every time I see a Black man, I'm looking at

God." He shakes his head and says, quietly, "Sometimes we don't treat each other that way."

I don't say a word. I simply listen, absorbing what he says. Despite everything I've heard about him, despite all the hateful rhetoric he's spoken publicly, I find myself caught up in his passion, his persuasiveness, the poetry of his speech, his melodic voice, his charisma. I know his language has caused a mess that's rippled through our culture, but I hear a message in that mess.

"I know you have to go," he says, "but before you do, I've always wanted to ask you something. Do you think you would ever have me on your show?"

It would have to be now, I think. As in right now. Because I'm about to leave the show.

"It would be good television," I say. "We both know that."

"I haven't done much television," Farrakhan says. "Yet. That could change."

"I need to talk to my co-executive producer, my partner, Marla Kell Brown. We make every decision together."

"Of course, I completely understand."

Louis Farrakhan and I shake hands again and then I get up from the table.

"By the way, Marla is Jewish," I say.

Farrakhan smiles. "I look forward to hearing from you, Arsenio."

The next day, I bring Marla into my office. She follows behind me, as always cradling an armful of folders.

"I met Louis Farrakhan and I want to bring him on the show," I say. "I know that's going to be an issue."

Marla drops her stack of folders on my desk and takes a long, deep breath. Finally, she says, "Booking the man the ADL considers America's most prominent antisemite isn't what most producers dream of."

A long silence.

"Paramount is not going to be happy," she says.

"Probably not."

"He says horrible things about Jews. And gay people and Black people, by the way."

"Which in part is why I want to have him on. There are some things my people need to hear about themselves. I also hate that Phil Donahue and Barbara Walters are allowed to sit down with him, but somehow Oprah and I can't talk to him? Or even be in a room with him, publicly?"

Marla says nothing. I push further.

"Why not rock the boat? Why not stretch this one time? I think it's important to present different views. And if he says something antisemitic, I'll call him on it. We will talk about it. We have to talk to each other. It's when we *stop* talking to each other that we have a problem."

Marla goes quiet.

"Look, he's an equal opportunity offender. He criticizes everybody. My audience shouldn't just hear the same saccharine voices they agree with. I know some hard brothers in my old neighborhood who only the minister can reach. No other late night show will talk about Black on Black crime or how we treat our women."

"We're going to hear that you're the wrong guy and this is the wrong format for this interview," Marla says. "And we can't interview Farrakhan in a ten-minute segment. We'd have to dedicate almost the entire show."

"I know."

"You will receive a tremendous amount of hate mail."

"I want to do this show, Marla. And I want to do it with you. But you can sit this one out."

"To be clear, as long as Paramount lets you, you're doing this show, no matter what."

"Yes," I say. "I think I should."

Marla waits only a single beat. "Okay, I'll produce the show. Because it's my job. And we're a team. But as a friend, I have to tell you, I'm really upset. You know that Paramount will greenlight the show because it'll be an even bigger publicity nightmare if they say no."

I lower my head and close my eyes.

My office door opens and closes.

I never see Marla leave.

Paramount signs off on Farrakhan. The suits at the studio announce the show well ahead of its airdate, but the pressure and criticism hits us hard and instantly. Marla takes the bulk of the hits as anger builds in the Jewish community. Rabbis across the country inundate her with calls. Even film critic Gene Siskel calls Marla. Incredibly, I never hear about the onslaught that Marla endures. She never tells me. As usual, she throttles the noise, keeps it contained outside my door. She protects me. We have a show to do every night and she keeps me focused on that.

Then during the run-up to the Farrakhan show, Irv Rubin, head of the Jewish Defense League, calls my assistant. He wants to meet with me. I take the meeting, and when word leaks that Rubin has met with me about Farrakhan, a whole different firestorm blazes. Rubin, it turns out, represents an extreme segment of the Jewish community, and those who don't like or agree with him start flooding our switchboard with complaints. It seems that by bringing in Rubin and booking Farrakhan, we've managed to polarize pretty much all Jewish people, everywhere.

As we prepare for the show, Marla works harder than I've ever seen her, immersing herself in research, completely engaged, meticulously planning, practically living at the studio, involved with every aspect of the show, neither of us getting a good night's rest leading up to the show, now scheduled in two weeks, for February 25.

I try to make her laugh. I remind her how Bill Clinton sat in with the posse, playing his saxophone. I mention that Minister Farrakhan started as a musician. Maybe he can sit in with the posse, playing his violin.

Nothing.

Crickets.

Not a snicker.

Marla's not in a laughing mood.

She can bail anytime, even the day of, and she knows it. She doesn't, though, and I know she won't. She doesn't have it in her to allow anything or anyone to prevent her from doing her job. She's that strong, that committed to the show, and to me.

The day of the show, I walk over to Pam Hyatt, who calls me "Sunshine," no matter my mood, even when I'm feeling down or sour, like when I've gotten death threats. Among the worst came a few years ago after I had on Lea DeLaria, the in-your-face lesbian comic, who referred to herself as a "big dyke" in her standup set. The morning after, Pam fielded dozens of irate calls and death threats.

"How we doing, Pamie?" I ask her now.

"Tons of calls, Sunshine," Pam says. "Running about half and half."

"Meaning?"

"Half support you for having on Farrakhan, the other half hate you, some want to kill you." Pam grins, shrugs. "Don't worry, I rarely give out your address."

"That's a relief," I say.

Pam laughs. "Have a good show, Sunshine."

Friday, February 25, 1994.

I drive onto the lot, turn toward my parking space, and practically slam on my brakes. In front of me, a squadron of men wearing suits and bowties stands on the roof of stage 29. I glance to the side and see several more men, also in suits and bowties, standing in doorways, blocking an alley between buildings—a platoon of bowtied bodyguards in front of me, behind me, above me. Not one of them carries a weapon and still the sight of them unnerves me. I get the message loud and clear—when it comes to protecting the minister, the Nation of Islam does not play.

When I get to my office, the air crackles, humming with anticipation and tension. Marla seems more fired up than ever, her usually supercharged motor on redline. She's all business, an attitude of "let's do this and get it over with" pulsing and real.

The day slogs along, sending off a slow, deliberate, slightly ominous vibe. I take a walk over to the stage and hear gospel singer Kirk Franklin rehearsing. Kirk will close the show tonight.

The clock ticks, time trudges, each minute feeling like an hour, and then I look up, and it's time to shoot the show. The doors to stage 29 open, the audience loads in, and we begin.

We start with a three-minute montage of snippets from Louis Farrakhan's speeches. He bellows, gesturing ferociously, pretzeling his body into nearly balletic movements in every clip we show. He rails against the white establishment for profiting from Black artists' and entrepreneurs' accomplishments and excoriates Blacks who don't fend for themselves or who commit crimes. He screams, "We *are* the music industry and we have *nothing*. You suck the blood of the Black community." Then he attacks his own, shouting that Black people are "no longer human beings but a race of animals."

After the three-minute Farrakhan rant, I appear seated, alone, in a pretaped opening. I wear wraparound sunglasses.

"Minister Louis Farrakhan," I say. "The controversial leader of the Nation of Islam. He's been called enlightened and inspirational. He's also been called racist and antisemitic."

I pause.

"Many people are thrilled that I'm having him with me tonight. Others are furious with me. But as the Public Enemy lyric goes, 'I gotta do what I gotta do.' I hope something positive comes out of the next hour."

I truly mean it.

Before I step onto the stage, I pray for it.

The screen rises, I step forward, my hands folded in prayer. I move toward the center of the stage and I feel my legs shake. A lump rises in my throat. I'm suddenly nervous. In the five-plus years of the show, I have never felt this way.

"Oh, wow," I say to the audience, most of whom are standing, applauding. "I need some love right about now."

The audience applauds louder, and then I say, "Let's get it on. We only got an hour. It's really time to get busy."

I then quote an author who recently sent me a personal note, "The only real defeat is when we stop talking to and listening to each other. I've said a prayer—"

I slowly shake my head and then I introduce Louis Farrakhan.

He walks out from the wings and hugs me. I return the hug, briefly, and then we break apart. He bows, and I lead him to the couch.

"Let's get right to it," I say. "Why do you think there has been so much resistance to me having you on the show? Not just from white people. I've had Black people tell me what you need to do is get sick on Wednesday. True story. You need to get sick on Wednesday and then cancel Thursday and Friday."

Farrakhan quotes Jesus, saying the truth will set you free, and then he states that the greatest fear of millions of people is Black people breaking out of captivity and becoming a free people. He tells me that he has received invitations to be interviewed by Phil Donahue, Mike Wallace, Forrest Sawyer, Barbara Walters, Tom Brokaw, Connie Chung, and Katie Couric.

"How about Oprah and Montel Williams?" I say, naming the only two other Black talk show hosts.

Farrakhan smiles.

"No," he says.

He says "they" think that being on my show, a "Black" show, he will get a free ride. "Their fear is that sitting with my brother, I will not be seriously opposed." He vows then that he will tell the absolute truth and says, "Ask me anything."

So I do.

"One question that comes out of the neighborhood," I say, "is who killed Malcolm X?"

Minister Farrakhan's lips merge into a thin line. No way he expected this to be my first question.

"Since the movie *Malcolm X* [starring Denzel Washington, directed by Spike Lee], there are a lot of people who say—" and I whisper, "'You know, Minister Farrakhan had something to do with that.' And I know you've heard it, too."

"I have. More so now than ever before."

For me, the show then takes an abrupt turn.

Minister Farrakhan launches into a passionate, detailed, and convincing defense of his innocence.

He recalls that in 1965, when Malcolm X was assassinated, nobody even remotely associated Louis X, as Farrakhan then called himself, with Malcolm's murder. Back then, the mainstream media reviled Malcolm. After his death, one major newspaper ran a headline calling Malcolm "The Apostle of Hatred." Eventually three members of the Nation of Islam were convicted of Malcolm's murder and sentenced to life in prison. Later, two of the three were found innocent and exonerated. But many in the media and in the community blamed the entire Nation of Islam, and as Farrakhan rose in power and became the Nation's leader, they held him responsible for Malcolm X's murder.

"They blame the *Nation*," Farrakhan says. "Now that's a big word. You can't blame the entire Nation for killing Malcolm X, just as you can't blame the pope in Rome for the actions of errant Catholics or rabbis for the actions of errant Jews."

For me, time stops.

A calm falls over me.

I have asked the question for my neighborhood, for my community, and for myself.

I continue the interview, I challenge him, I exhort him to explain the sometimes vile statements he's made, which he attempts to do in lengthy, sanctimonious rhetoric resembling a sermon. I confront him about his blatant antisemitism. I ask him to respond to being called the "new Black Hitler." He laughs and says, "I should dismiss it. I should not even dignify that foolishness with a response." The audience agrees with him and applauds. He continues, responding with very passionate language, saying, "If I am a righteous person, and that I am trying to be, I can never dislike, or hate, a person because of their faith."

We keep talking. He sermonizes, finding a groove the way that great orators do. His answers to my questions are never boring and never short. But time is flying. As we head toward the end of our conversation, I feel like I could use another hour at least to do this interview justice. I need a podcast, but the podcast hasn't been invented yet. We talk about the Bible, slavery, reparations. I ask him if he has any Jewish friends. "No," he says, simply. I want to follow up, maybe ask him about how he got along with his Jewish violin teacher when he was studying with her. He talks about being a minister for addicts and alcoholics, the homeless, the downtrodden, and those who have committed violent crimes, begging Black people to lift themselves up. He laments Black on Black crime, saying, "If we don't love each other, who then can we expect to love us?" and adds, "The burden is not on white people to change towards us. The burden is on us to change towards ourselves."

The day began as a slow march to this moment. The last hour has evaporated in a blink. Kirk Franklin performs, Farrakhan and I join him after his song, and the show ends.

I don't remember much after that. I'm vaguely aware of a phalanx of Minister Farrakhan's bowtied bodyguards hustling him away. My body suddenly feels heavy, every bone a weight. I feel as if I've gone through a heavyweight fight. Mental exhaustion pummels me. I head up the stairs to my dressing room and fall onto the couch. I study the ceiling. I think about meeting Minister Farrakhan that evening at Georgia's and what I've been through since. Now, it's over in a blink. I went through hell, but managed to step through the inferno, alive.

Was it worth it? Did I have to interview Louis Farrakhan before I quit the show?

I hear my mom yelling at me when I was little, *You're so hardheaded. Your problem is you don't listen.*

It would have been so much easier to take the advice of all those around me, to take the road most traveled. Did I let my stubborn ego damage my public image for life? I'll soon know. But as one of my Kent State professors said, "If you please everyone, you probably aren't doing anything special."

I tried to stay true to myself, to my Blackness.

Insatiably Black.

I have never felt more alone.

32

DADDY COACH

AFTER THE FARRAKHAN INTERVIEW, letters flood our office, calls overload Pam's switchboard. The reaction runs hot and evenly. Fifty percent embraces me, praises my courage in having Louis Farrakhan on. The other half excoriates me, screams at me, wishes me dead.

Then the fervor fades.

The world does not explode.

The show goes on.

And my misery intensifies.

I write several more drafts of my resignation letter, ball them up, shoot jump shots with them into the wastebasket.

I have to leave the show. I see that clearly. But I can't see beyond that. What will I do after I leave? How will I fill my days? What will be my purpose?

I sit down to write the letter. I stare at the legal pad. The blank black lines on the yellow page shimmer, stare back at me.

At the end of March, Magic takes on an impossible assignment, accepting a job that's doomed to fail before he starts—coaching the pathetic Los Angeles *Fakers*. He will coach exactly sixteen games, finishing with a record of 5-11. Winning five games with that team should qualify him for coach of the year.

One afternoon, I visit Earv, Cookie, and their youngest son, two-year-old EJ. I love EJ and adore the tender relationship I see between him and his dad. I first met EJ when I had him on the talk show, sitting with Earv, Cookie, and Earv's mom. Since then I've developed my own special relationship with EJ. I've even taken him on playdates with Jordan-Rose Brown, Marla's daughter. Today, I surprise EJ with a battery-powered, rideable Porsche. His first car.

As we talk, Earv and Cookie mention that EJ had never seen Daddy do his legendary job back in the day. I propose that I take EJ to watch Daddy coach a couple of games. We make arrangements for me and EJ to attend the next home game, a Sunday afternoon at the Great Western Forum. When Sunday comes, we pack snacks and EJ and I climb into the backseat of my limo, practicing the three words "Daddy's the coach" all the way to Inglewood. At the Forum, we take our seats on the floor next to the Lakers' bench, flanked by actress Dyan Cannon and Glenn Frey of the Eagles.

Earv, wearing a suit, comes out of the tunnel last, jogging onto the court after all the players and assistant coaches. He waves at us, and EJ waves back and hollers, "Daddy coach!" Magic blows a kiss to his son, waves again, and then instantly becomes all business, settling into his spot on the sideline. I watch the players doing layups and it's obvious immediately that they are not a playoff team. They're barely a professional team.

"They don't play like Daddy," I say to EJ, watching the Lakers blow two layups in a row.

"Daddy coach," EJ says again.

"He's gonna have to."

The first half starts and EJ watches Magic instead of the game, constantly shouting, "Daddy coach!" Magic, the ultimate competitor, stays locked in, pacing the sideline, yelling instructions, often burying his head in his hands or studying the floor when a player misses a dunk, or the point guard throws a pass a mile over a teammate's head into the crowd. Magic, the NBA legend who could play all five positions on a basketball court, seems completely baffled by the so-called professionals he's coaching who can't even execute the basic basketball skills he could do in his sleep. The first half ends, and the players, down by a million points, slink off the court and duck into the tunnel toward the locker room.

Later, cradling EJ into my chest, I wait for Magic at the mouth of the tunnel before the players, Laker girls, and coaching staff emerge for the start of the second half. The team appears, walking as if they're about to be executed, stepping onto the court to tepid applause. Everyone else associated with the team comes out of the locker room, except for Magic, and then, finally, his face frozen in frustration, his eyes glazed over, he appears, the last person out of the tunnel.

EJ screams, "Daddy!"

Magic stops.

Every blown shot, terrible pass, missed defensive assignment—all thirty minutes of ineptitude he's just endured and we've witnessed—disappears and the famous Magic smile spreads across his face. EJ squirms in my arms and reaches for his dad, nearly flopping out of my grasp.

"Daddy! Daddy! Daddy!"

Magic encircles him with his arms and clutches him, his precious son, showering his face, head, and arms with kisses. "Are you and Arsenio good?"

EJ beams. "Daddy coach."

Earv laughs and his laugh causes EJ to laugh. Magic hugs EJ, kisses him again, closes his eyes, and holds him, just holds him, rocking him gently, the love in his eyes immeasurable, the love pouring from father to son, a dazzling light between them. I am witnessing—*bliss*. A love beyond measure. And then I know, without a speckle of doubt—

This is it. This is what I want.

I want a son.

Earv is so emotional, so affectionate, so uninhibited.

He doesn't care who sees this love.

I want that, too.

I know my father loved me, but he never held me or kissed me the way Magic is holding and kissing EJ, never, not at home, in private, and certainly never in public.

I want that so much.

I want a *child*.

So, now I know.

I know what I want to do when I leave the show. I know how I want to fill my days.

I want to be a dad.

33

ALL SHE WROTE

I WRITE THE LETTER.

Thoughts and emotions burst from me, sentences spew, words flow, tumbling over each other.

I revise it, polish it, Cheryl proofreads my spelling and types it, then copies it, walks the letter to Kerry's office, and hands it to his assistant. On the envelope Cheryl has written, "Personal. Urgent."

April 6, 1994

Dear Kerry,

I can't remember a more complicated time in my life, and it's only April of this insane new year. But everything happens for a reason, and I don't believe God has brought me this far to leave me.

Cut to the chase . . . in a nutshell, all signs tell me that it's time for Arsenio to leave the late night party days behind. "It's Time" . . . I feel it in my heart. I would love to sit with you and decide what our approach toward this closure should be.

Until then, I would like to use a couple of these lines to personally thank you for being an honest and positive guy throughout our short association here at Paramount. Your aggressive proposals and offers for a seventh season were more than fair and I thank you for your faith in me. Unfortunately, for me, reality is knocking . . . and I'm going into retirement from the gab-fest game. These years at stage 29 have been a real-life dream come true . . . God has smiled on me.

Peace,
Arsenio

April 6, 1994

Dear Kerry:

I can't remember a more complicated time in my life, and it's only April of this insane new year. But everything happens for a reason, and I don't believe God has brought me this far to leave me.

Cut to the chase...In a nutshell, all signs tell me that it's time for Arsenio to leave the late night party days behind "It's Time"...I feel it in my heart. I would love to sit with you and decide what our approach toward this closure should be.

Until then, I would like to use a couple of these lines to personally thank you for being an honest and positive guy throughout our short association here at Paramount. Your aggressive proposals and offers for a seventh season were more than fair and I thank you for your faith in me. Unfortunately for me, reality is knocking...and I'm going into retirement from the gab-fest game. These years on stage 29 have been a real-life dream come true. God has smiled on me.

Peace,

Arsenio

AH/clb

When Cheryl gets back, I ask Marla to gather the entire staff on stage 29. She tells everyone to sit in the audience. I stand on the stage, toe my monologue mark. I take a deep breath, exhale, and say, "Hi, everybody. Cheryl just delivered a letter to Kerry McCluggage."

I feel a catch in my throat, then with my voice cracking, I say, "I'm leaving the show."

A collective—"*WHAT?*"

Followed by an explosion of sound—

Shouting.

"No, no, *no!*"

Voices clamoring, colliding, speaking over one another.

Expressions of shock, disbelief.

Sobbing.

I wait for the sounds to fade, and then I say, "This has been an incredible experience. I love you all. You're family. Most of you I'm going to miss in a way you'll never know."

Claudia Cagan, a talent coordinator, shouts, "Could you tell us which ones you're going to miss?"

Huge laugh.

Thank you, Claudia.

Softens the moment.

Slices through the pain we all feel.

Then someone says, so quietly her question comes out in a hush, but the impact silences everyone, "When are you leaving? How long do we have?"

"I don't know," I say. "I guess that's up to Kerry."

"You can't do this in a letter," Kerry says to me on the phone. "Come to my office after the show. We have to talk this through."

In his office, we discuss the end of the show, but I only remember fragments of conversation, disassociated words.

Kerry tries, in his low-key way, to convince me to continue the show, but I've made up my mind. I see the horizon. I see that the syndicated model for a late night show can never be as profitable as it once was. The business has changed in front of my eyes. He asks if I would consider staying on and producing a show for my time slot. I know how hard Marla works and I really don't want to take on that responsibility. Finally, Kerry and I come to a gentleman's agreement. We will release a joint statement explaining that I'm leaving the show. Then he asks who I think should replace me. It feels strange suggesting my successor, but I recommend two comics, Bill Bellamy, and a guy named Jon Stewart. Kerry eventually replaces me with a relative unknown, Stephanie Miller. Then Kerry and I talk about how we will approach our last shows.

"Between now and then," Kerry says, "let's make these final weeks a celebration. Let's book your favorite guests. Go out with a bang."

"*Yes*," I say, and we shake hands, and I think, as I leave Kerry's office, this meeting went surprisingly well.

Except this ain't Cleveland.

Or Kansas, Dorothy.

It's Hollywood, where handshakes don't count.

Kerry sits on the letter. Buries it. Never acknowledges it. Never shows it to anyone. Never indicates that I resigned and that I, alone, made the decision to leave. Instead, the Paramount PR machine concocts a much sexier ending and stalls when I ask how and when we should proceed with a joint statement. On April 18, less than two weeks after receiving the letter, Paramount announces that our last show will be May 27, 1994, around six weeks away.

I feel blindsided.

Then the calls start flooding my office phone, inundating me.

Michael Jackson calls. "I can't believe Paramount canceled you. It's so unfair. What can we do to stop this?"

"They didn't cancel me. I quit. Who told you Paramount canceled the show?"

"Everybody. They're saying it's because of your interview with Minister Farrakhan."

"No, no, that had nothing to do with it. I resigned. I wrote them a *letter*."

Reverend Jesse Jackson calls from Chicago. "I heard what they did to you. We should talk and figure out a way to correct this. This is very, very wrong."

"*They* didn't do it," I say. "*I* did it. I quit."

I can't keep track of all the people who call, offer condolences, express disbelief and anger, and vow to reverse what they see as both a personal and cultural injustice. The calls keep pouring in—Whoopi, Luther, Mariah Carey, Tommy Mottola, Quincy, and all my comedian friends, Jay, George, Howie, Sinbad, Roseanne, Bobcat. They all express outrage, and their outrage ignites my own. I'm furious that Paramount didn't acknowledge my letter at all and didn't offer me a more celebratory send-off. Instead, I stare at the calendar and can't believe what I see. Six weeks. That's all I've got left until the final show. No victory lap. No formal goodbye. No. A flurry of publicity announces the end of the show, and then, wham, the door slams.

Goodbye, Arsenio. See you. Nice knowing you.

I miss Dana at a time like this. Paramount would not have run game if she were still in the mix. She would've known what to do, how to handle my exit better, how to tell the world the truth.

The clock ticks down, April ends, May begins, I look at our schedule and feel a jolt of shock. We have twenty-three shows left. Then to my surprise and Paramount's dismay, the outrage that the show will be ending doesn't fade, it intensifies.

May 1, 1994.

I book a frequent guest, shock comic Bobcat Goldthwait, introducing him, "My next guest makes me seem sane by comparison." Bobcat strolls out wearing a leather jacket and a fedora. He slams himself onto the couch and in his craggy voice, says, "This is so sad. It's honestly so sad. I don't often get maudlin, but I'd like to thank you for having me on the show so much over these past six years."

"Thanks, man."

We shake hands and I say, "We go way back."

"Yeah, then I started thinking—what are you gonna do? I don't want to be rude or anything, but will you still be able to help my career?"

I crack up.

"Essentially what I want to know is, do I have to keep kissing your ass?"

I'm really laughing now, and then Bobcat suddenly stands on the couch.

"I feel," he says, waving his arms. "Why make it easier for the next guy? Are you really quitting?"

"Yeah, I am."

"Then let's cut the shit right now."

Bobcat turns and faces the back wall. He reaches inside his jacket and pulls out a can of spray paint. With the audience screaming, he starts spraying something in large black letters on the back wall, a word, and then a sentence, and then he steps back so everyone can read what he's written—

"*PARAMOUNT sucks.*"

"No," I say, pained, curled up in my armchair, my hands covering my face. "No, no."

Bobcat tosses the spray can to the side, leaps off the couch, picks up the couch cushions, runs to the end of the stage, and hurls them into the audience. He turns and dashes offstage, lifts the monitor next to Marla, throws it onto the floor, and stomps on it. Glass shatters and flies, a shard nicking Marla's leg. In the insanity surrounding us, I don't hear her yell.

I move to the side, stunned at Bobcat's manic outburst. "Bobcat, no," I say. "Enough."

I rush to him, throw my arms around him, subdue him as much as I can. He pushes against me, squirms, wriggles, tries to extricate himself from my grip around his waist, but I hold on.

"Okay, okay," Bobcat says, as I drag him to the couch, keeping my arms locked around him.

"We'll be right back," I say, as we go to commercial.

During the break, I release Bobcat, run backstage, and find Marla bleeding, dabbing at a gash on her leg.

"You okay?"

Marla shakes her head, murmurs, "He's insane."

During the break, I calm Bobcat and when we return from commercial, he sits on the couch, and I settle back in my armchair. "You tore everything up, man."

We talk civilly for a minute, Bobcat goes into a routine about joining the PTA at his kid's exclusive private elementary school, and going to a meeting for the school's upcoming fundraiser. "I suggested we sell crack," he says.

"Oh, man," I say.

"Not to our kids," he says. "To the public school kids."

The audience laughs and then Bobcat says, "I'm sorry. I just feel like breaking more stuff."

He stands and starts lifting another piece of the couch and the thought rushes in, *I have to do another show on this set in twenty-three hours.*

"No!" I say and I grab him from behind and yank him down onto the couch. I lock my arms and legs around him. We're both breathing hard, and finally Bobcat raises his hand in submission. When we go to the next break, I say, "I'll let you go, but you got to promise not to do any more shit."

Panting, he raises a finger. "I promise."

We end the show by briefly going into the audience, talking to a few audience members, but as the end credits roll, I think, *Twenty-two more to go. I hope I survive.*

One second after the show ends, Kerry McCluggage calls me. "You're killing me."

"Me? What do you mean?"

"Your friends are killing us on the air."

I've never known Kerry to show much, if any, emotion, but his voice rises and I can hear that he's pissed.

"You know." He pauses, takes a long breath before he speaks. "Most times when you are at the end of a road like this, when a show ends, you just part. That's it. No fanfare. It just ends. I'm letting you finish out the season, allowing you to do these shows, the shows you want, the guests you want, and you're killing me, every night."

"I'm not doing anything. I didn't know he had a spray can. I was as surprised as you were. I had no idea he was going to do that."

"But you know your friend."

I hate conflict. I hate confrontation. I hold back screaming at him, "You started this. If you had told the truth about how the show ended—if you had acknowledged the letter—my friends wouldn't be acting like this."

I don't say that. I want Paramount to let me do these final farewell shows, so I just seethe while Kerry fumes.

"It has to stop," he says.

"Yes, I know my friends," I want to scream. "*And it's not going to stop.*"

In retrospect, maybe I should have gone after Paramount for not being honest about how the show ended. Maybe I should have written another letter, saying how Paramount never publicly acknowledged my resignation letter. I do have a conversation with my lawyer about this, but he cautions me, "Why do you care? You're moving on."

I don't send a second letter. But I do care. And I do want my flowers. *Some*, that's all. I remember how Magic received a farewell tour when he retired. I picture him at mid-court in Milwaukee as someone rolled out a rocking chair for him, a gift to honor his retirement. Nice gesture. I guess I do want something like that.

Then, thanks to Queen Latifah, a few days before our final show, I receive my own symbolic rocking chair.

She organizes a hip-hop extravaganza, thirty rappers appearing together on my show. We call it the "Hip-Hop All-Stars Edition!" and we schedule it for the last ten minutes of the show. As the thirty rappers fill up almost every inch of the stage, I sit below the couch, on the lip of our set, watching Yo-Yo, Naughty By Nature, MC Lyte, A Tribe Called Quest, CL Smooth, Guru of Gang Starr, Das EFX, Wu-Tang Clan, KRS-One, and others rap for ten or fifteen seconds each, all of them praising me in rhyme. They call me the "biggest and the baddest," the "mastermind of all things," rhyming *Hall* with *all*, and then one of the rappers roars, "If not for Arsenio, there wouldn't be no late night TV." As I sit, I sway and grin, basking in this remarkable tribute, an immense display of love that douses me, fills me up. When the segment ends, I stand, and the rappers move toward me, and my eyes filling up, I hug every one of them. With drums booming, Ol' Dirty Bastard begins a closing chant, "The Black man is God, the Black man is God," over and over and over. I know Kerry McCluggage is watching this on his monitor. I bet he can't wait to get my Black ass off the Paramount lot.

I don't receive a rocking chair, or a gold watch, and Bette Midler doesn't croon "One for My Baby (And One More for the Road)," but I'll take my historic hip-hop all-star send-off any day.

Then we come to the end.

Friday, May 27, 1994.

Our last show.

This day—a day unlike any other—begins like every other.

I drive through the Melrose gate into the studio as usual. I pull into my parking space around eleven, get out of my car, take two steps toward my office, and stop. I stare at the massive, fake blue sky above me. The perpetually sunny sky, the sun ablaze every hour here at Paramount, no matter if it's stormy weather or approaching darkness. I feel myself walking then, as if on a mechanical sidewalk, gliding toward the office. I slide past stage 29. I'm here—and not here. That's how I feel the entire day—in some kind of trance, floating from place to place, almost as if a magnetic force is propelling me from my office to the stage to the dressing room, the unreality of this day distant, closed off, my emotions in check, not yet unleashed, not yet walloping me. I can't access *reality*, that everything I do today, every normal thing, every small thing I do every day almost by rote—sitting for my makeup, choosing my clothes, glancing through the cue cards, going over the segments with the director, planning every detail with Marla—everything I do today, I am doing for the last time.

We've planned this show carefully and yet I feel as if I'm an observer, watching my staff and crew at work from afar. I feel disconnected. *I wanted this*, I remind myself. *I made this choice.* But I miss every single thing and every single person already. The hour before the show, I barely speak. I can't find words. I nod. I smile. I whisper. I search for—I'm not sure what. The emotions start bubbling, but then I realize, I don't feel sad, or loss. I feel content. I not only wanted this end, I planned it.

It's time. We begin. Tonight, the hour show will rocket by in what seems like five minutes. I feel lightheaded as the opening we've chosen begins—

A clip from January 3, 1989.

My very first show. My very first guest.

Brooke Shields.

She sits next to me on the couch. I say to her, "You got a lot of press about some comments you made about being a virgin—"

She laughs. The audience laughs.

"How's that going?" I ask and the audience erupts.

The clip ends, we fade to black, and I appear, live, sitting on the stage, bathed in blue light.

"I'm going to miss this couch," I say. "I've interviewed everyone from Arnold Schwarzenegger to the pig, Arnold Ziffel. And now it's time. Time to conclude this chapter of my career."

I pause. "The party began January 3, 1989. My number one priority was to send you to bed five nights a week with a smile on your face and laughter in your heart."

We go to a montage of comedians, sketches, pratfalls, and punchlines.

Richard. Robin. Carlin. Cosby. Eddie. Seinfeld. Ellen.

Then I'm back live and I say, "Sometimes we had to keep it real."

A dramatic shift. Clips from the L.A. riots, streets on fire, buildings burning, people looting, then to gang members sitting in our audience, talking, really talking, beginning an L.A. gang truce on our show. Then shots of—Martin. Malcolm. Bill Clinton playing the sax. I confront Queer Nation. I interview Farrakhan. Magic announces he has HIV. Back to me, sitting on a stool.

"And not a day went by that I didn't hear the criticism, 'Arsenio, the show's too Black.' They would sweat me twenty-four/seven. I fought to put soul in America's bowl like never before."

A montage of Black performers, singers, rappers, athletes, jazz musicians, dancers, comedians, politicians, pastors, Maya Angelou.

Back to me, standing at center stage.

"Finally," I say, "I wanted to shake up late night, break the rules, liberate the bland, and most of all, keep it very, very unpredictable."

Now to a series of skits and spontaneous moments—me and Madonna, wrestlers, small people fighting, giants, magicians, Diana Ross and I making out, Diana slipping me tongue.

The opening montage runs ten minutes, and then I appear onstage again, and I say, "Let's get busy one more time."

The posse plays "It's Hall or Nothing," Burton Richardson belts out his usual opening, announces our guests, "Whoopi Goldberg and James Brown," declares that "we're saving the best for last," tells the audience in the studio and at home to "grab a slice of history," introduces me, holding the "O" on Arsenio beyond the range of any human voice, and then, for the final time, I bow my head, whisper my prayer, the curtain rises, and I step out to my mark on stage 29.

I feel calm.

This feels so right.

A smile slides across my face. I walk to the posse, and Mike and I grab on to each other and we hug, clinging to each other, not wanting to let go.

"I love you," we say simultaneously. We break apart, and turn away from each other, so we won't cry on camera in front of millions of people; the posse plays, and the audience stands and applauds for two straight minutes. The applause ebbs, then erupts, everyone looking past me as the screen rises again, and Luther Vandross steps out. Excitedly, I run to Luther, who appeared on my first show, and hug him.

"Marla," I say, looking off camera. "You did this. Thank you. Thank you, America."

"It's come full circle," Luther says. "I wanted to be the first one to congratulate you on all these years."

"Thank you," I say. "Wow."

"You should see the party that's going on backstage."

I laugh, thinking, *Yeah, there's always been something going on in the Green Room, even up to the last show.*

Then Luther points to me and says, "People love this man so unconditionally."

The audience roars.

"I'm so sad," Luther says, "because America is going to have a big chunk missing. But if there's one thing I do know it's that he knows what he's doing."

The audience applauds again and I ask Luther if he'll sing, a cappella. He pretends to object while Mike hands me a mic, and then Luther lets loose, singing from the depths of his heart, one of my favorite songs, "Let me hold you tight, if only for one night, let me keep you near—"

His voice and those words send me crashing to the floor. I'm spasming with joy. After a moment, I haul myself to my knees, but I am undone. He finishes the song, I stand and hug him again, and we go to commercial. We return from the break and I introduce my final musical guest ever, the "Godfather of Soul, the hardest working man in show business," James Brown, who belts two songs, "Cold Sweat" and the ballad "Try Me," accompanied by his dancers and his tight, powerful band. We follow that with a pretaped message from Arnold Schwarzenegger, who thanks me, praises the show, and invites me to appear in a movie with him now that I have some time on my hands. Then I bring out the "Godmother of Soul, the hardest working woman in show business," Whoopi Goldberg, who arrives onstage holding a bottle of champagne and two flutes. I pop the cork, pour the champagne, and offer a toast, "To those who have gone on before us. For Miles. And Sammy. All the brothers who paved the way. Josephine Baker and Billie Holiday."

I move through two segments with Whoopi, going into the audience with her, giving Wesley Snipes some love, saying hi to Quincy Jones, and, surprising me, Nancy Wilson, without whom I would have no career. As we make our way from one Black celebrity to the next—two of the guys from New Edition, the Pointer Sisters—Whoopi says, "All these Black people on television at one time. How scary is that for Paramount?"

Later, seated on the couch, Whoopi reads what the suits at Paramount wrote about the show in the trades. I appreciate what they wrote, though it seems slightly generic. Whoopi calls it bullshit, and tosses the paper over her shoulder, more smoke that Kerry and Paramount could have avoided if they'd been honest about my departure.

"They had no problem letting you go," she says. "Against all odds, you were not supposed to make it, but you did."

We return to the audience and then, to my disbelief at how fast this hour has gone, our time is up. I walk over to James Brown, but before

I introduce his last number, "Say It Loud," I pause in the center of a muted spotlight, and say my last good night, "I'd like to thank America. I'd like to thank all the talent in Hollywood who made this what it is. I'd like to thank my staff and crew. And most of all, I'd like to thank God. This has been the greatest five and a half years any man could ever dream of. I won't see you in twenty-three hours, but I will see you again."

As I'm speaking, I see James Brown in my peripheral vision, holding a brand-new bag, literally. Two bags, actually. Two bags of cookies. I'm so thrown, I lose my place in the cue cards, and then I start babbling something about James about to sing "Say It Loud," and he's holding up his cookies and he says, "If y'all will have some James Brown cookies, I will," and then he starts singing, "Say it loud, I'm Black and I'm proud."

Moments later, I'm in my dressing room. I don't remember walking here. I've space-shifted from the stage to here. I change into jeans and a simple white T-shirt and head for the door. While I'm gone, somebody will steal the clothes I wore while I was on-air saying goodbye to America and the watch Patti LaBelle and her husband Armstead gave me. We will eventually catch the thief—a studio guard!—and retrieve the clothes and the watch.

I leave the dressing room in a sort of daze. I find myself popping up everywhere—in the hallway, in the Green Room, in my office, not knowing how I've moved from place to place. I hug everyone, and then I'm holding a glass and someone pours champagne, and I see Milt Hoffman, my executive in charge of production, and Kim Swann, Claudia Cagan, Michael Wolff and Starr Parodi, Cheryl, Sandy, and Marla, and then I am aware of only her, and I think, *We did it!* Marla. My sister from another mister. My best friend. We hug and I whisper, "I never could have done this without you." I see tears trickle down her already moist cheek, and I whisper, "Where are you going to go now?"

"Home," she says. "I'm going home."

"Me, too," I say.

VIII
GOING HOME

34

DREAM

THIS WAS THE STORY of a dream.

As I said at the 2024 Emmys, "Most kids in Cleveland wanted to be a football star like Jim Brown. I wanted to be an old white man with a talk show."

I wanted to have a talk show like Johnny Carson.

That was my dream. A crazy, ridiculous, impossible dream.

My dream came true.

The Friday night after my last show, I walk into my new house in the Malibu Hills, my dream house. I step into my living room overlooking the ocean, lie on my couch, and fall into a deep sleep that feels like a coma. I sleep for the entire weekend. The few times I wake, I stare at the ocean, glimpsing Catalina Island in the distance, then fall back on the couch, listening to the gentle crash of the waves. *I had my own talk show and I live in paradise.* Pinch me.

Monday morning, still curled on the couch, I wake with a start. *I'm late, I have to get to the studio*, and then I realize, *I don't.* I lie back on the couch, and wait for the inevitable feelings to bash me—regret, fear, loss—but they don't come. Instead, I feel calm. I feel strong. I feel complete. A voice rings in my head, *You did it. You left on top. You wrote your own ending.*

What do I miss?

I miss the first five minutes of the show. I miss the curtain rising, stepping out onstage, my theme song playing at my back, tapping fingers with Mike, and I miss doing the monologue. I miss commenting on current events and getting laughs from the audience. I kept people connected. I became the forum for funny, outrageous stories. I was the Twitter of my day, but instead of the bluebird, I was the blackbird.

I don't miss interviewing celebrities who came on to plug their show, movie, or book, their publicist generating a list of generic questions that I had to ask. I don't miss that.

I still hang with Eddie, and Johnny Gill, and Earvin, and Jay. But mostly I hang out with Natalie, which is exactly what I want to do and where I want to be, at home, the two of us, enjoying each other's company. I'm living the life I want, the life I chose.

Since I ended the show, I've stayed in show business, appearing on sitcoms, game shows, talk shows, and my own Netflix stand-up special. From 1998 to 2000, I costarred with martial artist Sammo Hung in *Martial Law*, a comedy-cop show on CBS. I loved that show, but Sammo came down with terminal homesickness for his native Hong Kong, he went home, and CBS dropped the show. In 2003-2004, I hosted a revival of *Star Search*. I even had dinner with Ed McMahon, who told me that Johnny always respected me. He said that we were driving on the same highway, but in different lanes. He appreciated that I never tried to knock him out of his lane or overtake him.

In 2012, I became a contestant on *The Celebrity Apprentice*, hosted by Donald Trump. I played for the Magic Johnson Foundation, which Magic helped create for HIV and AIDS awareness. Early in the competition, after a rough episode, certain that Trump would tell me "You're fired," my fourteen-year-old son gave me a pep talk.

"Don't give up, Dad," he said. "Win this for us."

I did win, beating out Clay Aiken for the championship. I took my son's words to heart. His pep talk was the halftime speech that turned the whole game around. I won for my son.

Yes, my *son*. My former assistant Cheryl Bonacci and I continued our relationship after the show ended, and in 1998, I experienced the greatest moment of my life. Cheryl gave birth to our son, Arsenio Hall, Jr., whom we call Cheron, his middle name. The second I laid eyes on him, I fell deeply, immeasurably, unconditionally in love. I remember EJ, Magic's son, squirming in my arms as he reached for his dad at the Forum, and now I picture how Cheron used to squirm and reach for me, his dad. When I talk about him, what he means to me, the love I have for him, I burst into tears.

Cheron has now reached his mid-twenties. He's a good kid, with a kind and true heart.

What am I talking about?

He's a good *man*.

I feel beyond blessed. He is God's gift to me. I love him so, so much. I'm crying now as I write this.

Time passed, and, in addition to Prince, I lost so many of my mentors, artists who inspired me, people who saved me. Richard, fighting MS and other ailments, succumbed to a heart attack in 2005. Michael Jackson tragically died of a drug overdose in 2009. Whitney Houston passed away in 2012, and the lady who gave me my break, Nancy Wilson, passed in 2018. Robin Williams, breaking my heart, took his own life in 2014.

And, finally, there was Marla.

The woman who stood by my side, collaborated with me, fought every battle with me, protected me every day, every hour, for the six years of the show.

She kept her word. The last *Arsenio Hall Show* was the last television show she would ever work on. She and Steve, her husband, who deserves a medal for his patience and support, moved back to Highland Park, Illinois, outside of Chicago. The same year the show ended, Marla gave birth to Jason Brown, who became one of the most celebrated figure skaters in the United States. Jason earned a bronze medal in the 2014 Winter Olympics, and in 2015 won the United States National Championship. Marla and I have remained best friends. I am godfather to her three kids and she's godmother to Cheron.

When I was a kid, known as Arsenio the Magician, I passed out flyers that promised, "I make the impossible possible."

That's how I feel.

Reflecting on my life, I made the impossible possible.

The Arsenio Hall Show lasted nearly six years, changed the landscape of late night, changed my life, and brought new meaning to the term "color television."

I ended the show at my own time, on my own terms.

Few people can say "I lived my dream."

I can say that.

Fade *out*.

ACKNOWLEDGMENTS

MY GRATITUDE AND ETERNAL love to the original *ANNIE HALL*

Natalie Watkins-Hall
Mark Landesman
Marla Kell Brown
Lenard McKelvey
Corey Yamamoto
Joanne Colonna
Lon Rosen
Steve Levine
Mavis & Jay Leno
Leslie Sloane
Jessica Pierson
Howard Stern
Jessica K. Mooney
Earvin & Earleatha "Cookie" Johnson
Nicholas Ciani
Melissa Milsten

Don Hooper
Esther Newberg
Kim Swann
Nina Shaw
Makiko Ushiyama
David A. Hurwitz
Bobbie E
Kareem Black Photography
My incredible Simon & Schuster posse
El Cholo Restaurant [Santa Monica]